DISASTER AT THE BAR HARBOR FERRY

Disaster at the Bar Harbor Ferry

Ferry

Maine's Worst Maritime Tragedy

Mac Smith

Down East Books

Camden, Maine

DOWN EAST BOOKS

An imprint of Globe Pequot, the trade division of The Rowman & Littlefield Publishing Group, Inc.

4501 Forbes Blvd., Ste. 200

Lanham, MD 20706

www.rowman.com

Distributed by NATIONAL BOOK NETWORK

British Library Cataloguing in Publication Information available

Library of Congress Cataloging-in-Publication Data Is Available

ISBN 978-1-68475-049-8 (paperback : alk. paper)
ISBN 978-1-68475-050-4 (electronic)

♾™ The paper used in this publication meets the minimum requirements of American National Standard for Information Sciences—Permanence of Paper for Printed Library Materials, ANSI/NISO Z39.48-1992

This book is dedicated to Jordan, Olivia, and Xander, and to Kathy Adams.

Contents

Introduction

Sunday, August 6, 1899, is a date that for many years will be held in memory as signalizing the most dreadful accident that has ever occurred within the boundaries of the state of Maine.
—Bangor Daily Commercial, *August 7, 1899*

The story of the disaster at Mount Desert Ferry is the story of the deadliest accident that ever occurred in the state of Maine.

The story is more than the tale of two hundred people being thrown into the deep, chilly Maine waters when an overcrowded gangplank fell away under their feet, however.

The story of the disaster at Mount Desert Ferry is also about how those people came to be on this tiny, obscure piece of land in rural Maine, which had become the gateway to the ritz and glamour that only turn-of-the-twentieth-century Bar Harbor could provide. The story is about the citizens in a small town on the coast of Maine, whose hard work and the sacrifice of their quiet way of life made the Golden Age of Bar Harbor possible.

The story is about irony. In particular, it is a story of the working-class people of Maine spending their one day a week off from work traveling on the same rails and steamboats used by the Astors, Rockefellers, and Vanderbilts, and to the same destination.

The story is about patriotism and the celebration of victory at war. The story is about rumors, conflicting stories, and a herd mentality. The story is about heroism and cowardice.

The story is about the determination and self-sacrifice of the upper crust of Maine society to transform an elegant yet rural coastal resort hotel into a hospital in a location where the nearest medical help was at least an hour away.

The story is about the importance of waiting to learn the facts before making judgment, and the head-shaking disappointment at simple human error.

This story is about the ghosts of Maine's past and the erosion of her history. Though the disaster in 1899 attracted national attention, it is now mostly forgotten. The story of the disaster at Mount Desert Ferry is a chapter of Maine history that needs preserving.

And, yes, the story is also about two hundred people being thrown into the deep, chilly Maine waters when their overcrowded gangplank broke and fell away under their feet. It is about their lives, their survival, and, for twenty Mainers, their deaths.

The Sunday Excursion

It was a merry party of excursionists that left Bangor Sunday morning at 8:25 bound for Bar Harbor, the Newport of Maine, with the intention of seeing the vessels of Admiral Sampson's squadron. The weather could not have been improved upon and the eleven carloads of humanity thoroughly enjoyed the trip, until Mt. Desert Ferry was reached.

— Bangor Daily Commercial

When the 8:25 a.m. special excursion train to Bar Harbor left Union Station in Bangor on that beautiful Sunday morning, it was so full of people that passengers were hanging from its steps.

Though a day trip to Bar Harbor on a summer weekend would always be special, this was no ordinary excursion. An entire squadron of American military ships was also headed to Bar Harbor. The North Atlantic Squadron would be arriving that same day.

A visit to Maine by the US Navy's North Atlantic Squadron in itself was exciting, but this year was even more special. Adding greatly to the excitement of the visit was America's recent victory in the Spanish-American War.

"SEE THE FLEET THAT WON THE WAR

Bar Harbor, August 6, 1899"

The arrival of the fleet had been anticipated all week long. The Maine Central Railroad prepared to run several special-excursion trains, with a reduced fare, to Bar Harbor that weekend. Posters advertising the event had been put up in every town in the state in which the Maine Central Railroad ran, which were many. "Their arrival was known all over the state," wrote the *Bar Harbor Record*. "The big warships of the North Atlantic Squadron were, on the Sunday, indirectly the cause of the greatest number of deaths than occurred in our navy during the entire Spanish war."

It was Sunday, August 6, 1899. The weather was beautiful, not too hot for an August day, and the morning was filled with excitement. The nine hundred people filling the Maine Central Railroad's eleven passenger cars were jammed tightly in the seats and the aisles.

The 8:25 a.m. train out of Bangor was the first of four trips to Bar Harbor planned throughout the day. Everyone wanted to be on the first train, however, to not waste one second of that beautiful weekend day. The crowd was anxious to see the majestic, heroic gray warships as they sailed into Frenchman Bay. The passengers on the train were described as laughing and singing as the train slowly pulled out of the station, with conductor Fred Sanborn of Portland at the controls. "It was a merry party of excursionists that left Bangor Sunday morning at 8:25 bound for Bar Harbor, the Newport of Maine, with the intention of seeing the vessels of Admiral Sampson's squadron. The weather could not have been improved upon and the eleven car loads of humanity thoroughly enjoyed the trip," reported the *Bangor Daily Commercial*, "until Mt. Desert Ferry was reached."

People traveled alone, in pairs or groups, with family, friends, or coworkers. Many carried baskets with the day's lunch. Some carried parasols or satchels. A few people carried babies. Some parties were complete as they traveled together on the train, but many parties were incomplete and had plans to meet other members of their party at the wharf in Bar Harbor.

As was the convention of the day, most passengers had put on their better clothing for the day of travel. The scene was set in a news story by *Bar Harbor Times* Arts and Style editor Nan Lincoln:

There were pigeon-breasted ladies in fancy wide-brimmed, silk-swathed hats, giraffe-necked, pleated blouses and cinch waist skirts reaching to the middle of their high-button shoes. Escorting them were dapper, derbied men in boxy jackets, stiffly starched collars and cuffless trousers tapering to narrow, spit-polished boots. Giggling girls in middy blouses and ruffled pinafores with big bows perched like giant butterflies in their long, shining tresses, were chased by mischievous boys in baggy knickers and cloth caps. Everyone was in a celebratory mood.

Special-excursion trains had become common by 1889. With the growth and improvements of rail and ferry service, the Maine coast was growing in popularity every year as a tourist destination, both from within the state and without. Elegant resort hotels began springing up along the coast to provide lodging to the tourists, who would visit for an afternoon, a weekend, or the entire summer season, depending on their financial means. Special daylong events on the grounds of these resorts on the weekends would cater to the blue-collar workers of the state.

In the summer, the Maine Central Railroad would offer special-excursion trains, with lowered fares, to these coastal resorts. The entire tourist industry became a network of convenient transportation to beautiful spots along the Maine coast. The people of Maine were now able to travel to places in the state that they had only read about in the newspapers.

The popularity of the 8:25 special-excursion train that Sunday morning was not just a testament to the desire of the people of Maine to use their newly acquired disposable income and their recently gained weekends, but also to their patriotism.

Even with a growing number of resort towns available to Mainers, Bar Harbor was always a particularly popular destination. The island town held extra attraction to the people of the state this particular weekend because of the arrival of the US Navy's North Atlantic Squadron. One of the squadron's ships, the *Massachusetts*, had already arrived in Bar Harbor, on Thursday. The early arrival of the *Massachusetts* allowed her commander, Capt. Charles J. Train, to be at the wedding of his young daughter, Susie, a part-time Ellsworth resident, to a young lawyer from New York. After the wedding ceremony in Bar Harbor, the newly married couple would head to the quieter Mount Desert Ferry, just eight miles away by ferry in the town of Hancock, where they planned to stay at the elegant coastal resort hotel, The Bluffs, and where they would find themselves in the middle of the disaster at Mount Desert Ferry.

The rest of the squadron, commanded by Rear Adm. William T. Sampson, fifty-nine, would be arriving in Bar Harbor that Sunday morning from Rockland. This included the flagship *New York*, as well as the *Brooklyn*, *Indiana*, and *Texas*.

Knowing that a visit to the squadron during its weeklong visit in Bar Harbor would be popular, the Maine Central Railroad arranged its special-excursion trains to begin running from Portland to Mount Desert Ferry in Hancock two days before the fleet's arrival. The excursions were advertised in newspapers and with posters throughout the state:

SAMPSON'S FLEET AT BAR HARBOR

August 4–5–6–7–8–9 1899

The Maine Central Railroad will sell excursion tickets, August 5th through the 9th Round trip $2.00

Good until August 14, 1899

Special train will leave Portland 7:20 AM August 6

Arr Bar Harbor 1:55 PM August 6

SEE THE FLEET THAT WON THE WAR

Bar Harbor August 6, 1899

The ships of the United States Navy on courtesy call to the island of Mount Desert. Excursion rates.

See ticket agent at your station.

The Maine Central Railroad offered a special rate for the weekend—fifty cents would buy a round-trip to the famed Maine coastal resort.

This would not be the North Atlantic Squadron's first visit to Bar Harbor, but it was a significant one—the country had recently been victorious in the Spanish-American war, which the United States had entered after the sinking of one of its ships, the USS *Maine*. The part played by the North Atlantic Squadron in America's victory had helped honor that loss.

The Spanish-American War had begun with Cuba's revolt against Spain for independence. The United States relied heavily on Cuba for trade, and the USS *Maine* had been sent to the region to protect US citizens and interests, though US President William McKinley opposed entering the conflict. On the evening of February 15, 1898, a deadly explosion occurred inside the USS *Maine*, causing her to sink quickly and costing the lives of 250 of the 355 sailors aboard. "Remember the *Maine*" became the slogan being chanted across the United States as the country was officially drawn into what would be known as the Spanish-American War.

The sinking of the USS *Maine* was especially personal to the people of the Pine Tree State. Eight men from Maine served with pride aboard the state's namesake. Six of those men died in the explosion.

Frank Talbot was a twenty-three-year-old man from Bath. His grandfather had served in the navy for twenty years, his father spent three years at sea during the Civil War, and Frank himself joined the US Navy on December 26, 1897, one day after Christmas. Frank Talbot had only been in the navy for two months when he died in the explosion.

Talbot's last letter home was written the night before the USS *Maine* left Key West, Florida, for Havana, Cuba, and he indicated he was enjoying his work very much. "I would like to come home this spring, but I can't tell when I will get north again. We leave tomorrow for Havana. Goodbye. Your loving son."

Quartermaster 3rd Class Millard Harris of Boothbay was forty-eight when he died in the explosion. He left behind a wife, Agnes. Apprentice Seaman William H. Tinsman of Portland had grown up in East Deering, Maine, and had served on the USS *Merrimac* during the Civil War. He died in the explosion. Also from Maine were Fireman 1st Class Bernard Lynch and John H. Bloomer from the Portland area, and John Sweeney, from Bath. All died in the explosion.

Martin Webber, of Bar Harbor, and William Lambert survived the explosion.

The Spanish-American War lasted for ten weeks, before Spain surrendered on August 12, 1898. Approximately three thousand Americans died in the war, but many of the deaths were due to yellow fever and typhoid.

A year had passed since the United States' victory in the Spanish-American War. In Bar Harbor, the ships of the squadron would be open to the public for inspection, and on that Sunday, August 6, 1899, the people of the 8:25 train out of Bangor would have a chance to shake the hands of the brave sailors of the squadron, and to show their respect for those who were lost.

It was not just the great warships that drew the crowd to Bar Harbor that day, but also a chance to witness the grand arrangements being made by the members of Mount Desert Island's Summer Colony to welcome the officers of the squadron, done on a scale that could only be imagined by the wage earners and shopkeepers of Bangor and Ellsworth who would be visiting for just the day.

Several private events had been planned in Bar Harbor in honor of Adm. William T. Sampson, the commander of the squadron, in his role as the representative of the fleet. Members of the private Canoe Club on Mount Desert Island had been preparing a reception for the admiral and the officers of the ships at the Malvern Hotel, the most fashionable hotel in Bar Harbor at the time, located near the center of town. On Monday evening, the day after the squadron's arrival, the grand event would be held in the Malvern's ballroom and reception parlors, which were appropriately hung with flags and bunting, while palms and potted plants completed the decorations. All of Bar Harbor's summer society was expected at the event. "Seldom has the Malvern been so gay," reported the *Bar Harbor Record*.

Though grand plans had been made for the admiral and the officers of the squadron, the numerous enlisted men who would also be visiting Bar Harbor had not been forgotten. According to the *Bar Harbor Record*, the best honor to give an enlisted man was some time off.

> *While Admiral Sampson and his officers have been this feted, the "men behind the guns" have not been neglected. They are an independent sort of a crowd, anyhow, who will manage to get all kinds of pleasure out of their visit even if you don't give events in their honor. It is the great mass of jolly, sunburned tans, numerous enough to make a good-sized summer resort by themselves, that finds the most pleasure in the visit of the warships. They throng ashore like children coming out of school; they are omnipresent, everyone is their bureau of information, and they swarm about the town with mischievous smiles, alert for fun and trouble alike. Insurance on a first-class wheel was way down when Jack Tar got aboard it. It was huge sport to see the way those machines moved with the sailor boys at the helm. Horseback riding has also been a favorite pastime for the tars. It doesn't run in a sailor's blood to sit properly astride a spirited steed and some who didn't sit there long.*

"The pastimes and capers of the sailor boys ashore have given the town plenty of amusement," wrote the *Bar Harbor Record* the week after the squadron's visit.

A trip to Bar Harbor would not have been possible for most Mainers just fifteen years prior to the disaster at Mount Desert Ferry, nor would

Bar Harbor have been as desirable a destination. Without Mount Desert Ferry, Bar Harbor would not have had its Golden Age.

In the early 1800s, the natural beauty of Mount Desert Island was known only to a few people who did not live there year-round. Travel to Mount Desert Island from the mainland was almost nonexistent.

The few people who did visit Mount Desert Island seasonally included several talented, artistic painters, who were able to represent the island's beauty on canvas. As those artists sold their paintings throughout the country and told their tales of the beauty of this small area in Maine and the characters with which it was populated, curiosity about Mount Desert Island grew. A few tourists began to arrive to see if the landscape was as beautiful as had been represented by the paintings that adorned their grand homes in Boston, Philadelphia, New York, Washington, DC, and so many other places that produced the opulently wealthy families of the time.

"This bold scenery transferred to canvas . . . soon made the locality familiar to the residents of the large cities, and summer travel soon began to gravitate toward the eastern part of the island. This was the beginning of Bar Harbor as a seaside resort. It was through these views that the scenery along this wild and rockbound coast became somewhat familiar to the dwellers in the great cities and turned the tide of summer travel in this direction," wrote *Pen and Pencil*, a travel magazine from the time, adorned with elaborate drawings that depicted various Maine summer resorts.

Steamship travel had been available in Maine since 1824, when the Kennebec Steam Navigation Company unveiled Maine's first steamship, the *Maine*, at Bath. By the 1830s and 1840s steamboats were becoming increasingly popular, and travel routes were rapidly expanding along the coast of Maine, as were the number of the towns becoming home to elegant coastal resort hotels.

By 1855 the first hotel had been built in Bar Harbor, the Agamont House, by resident Tobias Roberts, who already kept a small store in town for the convenience of the few straggling settlers on that side of Mount Desert Island. Two years later the first regular steamship service to Bar Harbor began with the inauguration of the steamer *Rockland* for regular passenger service between Rockland and Bar Harbor. The steamer ran twice a week. Ten years later, in 1867, the Bar Harbor Public Landing was built, as was the Rodick Hotel, both built by Mr. Roberts. With regular, though limited, steamship service and a public wharf, the number of visitors to the island increased, as did the number of upscale hotels, which grew rapidly. The Grand Central Hotel was built in 1869, later to be enlarged several times. Built the following year was the Atlantic House, which burned to the ground and was rebuilt, even bigger, in 1873. The Newport was built in 1871.

"That Mount Desert Island, with Bar Harbor as a rallying point and business center, is to become an immense summer resort, no one who has become acquainted with its peculiar adaption to that purpose, can for a moment doubt," wrote *Pen and Pencil.*

Growth was steady on Mount Desert Island for the thirty years after the first hotel was opened in Bar Harbor. The tourists who had been spending their summer seasons in the grand hotels now were building "cottages" throughout Bar Harbor and across the island. "Now the palatial hotels, the millions of dollars invested in cottages, the almost fabulous prices at which real estate is sold in and around Bar Harbor, and the distinguished names . . . Vanderbilt, Blaine . . . indicate that this is to be the fashionable quarter of the Island," wrote *Pen and Pencil.*

The *Rockland* and its twice-a-week trip to Bar Harbor had been welcomed by the traveling public in 1857, but as the needs of the traveling public grew, the need for better ferry service was soon realized. The trip to Bar Harbor was still an indirect one, requiring travelers from Boston, New York, Philadelphia, and other points south to travel by train to Portland, embark on the steamship *Daniel Webster* to the city of Rockland, then transfer to the *Rockland* for the final trip to Mount Desert Island. The *Rockland*'s twice-a-week schedule was also becoming inadequate.

In addition to the public demand for more rapid and convenient service to Bar Harbor, there was also a need for service to the other island localities. With the growth of Bar Harbor had come the growth of the rest of Mount Desert Island, and coastal resort hotels were being erected everywhere, with each island town having its own appeal to the diverse group of summer colonists.

Twenty years after inaugurating service to Mount Desert Island, in 1877 the number of trips from Rockland to Mount Desert Island was increased to three times a week, and by the early 1880s additional stopping points were scheduled. A steamboat wharf was built at Try House Point in Bass Harbor over the winter of 1881–82, and the Kimball family built a wharf at Northeast Harbor the following year for the arrival of the steamboat in that village. Seal Harbor's steamboat wharf was inaugurated on August 15, 1882.

Though attempts were being made to improve travel to Bar Harbor, the route was still convoluted, requiring many transfers, all of which cost time and convenience. A new travel demand was also growing among the members of Mount Desert Island's summer colony, something for which they were willing to pay good money—the summer colonists wanted to travel in elegance.

Around the corner there is always a better mousetrap just waiting to be built, just waiting to revolutionize an industry. Mount Desert Ferry was that mousetrap.

The idea for Mount Desert Ferry came from the Maine Central Railroad, which was attempting to meet the increasing demands from the increasing number of people traveling to Mount Desert Island every summer season. The Maine Central Railroad had been created through the consolidation of several small Maine railroads after the Civil War and the merger of two large railroads, the Androscoggin and Kennebec Railroad and the Penobscot and Kennebec Railroad. The railroad had been in operation for twenty-six years when it built Mount Desert Ferry in 1884.

The Maine Central Railroad showed that it was serious about the ever-growing ferry service with the purchase of the Portland, Bangor, Mt. Desert and Machias Steamboat Company in 1881. Two years later plans were announced for the construction of Mount Desert Ferry, the cornerstone in the train-and-ferry service planned by the railroad. An area of land in the town of Hancock would be the terminus of the Maine Central Railroad's new Waukeag Line. The new railroad line would extend from Bangor to Brewer, from Brewer to Ellsworth, and then another ten miles to Hancock, for a total of forty miles of new track, which would be constructed by the Maine Shore Line Railroad.

The plan was to create a train route from as far south as Philadelphia that would run to Hancock without any need for passengers to transfer to another vehicle. The final ten miles of the trip, from Hancock to Bar Harbor, would be traveled by steamboat. The ferry would service several towns on Mount Desert Island and would run almost daily. The Pullman cars of the Bar Harbor Express as well as the ferries that would carry the passengers would be befitting of the social status those passengers represented. Mount Desert Ferry would cater to every demand of the public traveling to Mount Desert Island.

The project would be costly. Before the rails could be placed, there would need to be surveys, land acquisition along the forty-mile stretch, demolition, excavation. The men building the new rail line, many of them immigrants, would need to be housed and fed. Maine Central Railroad was backing part of the project, but the towns along the new railroad line were asked to help with the cost. Maine Central argued that the towns involved would reap benefit from the extension of the rail line, the main mode of transportation in the late 1800s. In February 1883 Ellsworth voters pledged ten thousand dollars to the Maine Shore Line Railroad for the project, while Bangor voters pledged twenty thousand.

Construction of the new rail line moved quickly after that. Just a month after Ellsworth voters pledged their financial support, in March 1883 a survey of the land between Brewer and Ellsworth was commissioned to determine the best possible rail line route. Two months later railroad workers began to grade the land.

As the line was being constructed, work was also under way in Hancock, with the construction of the train station, the ferry wharf, and the extensive facilities needed to support the trains and passengers. A private developer had also leased part of the land at Mount Desert Ferry and was beginning construction on an elegant summer coastal resort hotel.

The 41.3-mile line of track was completed the following year. On June 28, 1884, the first passenger train ran the new Waukeag Line of the Maine Central Railroad to Mount Desert Ferry. The following day, the

Maine Central Railroad steamer *Sebenoa*, which would soon be joined by the *Sappho*, made the first of many steamship runs from Mount Desert Ferry to Bar Harbor.

Twenty-seven years after the establishment of steamship service to Mount Desert Island, the demands of the traveling public had been met. "No longer as in days gone by, is the visitor obliged to cross the Island from Southwest Harbor by the circuitous route, through Somesville nor, as later, to depend upon a single line of steamers, making the trip two or three times a week, to reach Bar Harbor, for since 1884, there is an all-rail route to within eight miles of Bar Harbor wharf, and safe ferry boats always in waiting to convey passengers across the intervening space, known as Frenchman's Bay," wrote *Pen and Pencil*.

During the first year in operation, eleven thousand passengers passed through Maine Central Railroad's newest terminal to Bar Harbor. The success of Mount Desert Ferry proved her necessity. "Already is Mount Desert Ferry a port of entry," wrote *Pen and Pencil* magazine.

With improved facilities for reaching Bar Harbor, the influx of visitors to Mount Desert Island increased at a phenomenal rate. The other railroad lines in the state arranged their timetables to align with that of the run of the Maine Central Railroad's Waukeag Line to Hancock. Private boat owners in Frenchman Bay would hire themselves out in the summer for personal excursions to Mount Desert Ferry, arranged to coincide with the timetable of the train and the steamships. "Steamer Electra, Capt. E. True runs to the various ports in Frenchman's Bay every weekday in connection with the Maine Central RR," read an advertisement from the time in the *Bar Harbor Record*.

The everyday scene at Mount Desert Ferry after its opening was described as quite lively. "Since the opening of the Mount Desert Branch of the Maine Central Railroad, a new impulse has been given to the travel in this direction, and the number of visitors to Bar Harbor has more than quadrupled within the last two years, and is yearly increasing," wrote *Pen and Pencil*.

The year after Mount Desert Ferry opened, the number of train passengers had increased by 50 percent, and the *Sebenoa* transported 12,999 passengers. During the third year in operation, ferry traffic was growing at such a pace that a second steamship was added to the Frenchman Bay run. The 149-foot steamship *Sappho* helped carry the thirty-one thousand passengers that went through Mount Desert Ferry that year. As the ferry service continued to thrive, stops were added in Seal Harbor, Northeast Harbor, Southwest Harbor, and Manset.

The number of passengers on the Mount Desert branch of the Maine Central Railroad was far higher than on any other branch. According to the annual reports to the stockholders of the Maine Central Railroad, during the fiscal year ending October 1, 1892, total passenger revenue from the Waukeag Line to Hancock was $71,718, equal to approximately $1.7 million in today's economy. Passenger revenue accounted for about 37 percent of overall income, with freight revenue making up the rest.

The *Sebenoa* also hauled 254 tons of freight the second year that Mount Desert Ferry was in operation, generating $27,621 in freight revenue alone, the equivalent of approximately $750,000 in 2021. Railroad officials would tell the newspapers that more lumber was being transported to Bar Harbor than to any other location the same size in Maine. This being the Golden Age of Bar Harbor, the building of extravagant summer cottages and elaborate private clubs and other buildings was at an all-time high. Also shipped in large quantities were granite and coal, and later, perishable products, after refrigerated railcars came into use.

The small station at Mount Desert Ferry was bringing in five million dollars annually to the large state railroad. By the end of the first year that Mount Desert Ferry was in operation, the Maine Central Railroad had leased the rail line between Brewer and Hancock from the Maine Shore Line Railroad, and four years later Maine Central bought out the Maine Shore Line altogether.

Much of the popularity of the train passenger service to Hancock was due to the elegant Bar Harbor Express.

The Bar Harbor Express made its inaugural run from Boston to Mount Desert Ferry on June 29, 1885, the year after Mount Desert

Ferry opened. The luxurious train ran only in the summer, and in its first few years of service it ran northbound on Monday, Wednesday, and Friday, and southbound on Tuesday, Thursday, and Sunday. There was no Saturday service because the social calendar mandated that if one were already on Mount Desert Island on a Saturday, one would want to stay the entire weekend.

Travel on the Bar Harbor Express mirrored the elegance found in the grand cottages erected on the island during Bar Harbor's Golden Age. Due to the wealth and stature of those spending their summers on Mount Desert Island, the Express became a premier example of train travel during the late 1800s. The *Mount Desert Herald* described the cars of the Bar Harbor Express as "perfect beauties, being finished on the inside in blue and gold, the curtains and seats and all the cloth trimming being of a beautiful blue and the woodwork carved prettily and gilded. Electric buttons between each window call the porter to each seat, there being room for thirty in the car. A charming compartment in one end of the car allows the gentlemen to smoke . . . the ceilings of the cars are stained in imitation mother-of-pearl."

Passengers could leave Boston in elegant palace cars at nine o'clock in the morning, and before eight that same evening be at their hotel or cottage at Bar Harbor. The other option available to passengers was to leave Boston at seven o'clock in the evening by sleeping car, arriving in Bangor at five-thirty the following morning and at Bar Harbor at eight-thirty.

It was not uncommon for such famous families as the Vanderbilts, Pulitzers, and Morgans to ride the Bar Harbor Express to reach Mount Desert Island. Track crews worked throughout the spring to ensure that the rails were in perfect working order and to guarantee that "not a drop of coffee or champagne were spilled." The president of Maine Central Railroad would ride the entire route prior to the opening of the summer season to see that the ride was smooth and functioning well.

The Bar Harbor Express featured special accommodations for the servants of its passengers, and some families traveled in their own private Pullman cars attached to the regular train, the unofficial record being twenty-one private cars in one day. In 1888 the Vanderbilts traveled to Mount Desert Ferry on the Bar Harbor Express, but since their private car was over seventy-three feet long, it did not fit on the turntable at the train station in Hancock and had to be taken all the way back to Newport, Rhode Island, in order to turn it around so that it faced the correct direction for the eventual trip home.

Due to its success, the route of the Bar Harbor Express would be expanded south to include New York's Grand Central Station and Philadelphia's Broad Street Station.

An event that would recognize and celebrate the success of both Mount Desert Ferry and the town of Bar Harbor occurred on August 8, 1889.

The building of Mount Desert Ferry had promoted rapid growth in Bar Harbor and across Mount Desert Island over its first five years. Along with the summer residents came the symbols of the society they represented. Elaborate cottages, private clubs, and cultural centers arose all over Bar Harbor. Over time the names and titles of the summer visitors grew more grand.

Bar Harbor would truly feel the jewel had been placed in her crown when, in the summer of 1889, it was announced that a sitting president of the United States would arrive there, via Mount Desert Ferry, for a weeklong vacation.

Mount Desert Ferry had been in operation only five years when President Benjamin Harrison, the twenty-third president of the United States, arrived in Hancock aboard a special, private running of the Bar Harbor Express.

President Harrison and his party were met at Mount Desert Ferry by US Secretary of State James G. Blaine, from Augusta, at whose cottage the president was to spend his vacation, and Henry Cabot Lodge, a US congressman from Massachusetts. The crowd gave the president three cheers before he and the rest of the presidential party boarded the *Sappho*, which would serve as the presidential yacht for the duration of Harrison's weeklong visit. "She was beautifully and tastefully decked with bunting . . . and resembled more a small floating palace than anything in the ferry boat line," wrote the *Bar Harbor Record*.

President Harrison would be celebrated at various functions in Bar Harbor, including a huge private party at the home of a summer resident.

The event was one of the most glamorous in Bar Harbor's history and was attended by both national and international summer visitors, including various ambassadors and diplomats. This was not only a celebration for the president, but a celebration of the success of the resort town of Bar Harbor itself. "At the tables outside were represented the social position and wealth of the summer colony," wrote the *Bar Harbor Record*. "No one of note seemed to be omitted."

During the trip, the presidential party would ride the *Sappho* from Bar Harbor to Somes Sound in choppy, foggy seas. A few minutes after departure, stricken with seasickness, few of the presidential party could speak. "The President tried to keep up appearances but in a short time had to withdraw like any other seasick mortal," said the *Bar Harbor Record*. "In short, the Somes Sound trip was a failure."

President Harrison would also depart the island through Mount Desert Ferry the following week upon the completion of his visit.

"Bar Harbor has had a visit from a real live President and has survived it," wrote the *Record*. "Mr. Harrison's first experience of Mount Desert has been delightful; and how could it be otherwise, with so many of the wealthiest and most influential in society ministering to his pleasure and vying with each other for the honor of entertaining him. Though courted and feted by the gay and fashionable, his courteous dignity of manner has left a profound and grateful impression on the great heart of the people; and the inhabitants of Mount Desert will regard President Harrison's visit to Bar Harbor as one of the most interesting and pleasant events in the history of the island."

This was not Bar Harbor's first visit by a sitting president, though it was the first extended vacation. President Chester A. Arthur, who had ascended to the office after the assassination of President James Garfield a year previously, passed through Bar Harbor on a trip to Bangor on September 12, 1882. "President Arthur was here for a day during his administration, but presumably because he was what might be called an accidental president, his presence did not create much of a flutter in society circles," wrote the *Bar Harbor Record* of the president's day on Mount Desert Island.

Eleven years after President Harrison's visit, in July 1910, President William Howard Taft would also travel through Mount Desert Ferry during a visit to Mount Desert Island.

A vacation at Bar Harbor by a US president gave the up-and-coming resort the social status that was so important to its summer colony. President Harrison visited both Newport and Bar Harbor that year. Bar Harbor had arrived, thanks to Mount Desert Ferry.

The Overcrowded Gangplank

It at once became apparent to the excursionists that they could not all go to Bar Harbor in the Sappho at one time and then began the mad rush to get aboard in order that not one minute of the anticipated pleasure at Bar Harbor should be wasted.

—Boston Globe

It would be almost ten years to the day after President Harrison's visit to Bar Harbor that the disaster at Mount Desert Ferry occurred.

While the Bar Harbor Express was making travel from out of state more convenient and luxurious, the creation of Mount Desert Ferry also gave people in the far-flung corners of rural Maine the chance to travel to Mount Desert Island. The Maine Central Railroad was now able to use its network of rail lines, combined with the networks of other rail lines in the state, to reach deeply into rural Maine for its special excursions. Regardless of the rail line traveled, all train passengers would end up on the Maine Central Railroad for the final leg of the trip to Mount Desert Island.

When it became known that the North Atlantic Fleet would be visiting Bar Harbor in August 1899, several transportation businesses, large and small, began organizing excursions to Mount Desert Island for that weekend, from the smallest boat owner in Frenchman Bay to several "monster excursions" organized by the railroad companies in the state. Another large Maine railroad, the Bangor and Aroostook Railroad, brought people from as far away as Caribou, Fort Fairfield, Presque Isle, and Houlton. Other passengers arrived from Bucksport, Brewer,

Ellsworth, Orono, Hancock, and many other small towns and large cities that lined Maine's extensive railroad system. That day there were fifty-three passengers from Portland, forty from Augusta, and several from Waterville.

The majority of passengers on the 8:25 train on that Sunday morning in August were from the city of Bangor. Those passengers represented the Queen City that Bangor had become at the turn of the century.

The modern city of Bangor in 1899 had its beginnings in the mid-1800s, and the city grew along with its lumbering and shipbuilding industries. Bangor had the perfect geography and climate for lumbering and shipbuilding, and the area was populated with hard-working, fun-loving, and industrious people.

Geographically, Bangor is located on the shores of the Penobscot River and was surrounded by forest when it was settled. Trees in the Maine woods were cut down to logs and floated to Bangor, where they were processed at the city's water-powered sawmill and shipped to any place in the world from Bangor's busy port. Bangor's lumber and shipping economy reached a high point in the 1870s. Industry was so great that in the 1880s Bangor was pronounced "The Queen City of the East."

The 1890s saw Bangor's streets paved, and sewers, telephone service, electric utilities, and street railways built. The Bangor Street Railway was chartered in 1887. In 1896 the Bangor Symphony Orchestra was founded (it continues as the oldest community orchestra in the country). The standpipe on Thomas Hill was built in 1897.

The growth of lumbering and shipbuilding and other industries spawned further growth in Bangor and led to a need for support positions such as merchants, clerks, and people trained in business skills such as stenography and typing. Bangor had grown to a more diversified, regional service-oriented economy, not as dependent on the lumbering and shipbuilding trades as it had once been. Bangor citizens were now finding jobs in other areas, including communications, transportation, general supply, pulp and paper, and manufacturing. Factories were in abundance in the Bangor area, and across the state, and Maine was known worldwide for its manufacture of shoes and moccasins.

The Maine Central Railroad was a major contributor to Bangor's growth. Bangor became a major terminal for the rail line, which conveyed products from northern and eastern Maine to other points in the state and across the country by rail and sea. The Maine Central Railroad was a major employer in Bangor and throughout the state.

With the transformation of Bangor came two new conventions for the inhabitants of the city, both of which contributed to the disaster at Mount Desert Ferry: a more standardized work schedule, which included every Sunday off, and spending money.

On the farms of Maine, from where many people had come to work in Bangor, nature dictated when jobs had to be done. In the city, however, there was more adherence to schedules and timetables, clocks, and watches. Sunday, the day traditionally set aside for religious observance, became the day off for the working class of Bangor. This regular day off and the spending money the jobs provided, combined with the Maine Central Railroad's ability to provide transportation to popular places such as Mount Desert Island, led a handful of Bangor residents to the special-excursion train out of Union Station that Sunday morning in 1899.

The names and occupations of a few of the passengers that were on the 8:25 train are reflective of the city that Bangor had become in 1899:

- Charles Adams was a lumber company executive, serving on the board of the Stillwater Log Driving Company and the Mattawamkeag Log Driving Company, among others.

- Mr. George Derwent was a newsagent employed on the Maine Central Railroad's trains running out of Bangor. He and his wife, Lillian, were newlyweds.

- Howard Stone was employed in the ticket office of the Maine Central Railroad's Bangor station.

- Lincoln Bragdon was one of many Bangor merchants aboard the special-excursion train. On Sunday, the shops were generally closed.

- William Miller ran a large hardware store.

- Elmer Nichols and Ida Edminster, young and in love, both worked at the Ida C. Nichols Dry Goods Company.

- Miss Lena Smith and Mr. Fred Tuck were engaged to be married. Mr. Tuck was a carpenter.

- Miss Gertrude Veazie was a buyer at a shoe company.

- Ellen Billings was a well-known hairdresser for Bangor's upper crust of society.

- Miss Grace Sumner, fifteen, was a recent graduate of Shaw's Business College and was to have taken a position as a stenographer the day after the disaster.

- Miss Lizzie Ward, nineteen, was a domestic.

- Walker B. Smith was a shoe factory employee in Bangor.

By the time the 8:25 a.m. train out of Bangor arrived in Ellsworth, it was already running late. It was 9:41 a.m., and waiting at the Ellsworth station were another four hundred passengers, all just as anxious as their Bangor neighbors to see the ships of the North Atlantic Squadron.

Much like at Bangor, the people waiting at the station that day were primarily Ellsworth's blue-collar workers and merchants in small business operations.

Irving Bridges was a farmer from Hancock who spent much time in Ellsworth. A widower, Mr. Bridges was traveling to Bar Harbor not to see the squadron, but to see his fiancée, Miss Marshall. Mr. Bridges traveled in a large party, including two of his sisters, Louise Bridges (called Lou) and Mrs. Mabel Davis. The Bridges sisters were members of the International Association of Rebekah Assemblies, Nokomis Rebekah Lodge, Ellsworth Chapter. Though not a formal outing, many members of this community-service organization were traveling aboard the train with the Bridges family. This group included Mrs. Maude Raymond; Miss Julia Billington, who provided singing at Rebekah meetings; and Mr. and Mrs. A. W. Curtis and their daughter, Mrs. Bertha Estey. Mrs.

Estey was a newlywed who was taking the day off from helping her husband at his laundry business in Ellsworth.

Mrs. Addie Stover was a wife and mother who was raising her three children by herself in Ellsworth while her husband supported the family by working fifty miles away, in Jonesboro.

Willie Downes, a teenage boy, was traveling with his mother.

Also waiting at the station in Ellsworth were twenty members of the Maine Press Association, who in fact were not meant to be on the train to Mount Desert Ferry that day. The previous day they had successfully completed their annual weeklong excursion along the Maine and Canadian coast. This Sunday excursion to Bar Harbor was an impromptu addition to their recent travels.

Newspapers and journalists were universally well respected in this era. As the only real means of broadcasting, newspapers were relied upon for information as well as entertainment. All the cities in Maine had at least one daily newspaper, and many small Maine towns had a weekly publication. From this multitude of newspapers grew the Maine Press Association.

The Maine Press Association was founded in 1864 and today is one of the oldest professional news organizations in the nation. Its goals were, and are, to promote and foster high ethical standards and the best interests of the newspapers, journalists, and media organizations in the state of Maine that constitute its membership; to encourage improved business and editorial practices and a better media environment in the state; and to improve the conditions of journalism and journalists by promoting and protecting the principles of freedom of speech and of the press and the public's right to know.

The members of the Maine Press Association were well-respected journalists. US vice president and Maine resident Hannibal Hamlin was an honorary member. Vice President Hamlin had spoken at the association's annual meeting only two years before. He told the news people at that meeting how he had worked as a chore boy in a newspaper office when he was young, "in a country printing office before rollers were introduced." The Maine Press Association was so esteemed that it served as the inspiration for similar organizations, such as the Maine Amateur Press Association, established in 1894.

The Maine Press Association met on a semi-annual basis, and in the summer the members would take great excursions. The leader of the twenty members who traveled to Mount Desert Island that Sunday was Chester W. Robbins, thirty-one, of Old Town. A year before, Mr. Robbins had begun a newspaper in Old Town, the *Old Town Enterprise*, which is still in existence under the name *Penobscot Times*.

Mr. Robbins was quite fond of the Maine coast, and of travel. He also seemed to be a practical, resourceful, and organized man. Mr. Robbins would combine his love for travel and his proficiency at organization to arrange and lead the Maine Press Association's annual excursion that year, as he had done for the previous three years.

The excursion, which led several members of the association to the disaster at Mount Desert Ferry, had started in Portland the previous Monday, July 31, when a delegation of that city's newspaper representatives and their wives left by rail for Bangor. Meeting the rest of the state's delegation there, the group of forty-six association members left the city for Machias, where they spent Tuesday. On Wednesday they visited Calais, where they were entertained at the St. Croix Club, which was managed by the father-in-law of one of the Maine newspapermen. Thursday was spent in St. Andrews, New Brunswick, followed by a return trip to Maine, visiting Eastport, Lubec, and other places along the rail line.

While on this particular excursion, Mr. Robbins's nephew, also named Chester Robbins, would run the *Old Town Enterprise* in place of his uncle. The younger Robbins ran the following paragraph in the August 2, 1899, edition of the newspaper, in the middle of his uncle's trip: "The Maine Press excursion this week over the Washington County RR to Machias, Calais and Eastport has been a very enjoyable trip, so writes the editor of the ENTERRPISE, who will furnish in the next issue a more extended account."

At the end of the weeklong excursion, on Saturday, the forty-six members of the Maine Press Association arrived in Ellsworth via the Washington County Railroad. During the day they were driven about town, then brought to the Nicolin Hotel at about 5:00 p.m., where a light meal was served. In the evening, through the courtesy of the managers of the Morrison Comedy Company, the group attended a performance at Hancock Hall. The association members described themselves as highly pleased with the treatment they received.

Saturday night was to have been the conclusion of the weeklong excursion for the members of the Maine Press Association. The twenty-six members who returned home Sunday morning as originally planned made the correct decision in hindsight. The remaining twenty, however, opted for one more adventure. Chester Robbins and nineteen other members of the Maine Press Association excursion party decided that being so close to Bar Harbor, and with the trip so convenient, the chance to see the victorious North Atlantic Squadron was just too good to pass up, and soon they were waiting at the Ellsworth train station that Sunday morning along with the many other people from that city.

"It was twenty of this party of forty-six who decided to stop over at Ellsworth and visit Bar Harbor on Sunday. Thirteen of the twenty were among the unfortunate two hundred who were precipitated into the water by the breaking of the slip," wrote Mr. Robbins in his newspaper after the disaster.

The twenty members of the Maine Press Association and their guests waiting at the Ellsworth train station that morning were:

- Horace E. Bowditch, forty-four, *Kennebec Journal*, Augusta.
- Mr. and Mrs. R. M. Campbell, Ellsworth. Mr. Campbell was the editor of the *Ellsworth Enterprise* and owner of the Campbell Publishing Company.
- Mr. Charles F. Flynt and his wife, Ida. Mr. Flynt was the editor of the *Kennebec Journal*. He had just joined the Maine Press Association that year.
- Arthur E. Forbes, thirty-seven, editor of the *Oxford Democrat*, South Paris. Mr. Forbes would be the last owner of the *Oxford Democrat*.

- Charles B. Haskell, thirty-three, and his wife, Alice, thirty-two, of Pittsfield. Mr. Haskell was the editor of the *Pittsfield Advertiser*.

- Louis O. Haskell, thirty, and his wife, Etta. Mr. Haskell worked on the *Pittsfield Advertiser*. He is believed to be a cousin to Charles Haskell.

- George D. Loring and his wife, Anna, both forty-six, of Portland. Mr. Loring was a printer and bookbinder.

- Mr. and Mrs. Jesse H. Ogler of Camden. Mr. Ogler was the editor of the *Camden Herald*.

- Mr. C. W. Robbins and his wife, Rachael, both thirty-one, of Old Town. Mr. Robbins was the editor of the *Old Town Enterprise*.

- Mr. Chester M. Robbins, nephew of the *Old Town Enterprise* editor, Chester W. Robbins, who joined the party in Ellsworth specifically for the trip to Mount Desert Ferry.

- Miss Grace Gatchell, twenty-one, Old Town. Miss Gatchell was a guest of Mr. and Mrs. Robbins.

- Fredrick M. Thompson, *Courier-Telegram*, Portland. Mr. Thompson would become the proprietor of the Thompson Art Co. and was well known in the art world.

- Mrs. F. H. Thompson, Portland. Mrs. Thompson was Fredrick Thompson's mother.

- Mr. Charles E. Williams, thirty-nine, Portland. Mr. Williams was with the printing firm Harris & Williams Job Printers.

When the train from Bangor arrived in Ellsworth, the members of the Maine Press Association embarked somewhere between the first and middle sections of the train. Those twenty people found themselves without seats—by now it was standing room only on the crowded train.

From Ellsworth it was just ten more miles of track. Normally these railroad tracks transported affluent people from faraway places, people whose disproportionate wealth and resultant way of life was bedazzling, as portrayed on the society pages of the newspapers every day.

The people on the 8:25 a.m. train and the people of Bar Harbor's wealthy summer colony had one thing in common—each would make just one trip to Mount Desert Island that year. The difference was that for the members of Bar Harbor's summer colony, for whom the rail line had been built, their one trip to Bar Harbor would last for the entire summer. For the people of Bangor, Ellsworth, and other areas of Maine that day, their special trip to Bar Harbor would have to end by the time of the day's last train, in order to be home for the beginning of the workweek the following day.

On this Sunday, however, the Waukeag Line of the Maine Central Railroad, including the elegant *Sappho* waiting at the wharf, belonged to the everyday person of Maine. Today they were the Astors and the Rockefellers. Today they were President Harrison.

As the train left the Ellsworth station for the last ten miles of the trip, the crowd aboard maintained their spirit of joy and merriment, though they were growing anxious to reach Mount Desert Ferry and to be first on the *Sappho*. The anxiety was due in part to a rumor.

At some point, as the two engines and eleven passenger cars of the 8:25 train carrying 1,300 passengers rumbled over the forty-two miles of track between Bangor and Mount Desert Ferry, a rumor had begun circulating among the passengers that there would not be enough space on the steamboat *Sappho* to take the entire load on its hourly run to Bar Harbor. In fact, according to the rumor, there would only be space enough on the *Sappho* to take one-third of the 1,300 train passengers.

Taking one look at the people standing crammed in the aisles and hanging from the steps outside the train made the rumor seem quite believable, whether true or not.

"This news spread rapidly through the train," reported the *Bar Harbor Record*.

The rumor that started on the train that morning would complete a chain of events that had started two months previously, with the building of a new gangplank at Mount Desert Ferry.

The passengers on the train were anxious to be on the first ferry crossing Frenchman Bay. Under ideal circumstances, even if the entire load of train passengers could travel on the first ferryboat, the 1,300 passengers would not arrive in Bar Harbor until after 11:00 a.m. Half the day would be gone by the time they stepped off the *Sappho* onto the island.

Like most rumors, no one quite knew where it started. All in all, though, the origin of this bit of misinformation really did not matter to those who were about to witness and experience the gruesome events that followed.

Whether the rumor was true or not cannot be pinned down with certainty. The Maine Central Railroad seems to have been an honest company. However, after years in business, its executives had become experts at public relations. They knew how to carefully pick and choose their words.

Franklin Wilson, president of the Maine Central Railroad, said in an interview after the disaster that he thought there was no necessity for anxiety on the part of the train passengers. He disputed the estimated number of passengers on the train, saying that only 968 tickets had been sold. He said the company had arranged for all the water transportation necessary to transport the passengers of the train, and a good deal more. President Wilson told the press that three steamers had been put in service by the Maine Central Railroad to accommodate the extraordinarily large crowds anticipated for the trip back and forth to Bar Harbor that day.

Technically there were three ships available for the transport of passengers. The first transport ship, the *Sappho*, was at the wharf and was the ship scheduled to carry all the passengers from the 8:25 train. The *Sappho* had a capacity of 1,200 people.

In addition, a second ship, the *Sebenoa*, was also at the wharf. The older *Sebenoa* was capable of accommodating four hundred passengers. There was also a third ship, which was on call in Bar Harbor. For the passengers of the 8:25 train who might be forced to rely on the third ship, it would mean a delay of forty minutes, at the very minimum, as the ship chugged across Frenchman Bay to Mount Desert Ferry.

Though Mr. Wilson's claims of the passenger capacity that morning were technically true, there were some problems with the railroad's arithmetic—whether the number of passengers was 968 or 1,300.

Regardless, it would take time for the *Sappho* to load 1,200 passengers. For those who would have to wait for the second ship, the *Sebenoa*, this would mean waiting for the *Sappho* to depart the wharf and the *Sebenoa* to take its place, and for the gangplank to be again properly positioned and arrangements made to take on the remaining passengers.

The other problem with the calculations is that there were many people already on the wharf waiting to board the *Sappho*, who had arrived before the 8:25 train. The visit of the North Atlantic Squadron, so soon after its victory at war, was a huge draw for Maine's blossoming tourism industry. All weekend private boats were pressed into service, their owners taking the opportunity to earn extra money to make it through the upcoming winter. Passengers had been landed at Mount Desert Ferry all weekend long, including Sunday morning, in conjunction with *Sappho's* departure and arrival schedule. Also waiting were guests of The Bluffs, the resort hotel at Mount Desert Ferry, many having come to the hotel specifically to make a weekend out of the event.

The 8:25 train out of Bangor began approaching Mount Desert Ferry at 10:20 a.m., thirty-nine minutes after leaving Ellsworth, and almost two hours after leaving Bangor.

Despite the lateness of the train, the rumors, and the general discomfort of the overcrowded passenger cars, or perhaps because of it, the mood aboard the train was described as celebratory as it approached Mount Desert Ferry. The passengers were nearly to Bar Harbor, and there was relief in the air that the trip was almost over, at least for the ones lucky enough to board the *Sappho* before it was full.

The train rounded the last small corner along the tracks in Hancock, and Mount Desert Ferry hove into view. As the train was arriving, arrangements to receive passengers had been completed aboard the *Sappho*, and railroad officials were just opening the gates to the gangplank for the passengers already waiting on the wharf.

Arriving at Mount Desert Ferry and seeing people already boarding the *Sappho*, combined with the general excitement of the day and the rumor that had circulated on the two-hour train trip, had an unsettling effect on the anxious passengers of the 8:25 train. There were already too few spots on the *Sappho*, and they appeared to be dwindling by the second, right before their eyes.

"The 8:25 train out of Bangor was crowded to the platforms, and it rolled into this station about 20 minutes behind the scheduled time of arrival," wrote the *Boston Globe*. "It at once became apparent to the excursionists that they could not all go to Bar Harbor in the *Sappho* at one time and then began the mad rush to get aboard in order that not one minute of the anticipated pleasure at Bar Harbor should be wasted."

The rush for the gangplank began even before the train had come to a stop.

The layout of the wharf structure at Mount Desert Ferry, though not flawed, contributed to the cause and enormity of the disaster that Sunday morning.

The wharf at Mount Desert Ferry was somewhat unusual in that it was built to run parallel with the shore, not running directly out from shore into the water as did many docking systems. The wharf had two slips that ran from the wharf into the water, at which the steamships would dock. A gangplank would be run directly from the wharf to the steamship that was being loaded, between the two slips.

The term "slip" can be confusing. In 1899 the slip meant the gangplank. Today it refers to the wooden structure that ran from the wharf to the water, at which one end of the steamer would rest during loading.

The wharf was two hundred feet long and sixty feet wide, built over the water of wooden pilings covered with planks. The railroad tracks ran down the middle of the wharf. Trains came to rest just before reaching the end of the wharf, which had heavy bumpers built onto its farthest end to stop any runaway train from going directly into the water.

The wharf at Mount Desert Ferry had been designed with the convenience of its high-society passengers in mind. On the shore side of the tracks on the wharf was the long freight depot, and on the water side the passenger depot. The positioning of the parked train left the passenger coaches under a wooden shed-like structure with a wooden awning overhead as protection against the moody coastal Maine weather. The unusual layout allowed train passengers to conveniently disembark directly onto the wharf, just a few feet away from the gangplank that led to the *Sappho*.

The wood and metal gangplank, which the passengers crossed from the wharf to the awaiting ferry, was thirty feet long and ten feet wide. The part over which the passengers would walk was made of two-inch wooden planks. Five four-by-twelve-foot timbers, set vertically, ran the length of the gangplank underneath, as did three metal rods, attached by bolts at the ends of the gangplank. The gangplank was hinged on the wharf end, and the ship end was supported by pulley chains, by which it was raised and lowered to suit the tides.

On this Sunday morning, the end of the gangplank that lay on the deck of the *Sappho* had quite an incline, as the tide was high.

At the other end of the gangplank, so tantalizingly close to the arriving train passengers, lay the elegant steamship *Sappho*. Maine Central Railroad had built a number of steamships specifically for the Mount Desert Ferry–Bar Harbor run, made especially luxurious for their elite Summer Colony clientele. The 140-foot *Sappho* was the best appointed of these vessels. Designed specifically for the short trips between Mount Desert Ferry and Mount Desert Island, she had no staterooms. The passengers whom the *Sappho* normally carried were considered living history.

The Maine Central Railroad had known how popular the excursion trains were going to be that weekend. Company president Wilson said that when it became known that the warships were to be at Bar Harbor on Sunday, the railroad made every arrangement to accommodate the expected large crowds who wished to avail themselves of the special-excursion rates. General superintendent Morris McDonald was directed to travel from Portland to Mount Desert Ferry on Saturday to take personal supervision of operations that weekend in anticipation of the extraordinarily large crowd.

According to Mr. Wilson, careful instructions were sent during the week to all employees of the railroad to do everything in their power for the comfort of the visitors. The trains moved with the greatest regularity and everything seemed to be going along like clockwork, noted Wilson. It was not until the early excursionists left the cars and began to cross the gangplank at Mount Desert Ferry that any trouble began.

"At this spot things took a most serious turn," said Wilson.

On the wharf, officials of the railroad and travelers already waiting to board the *Sappho* watched in horror as passengers began jumping from the still-moving 8:25 train. "The many who wished to cross with the first, started a rush for the slip," reported the *Bar Harbor Times*. Wrote the *Waterville Mail*, "In that rush, death came."

According to President Wilson, general superintendent Morris McDonald, was on the wharf when the train arrived that Sunday morning, personally supervising operations to take care of the expected large crowd. He and the other railroad officials under him were in charge of the transfer of the excursionists from the train to the boat and made every arrangement to keep the crowd from rushing aboard the steamer and causing a panic. Mr. McDonald said there were four men at the entrance of the gangplank endeavoring to keep people orderly, and to make them walk slowly and in moderate numbers down the gangplank.

The crowd from the train had quickly covered the short distance from the wharf onto the gangplank, pushing and jostling each other good-naturedly but ever eager to be among the first to embark on the *Sappho*. "It was like a great flock of sheep, and everyone was trying to get on the steamer first," said Horace Bowditch of the Maine Press Association.

For many, the rush for the gangplank was just part of the fun and adventure of the morning. "Maine Press excursionists were right in the center of the crowd," said Charles E. Williams of the Maine Press Association. "We were all pushed and hustled along by the crowd and were in the best of spirits—laughing and joking amongst ourselves and planning for a pleasant day's outing over at the Harbor."

According to Mr. Wilson, the officers of the *Sappho*, when they saw how the crowd was acting, did everything in their power to check it. The mate and the crew of the *Sappho* tried to reason with the people and almost resorted to force to keep them back. But they just could not check the jostling, pushing crowds. In the rush of train passengers, the officers were swept back by the weight of the crowd. The herd mentality of the crowd had taken over.

Despite all efforts on the part of the employees of the railroad to persuade the passengers to move in an orderly way, the crowd surged onto the gangplank and began to board the *Sappho* with the "wildest kind of a rush." Many passengers began crowding under the railing of the wharf and jumped directly down onto the gangplank. People jumped over the sides of the *Sappho* and clambered onto the lower decks, while the living, seething mass of eight hundred to one thousand people still on the wharf were pushing and struggling to reach the boat slip.

Some blame for the impatience of the crowd was given to the angle of the gangplank, its ship end being extremely high due to the high tide that day, which slowed down the ship's embarkation process.

For the first of the passengers reaching the gangplank, things were still merry. Some passengers were singing; others were calling to friends and family, many of whom were separated in the rush from the train. The merriment started to ebb, however, as the gangplank became full of people. For the passengers near the wharf-side entry of the gangplank, the impatient among them were clamoring for more haste in getting aboard the *Sappho*. They continued to try to push onto the gangplank themselves. "[T]hose anxious to be first aboard crowded on to the platform of the slip until there was not room for any more to squeeze in. Those in the rear of this torrent of humanity pushed and yelled for those ahead to move on," wrote the *Boston Globe*.

The people who were crowded on the gangplank, now in danger of being crushed or pushed into the water below, called to those still swarming on the wharf to wait. Singing and laughing started to give way to calls of frustration and concern.

It has been estimated that anywhere from a few to two hundred people had made it aboard the *Sappho* by this time, with another two hundred people packed together like sardines on the gangplank, and the remaining six hundred to nine hundred people trying to push their way aboard the gangplank, anxious not to be left waiting at the wharf.

"Don't push!" cried those on the end of the gangplank nearest the wharf, who had no place to go. They began trying to push the crowd on the wharf back from them, but they were no match. The inpatient crowd on the wharf continued to push their way onto the gangplank.

Suddenly, from the gangplank came a slight quiver and then the harrowing sound of grinding timbers.

"All at once it seemed to me as though the slip was settling beneath my feet, and it was slow at first and I scarcely thought anything of it," said Mr. Williams. He added that members of the Maine Press Association excursion noticed an unusual commotion in the center of the slip, where they stood, while frightened faces were seen to turn quickly and frantic struggles were made by those in the center of the crowded gangplank to turn back toward the wharf, which was quite impossible given the crowd on the wharf pushing to get onto the gangplank.

A second later there was a loud sound that rang throughout Mount Desert Ferry, a snap, like the breaking of a chain, but very loud, like the firing of a cannon.

Witnesses described that the sound was followed by a woman's scream: "For God's sake give way, the slip is breaking!"

The Deadly Rescue

The terrible scene of the next few moments is indelibly printed on the minds of all who witnessed it.

—Ellsworth American

Two hundred people, feeling the gangplank giving way under their feet but trapped by the crowd, had no place to go but down.

The first few shrieks quickly swelled into a chorus of cries coming from the center of the gangplank as the people standing at the breaking spot disappeared from view into the cold waters below.

"The slip broke with a noise like a boiler explosion, and nearly every one's first thought was that the engine boiler of the ferry steamer had blown up, and the boat hands rushed in that direction. In a second, however, a terrible shout went up and one of the most frightful scenes ever witnessed was seen," wrote the *Boston Globe.*

With the center of the structure broken, the ends of the gangplank nearest the break started falling in the water. People who had already passed the center of the gangplank but had not made it onto the *Sappho* started to slide down to the break in the gangplank, their feet futilely attempting to stem the tide and to ascend the inclined plane, which every instant grew steeper and steeper. Some people were left clinging to the broken gangplank, the broken ends now poking down into the water.

Approximately a dozen people were able to jump directly from the gangplank to the side of the *Sappho*. Mr. J. H. Deahan and Mrs. Dutyl of Bangor caught hold of the side of the steamer when the slip broke and hung there until pulled aboard. Horace Ashley of Sullivan, who was the summer gardener at another coastal resort hotel, the Kimball House in Northeast Harbor, was on the gangplank when the crash occurred. The shock threw him off his feet, but he was able to land on board the *Sappho*.

Those who had been lucky enough to have crossed safely to the *Sappho* turned to see the long slip, black with people, part in the middle and the struggling crowd fighting and clawing one another in a desperate effort to not disappear into the deep water around the pilings.

On the wharf side of the broken gangplank, the passengers on the structure were horrified at the gaping orifice before them, through which so many had already fallen. They attempted to keep their feet from sliding to the hole, to hold themselves on the edge of the precipice. Their effort was in vain.

When the break occurred, the people at the shorter, steeper end of the break, on the steamer side, were the first dropped into the water. The larger end of the broken gangplank, the wharf side, was at less of an incline, and when the passengers on that end started sliding and falling into the water, they landed on top of the people who had been thrown in from the steamer side of the break.

"It was only the matter of a second and the landing stage had been completely cleared of people and the broken parts swung easily on their hinges, forming a V shaped opening, through it could be seen the many terrified excursionists fighting for life," wrote the *Bar Harbor Record*.

The crowd on the wharf, numbering approximately nine hundred, was so dense and eager to board the *Sappho* that people just twenty feet away from the gangplank did not at first know what had happened. Those who had witnessed the disaster cried out, "[T]he people are overboard," in an attempt to stop the pushing. Those in the back of the crowd mistook the screams and cries of distress for horseplay and continued their merry shoving, sending more people from the side of the wharf into the water. Approximately fifty people were accidentally pushed into the water after the breaking of the gangplank.

The 250 people thrown into the water were all desperate for escape. They were penned in by the pilings of the wharf at one end, the *Sappho* at the other, and the pilings of the two slips of the wharf on each side. As described earlier, the pilings of the slips and wharf were boarded over with planking. With the high tide, giving the water in the pen a depth of sixteen feet, there was too much water to simply stand up, and too much distance from the top of the water to the wharf to simply climb out to safety. The pilings of the wharf were covered with moss and algae and made smooth and slippery by the daily tides, making them impossible to climb. There was an opening between the wharf's pilings that had not been covered with boards, but that opening was toward the bottom of the pilings and underwater.

The victims were penned into a very small cage. In their panic they clutched one another in an instinctual, deadly fight for life. Due to the concentrated area of the disaster, the crowd on the wharf and the *Sappho* were forced to watch the death struggle unfolding in front of them. "The terrible scene of the next few moments is indelibly printed on the minds of all who witnessed it," wrote the *Ellsworth American*.

Many in the crowd instantly fled the danger of the wharf, fighting their way through the crowd and away from the horror unfolding in front of them. "The pen was filled with people, and only those near the slip knew what had happened. Many of those who saw the crowd thrown into the water were so horror-stricken that strong men, as well as women, lost their presence of mind and all fought like demons to get away from the danger. People went mad with fear; back in the crowd still safe upon the wharf men struck out, leaving the scene, right and left fighting their way from the terrible sight," wrote the *Boston Globe*.

For almost a full minute, the remaining 1,000-plus people left on the wharf and on the deck of the *Sappho*, watching the 250 men, women, and children clawing for their lives, failed to register what was happening. "People left on the wharf were stupefied, failing at first to realize the enormity of the tragedy they were witnessing," wrote the *Portland Daily Press*. "The awful nature of the accident was not comprehended for at least a minute by those who were the last to leave the train although the scene changed instantly from one of holiday gaiety to a death struggle."

From the pen of struggling victims, wails from the women and children mingled with the hoarse shouts of men. The enormity of the accident soon started to register with the crowd, and the desperate cries for help from those in the water brought those who were ashore back to their senses. Once the gravity of the situation was realized by the crowd, the wharf and the *Sappho* became wild with excitement.

"Indescribable confusion prevailed," said the *Boston Globe*.

In the panic, the initial, unorganized rescue attempts were responsible for some of the deaths that occurred in the pen. People on the wharf began to throw heavy items such as planks and deck chairs into the pen. These wildly thrown items struck those struggling in the water, stunning them, and causing them to drown.

Two witnesses, Mr. Collier and Mr. Vance, told how one man and his wife fell into the water from the broken gangplank. The man managed to clutch a rope with one hand, and with the other seized his drowning wife's head as she came up from under the water for the second time. At the same instant, a plank was thrown from the wharf, which struck her across the forehead, sending her under the water for a third time, not to come back up. The deaths of two victims, Bertha Estey and Lillian Derwent, were attributed to these initial rescue efforts.

"They threw into the water whatever they could lay their hands upon. Some heavy lumber that was cast down struck people upon the head, stunning them. For the moment, any sensible attempts at rescue were forgotten and men looked on in a wild fashion at the many who were crushing down the weaker in the watery hole of death," reported the *Bar Harbor Record*. "All sensible attempts were forgotten."

A few brave fellows initially stripped off their clothing and plunged into the water to assist the weaker victims, but their attempts were unavailing and dangerous, for the drowning ones clutched at them and endeavored to pull them down. It soon became apparent to those on the scene with more level heads that a better-organized rescue effort would need to be launched to prevent more of the unnecessary deaths that were occurring and to be effective at saving as many of the 250 people as possible.

According to many sources, it was Capt. Edgar Dickson of the *Sappho* and other Maine Central Railroad employees who started and were most effective in the rescue effort on the *Sappho* side of the pen. "[T]he cooler heads in the crowd, more especially among the officers and crew of the steamer, asserted themselves and the work of rescue began," wrote the *Portland Daily Press*.

Captain Dickson and Frederick Sanborn of Portland, the conductor of the 8:25 train, organized a rescue party from the crews of the *Sappho* and *Sebenoa*. In a few minutes, ropes, ladders, and deck chairs were extended out from the *Sappho* to the terrified men, women, and children in the water. As each instrument was grabbed by a person in the water, that person was pulled to safety as quickly as possible.

Captain Dickson and Mr. Sanborn found a ladder, which they extended over the side of the deck of the *Sappho*. While the two men held each side of the ladder, sixty people were eventually able to climb to the safety of the ship.

The strain on Captain Dickson and Mr. Sanborn was extensive. Many of the sixty people they rescued with the ladder were too weak to climb it on their own, so the two men would pull up the ladder until one of them could reach down and drag the person to the deck. As some of the victims reached the safety of the ladder, their weight would be added to by two or three other victims grabbing hold of the person trying to climb to safety. The two men were often attempting to pull up the weight of two or three water-logged, panicking persons at a time. The muscular strain was so great and the act such a feat of strength that Captain Dickson and Mr. Sanborn suffered considerably from their efforts. After all the living had been rescued, it was said that Fred Sanborn was so tired and stiff he could barely move. His body and arms were a mass of bruises and cuts. Captain Dickson was described as being in not much better shape.

"The station employees and railroad men are working like Trojans, while the crew of the SAPPHO are saving many lives, pulling people from the water with boat hooks and oars and throwing life preservers in every direction," wrote the *Bangor Daily Commercial*.

The hero of the rescue on the wharf side of the pen was Chester W. Robbins, editor of the *Old Town Enterprise* and leader of the Maine Press Association expedition.

Chester Robbins was one of the thirteen members of the press association who went into the water with the breaking of the gangplank. He had been able to escape the water quickly. Instead of heading for the warmth and safety of The Bluffs Hotel, just one hundred yards away, where the other survivors were being taken, the newspaper editor decided to strip off his clothes, grab a rope, jump back in the water, and start pulling people to safety. Chester W. Robbins was not going to leave anyone behind.

The key to successful rescue efforts on the wharf side of the pen involved setting up an efficient operation. Planks were held down from the wharf to the people in the water, who were kept afloat that way. As fast as possible, a man in the water brought a rope to each person clinging to a board, tied the rope around them, and the person would be pulled to the safety of the wharf. The rope would be untied and lowered into the pen again and again.

"When C. W. Robbins of the Old Town Enterprise, who had a narrow escape from falling into the water himself, saw the extent of the accident, he hastily stripped off his outer clothing and climbed down through the mass of broken timbers and planks to the surface of the water, and then tying a rope around his chest descended into the center of the strife," wrote the *Bangor Whig and Courier*. "One by one he would take persons, tie a rope around them and let them go, and by the time one head reached the wharf, Mr. Robbins had another supported, ready to be lifted on to firm footing. It was estimated by other workers in the rescue that fully thirty bodies, conscious and unconscious, were brought out the well in this way."

Many people who had been submerged underwater found themselves under the wharf when they came up for air. The pilings on the outside of the wharf had planking over them except at the bottom. Though they were safe from the other struggling passengers under the wharf, the area held its own danger. It was dark, and the cold, wet, tired, and traumatized train passengers who found themselves there clung desperately to the smooth pilings, hoping that the last of their strength would hold out until it was their turn at rescue.

With the major rescue operations being conducted by Captain Dickson at one end of the pen and Chester Robbins at the other, individual groups of people were doing what they could. Among the rescuers who risked their own lives were the men of Hancock, the home of Mount Desert Ferry.

William Jellison, thirty-five, of Hancock was employed at Mount Desert Ferry as a freight agent. The accident was unfolding in Grant Cove, almost at the spot where Grant Cove met Jellison Cove, which was named after William Jellison's ancestors.

Mr. Jellison was described as being one of the first to begin the rescue work by throwing a rope to the drowning. The rope was not effective, as it slipped through the hands of the people who tried to grasp it. Mr. Jellison next procured a ladder, which was let down into the pen and became the means of saving many lives. His actions in beginning an effective rescue effort were described as the impetus that snapped others at the scene into action. "One of the quick-witted among those on the wharf, William Jellison, baggage master at the station, ran for a ladder. Jellison is an old sailorman, and the ladder he thought of was the most useful of all the things brought to aid the rescuers," wrote the *Boston Globe*.

Frank Kelly, twenty-eight, also of Hancock, was one of the brave men who voluntarily swam under the dark wharf to help rescue people. The danger in the pen was known; the danger under the wharf was not. Mr. Kelly saved eight people from the dark waters under the wharf.

"There were noble heroes and cool heads in that crowd of excursionists," wrote the *Ellsworth American*. "Men who, more fortunate than their fellows, succeeded in reaching a place of safety, risked again their lives, and in more than one instance lost theirs for the sake of others. The stories which could be told of the deeds of heroism in those terrible minutes would fill many pages."

The people that became unexpected rescuers that morning came from all over the state. The heroics of those passengers from Bangor were documented in that city's major newspaper, the *Bangor Daily Commercial*.

Charles F. Ward, fifty, of Bangor was one of the fortunate people who had made it aboard the *Sappho* before the gangplank broke. Mr. Ward saw boards being thrown into the pen and knew people would be killed that way. He asked for a rope but did not get one. Mr. Ward said everybody in his vicinity seemed to be completely paralyzed with fear.

Mr. Ward took matters into his own hands. He broke in the door of a closet on the *Sappho* that contained ropes, bringing them to the deck for use in the rescue. According to the *Bangor Daily Commercial*, Mr. Ward, an ex-alderman of the First Ward for that city, was one of the modest heroes of the disaster at Mount Desert Ferry. "He hasn't said anything about what he did for humanity down there, but his friends are gradually finding out the truth," wrote the newspaper.

Lincoln G. Bragdon, thirty-eight, was a dry goods merchant from Bangor. He was aboard the excursion train with his wife and son. The Bragdon family were among the first people to go into the water when the gangplank broke, which meant many more desperate people toppled in on top of them. In the water, Mr. Bragdon was able to get ahold of his son. Suddenly, a large man grabbed the boy and tore him from his father's grip in a desperate attempt to buoy himself up in the water. Mr. Bragdon was able to rescue his son from the man, but in the struggle, Mr. Bragdon was separated from his wife and son. Eventually Mr. Bragdon was plucked from the water by means of a rope. His wife and son were nowhere in sight. For forty minutes it was thought that Mrs. Bragdon and the boy had drowned. Mr. Bragdon was described as being nearly insane with grief.

Dennis Sullivan, thirty-two, a telephone lineman from Bangor, stood at the side of the broken gangplank with a rope, one end of which was made into a noose, and this he lowered into the pit and with it took out seven or eight persons. The first one taken out was Mr. Bragdon's little boy. The noose of the rope was slipped under the boy's arms, and the strong arm of Mr. Sullivan pulled the boy safely to the wharf. Mrs. Bragdon was next saved. "It was noble work," wrote the *Bangor Daily Commercial*.

Both Mrs. Bragdon and her son were described as being "half dead" after they were pulled from the water. Later that day Mrs. Bragdon was able to tell her story. After Mr. Bragdon had been separated from the family, Mrs. Bragdon and her son had been able to stay together. They spied a board nailed to a piling on the outside of the wharf. They clung to this board for more than half an hour before being rescued by Mr. Sullivan.

Mrs. Bragdon bore up well under the severe shock until she reached her home in Bangor. There, she broke down and couldn't sleep without crying out and experiencing again all the sensations of drowning.

Charles H. Adams, thirty-nine, of Bangor, and his wife had just entered the gangplank and were able to get back on the wharf as the gangplank fell into the water. Mr. Adams started instantly for a neighboring pile of boards, secured one, and reached it down to those below in the water. John H. Stone, a Bangor merchant, was the first to catch hold of the board, but then two others also took hold of it. Mr. Stone finally got onto a ladder by himself, but was so exhausted that he was unable to get onto the wharf without assistance.

Charles McAvey, thirty-five, of 178 Date Street in Bangor ran a grocery store and bakery. He had been injured in a Maine Central Railroad accident in Orono two years previously. Mr. McAvey was later described as having behaved with conspicuous bravery and coolness in the disaster at Mount Desert Ferry, being among the most prominent of a band of men who were instrumental in the rescue of twenty people.

Corey Tingley, nineteen, who was employed by grocer Fred T. Hall in Bangor, showed great heroism and rescued nine persons unaided. Mr. Tingley was reported to be in the water from the time the accident happened until twelve o'clock, more than an hour.

Charles H. Parsons, twenty-seven, of Houlton, conductor on the Bangor and Aroostook Railroad, found himself in the pen after the breaking of the gangplank. After extricating himself from the mass of bodies in which he found himself, he worked to save the lives of several other people.

Howard Stone, a well-known young Bangor man who was employed at the Maine Central Railroad ticket office in that city, succeeded in getting four people to safety.

Blanford Greene, twenty, of Brewer was a guest staying at The Bluffs. Blanford was credited with risking his life by going into the water with a piece of rope and saving a dozen or more people. He also assisted in recovering several bodies.

Other men from Bangor who helped save lives and restore consciousness to those who were brought ashore included E. C. Ryder, an alumnus of the Waterville Classical Institute; George S. Chambers, one of Bangor's best-known citizens at the time, who was active in the lumber business and served as the treasurer of the Eastern Maine Music Festival; John M. Oak, who was active in Republican politics; an unnamed farmer from Aroostook County, who was credited with saving eight lives; and Miss Gertrude Veazie, twenty-four, of Bangor, who was described by the *Bangor Daily Commercial* as being "one of the few women who succeeded in saving other lives besides their own."

Gertrude Veazie was born in Bangor and was a graduate of Bangor High School. After graduation she went into the shoe business, graduating from the Cousins School of Salesmanship and Service in New York. She received her early training from G. E. Homestead, a well-known shoe distributor in Bangor. After several years at the Homestead store, Miss Veazie became associated with the E. C. Nichols Company, where she advanced to the position of shoe buyer.

In later years, after the disaster, Miss Veazie would serve as the superintendent of the Good Samaritan Home in Bangor. She was active in her community, working with young people at the Second Congregational Church at South Brewer. Miss Veazie served on the Bangor Business and Professional Club and acted as the collector of the annual membership fees for the Brewer Free Public Library Association, her duties including going door to door to collect the library's annual one dollar membership fee.

Miss Veazie was accompanied on the excursion train that day by her sister, Mrs. Bright, and a companion. They all went down when the gangplank broke. After falling into the pen, Miss Veazie could see that her sister was unable to stay above water and was drowning before her eyes. Miss Veazie made her way through the struggling crowd, reaching her sister and her companion, and keeping them above water until rescue came from the wharf.

Gertrude Veazie was one of the last people taken alive from the water that day.

Thirteen members of the Maine Press Association who had traveled to Mount Desert Ferry had been in the center of the gangplank when it broke and found themselves in the middle of the water. In addition to Chester W. Robbins of the *Old Town Enterprise*, other members of the association were also hailed as heroes.

R. M. Campbell, editor of the *Ellsworth American*, was credited with saving nearly a score of people from watery graves. "Mr. Campbell of the Ellsworth Enterprise was another of the heroes of the day, for he, like Mr. Robbins, was active in saving life and I think that it would be difficult to say which of the two saved the most lives," wrote the *Bangor Daily Commercial*.

Mr. Jesse H. Ogler, editor of the *Camden Herald*, was credited with doing effective work in the rescue operation. Mr. Ogler was stationed on some broken timbers under the wharf, from where he helped rescue passengers struggling in the water. Mr. Ogler was reported as being "seriously depleted" from his rescue work and received medical care at The Bluffs.

Charles Flynt of Augusta was the owner and publisher of the *Kennebec Journal*. He and his wife, Ida, were in the center of the gangplank when the accident occurred and were thrown into the middle of the seething mass of people. Mr. and Mrs. Flynt clung together desperately, struggling to keep each other above water. The two were able to grab a plank, either nailed to a wharf piling or extended from the wharf by a rescuer above, and they found the strength to sustain each other until rescued by Mr. Robbins.

"I suppose I was in the water but a few minutes but it seemed half an hour at least," said Ida Flynt. "Mr. Robbins certainly saved my life as I could not have stayed above the surface much longer when he thrust a plank under me. I had an arm about my husband and gave him some support by placing my foot under his leg. With the assistance of the plank, we were able to keep up until we were hauled out by the people on the wharf above us."

Charles Williams, a newspaper printer from Portland, saw Mr. Flynt holding up his wife, who he described as a large woman, and also keeping above the water a young lady who was with them. Mr. Williams described Mr. Flynt as being not a robust man. Mr. Flynt saved both women and refused to leave the water, despite chance after chance to do so, until he had saved three or four more women near him. "This nearly cost him his life," said Mr. Williams.

Mr. Flynt was unconscious when rescued from the water and carried to The Bluffs. That night he was too sick to be seen, and he was one of fifteen disaster survivors to spend the night at The Bluffs Hotel due to their medical condition.

Mr. Flynt later stated that his sensations were extremely difficult to describe, but that he expected every minute in the pen would be his last.

The Lack of Doctors

*Spaulding was as near dead as he ever will be and get back again, and
30 minutes of work on him were required before a feeble groan suggested the rekindling of the dying spark. He had an immense amount
of water inside, but at the end of an hour and a half he had revived
sufficiently to say, "O, for heaven's sake, let me alone."*
—Boston Globe

Those who fell into the water were pulled out mostly by the sheer human
strength of those lucky enough to remain safely on the wharf or on the
Sappho. The pen itself had been cleared of survivors within approximately
thirty minutes. Many people were still stuck under the wharf, clinging
desperately to the slick pilings for life. That portion of the rescue would
go on for a full hour.

Pulling the 250 people out of the water at Mount Desert Ferry was
just the beginning of the rescue effort. "As fast as the people were pulled
from the water, they received such attention as their case required. The
injured were taken to Hotel Bluffs. Many taken from the water were
brought back to life only after much work over them," wrote the *Ellsworth American.*

From the water, the survivors went one of three places. Those who were
simply wet and bedraggled walked to The Bluffs Hotel, just one hundred
yards away overlooking the train station. Those suffering from physical or
psychological injuries were carried on cots or escorted to the hotel.

Those survivors who required immediate lifesaving medical attention were treated on the wharf and shore of Mount Desert Ferry. Many in this group of people had water in the lungs from their immersion in the water and were unconscious, some nearly dead. Of those who were able to be revived, it was only after much difficulty.

The third set of survivors included those who had been rescued on the *Sappho* side of the pen. Due to the broken gangplank and lack of opportunity to reposition the *Sappho* at the other slip, those rescued by the *Sappho* were required to stay aboard the ship and complete the voyage to Bar Harbor, regardless of medical condition. Among the survivors aboard the *Sappho* were three women who died during that crossing.

All the survivors were described as being "exhausted from their struggles and nearly all the women suffered nervous collapse," wrote the *Boston Globe*. "Every attention was given them, however, and all that was possible was done to aid the unfortunates."

Railroad officials at Mount Desert Ferry quickly sent telegrams and made phone calls to Bar Harbor, Ellsworth, and Bangor, requesting any available doctors to report to Mount Desert Ferry as quickly as possible. Upon hearing the news, Maine Central Railroad president Franklin Wilson, who was at his summer home in Bar Harbor at the time of the accident, gave orders to the employees of the Maine Central Railroad to expend the utmost exertion in relieving the distress of the victims of the disaster.

The remote nature of Mount Desert Ferry, which was its blessing, was now also its curse. The town of Hancock and the surrounding areas on the mainland, including Ellsworth, had no medical facilities other than a few local doctors. Maine Coast Memorial Hospital, which would have been only ten miles away by train, would not be built for another fifty-seven years. Blue Hill Memorial Hospital would not be built until 1922.

There was a hospital on Mount Desert Island. The Bar Harbor Medical and Surgical Hospital was built in 1898, just a year before the disaster. The building was forty-six by eighty-four feet, with a capacity of only ten beds, five in private rooms. Though this new hospital was a symbol of Bar

Harbor's growth, its limited capacity was not capable of handling all 250 victims of the disaster at Mount Desert Ferry. Though not recorded, the new hospital in Bar Harbor may have played a role in the treatment of survivors who traveled aboard the *Sappho*.

Mount Desert Ferry was on its own.

With no other options, the people at Mount Desert Ferry and the guests at The Bluffs Hotel took matters into their own hands. They were determined to do all they could to save the lives of the people that fate had thrust into their charge.

There were four doctors known to have been on the scene when the disaster occurred, one of them a dentist. All four had arrived at Mount Desert Ferry on the 8:25 train. Two of them had been thrown into the water with the breaking of the gangplank, one of which was injured.

Dr. Frank Whitcomb was a dentist in Orono. Along with his wife, Ella, and son, Robert, and some friends, Dr. Whitcomb was on his way to Bar Harbor to visit relatives. The Whitcomb party found themselves in the water after the breaking of the gangplank. Though badly injured, Dr. Whitcomb saved his wife and son and two other women. Dr. Whitcomb and his family would continue the trip to Bar Harbor, where Dr. Whitcomb stayed an extra length of time due to an injury to his knee suffered in the accident, ambulating with the use of crutches. Whether Dr. Whitcomb was able to provide medical care at Mount Desert Ferry is not recorded.

Dr. Watson S. Purington of Bangor had been out of medical school less than a year when he was pressed into service at Mount Desert Ferry. A graduate of Dartmouth College, Dr. Purington, along with his fiancée, Miss Nellie Jenness, were crossing the gangplank to the *Sappho* when the accident occurred, and they were plunged into the water. Dr. Purington was able to grasp a beam that was connected to the wharf. While clutching the beam he guided four persons, including his fiancée, to safety. Dr. Purington and Nellie Jenness were among the last of the survivors pulled from the pen that morning. After recovering sufficiently from his own experience, Dr. Purington went to the aid of the survivors in The Bluffs, working all day and night with them.

In an interview with the *Bangor Daily News* in 1962, Dr. Purington, then eighty-nine years old, said he hoped that he would never again have to go through as tragic an experience as the one at Mount Desert Ferry.

Dr. William P. McNally, thirty-two, of York Street, Bangor, was on the excursion train but had not been on the gangplank when it broke. Dr. McNally not only provided medical assistance on shore but remained at The Bluffs overnight to render the medical attention required by the fifteen survivors who were too ill or injured to move home that evening.

Dr. Ora Pease, fifty-three, of Old Town had been on the special excursion train but was spared from going into the water. Dr. Pease quickly went to work directing the resuscitation efforts of those pulled from the pen with water in their lungs, many near death.

"George Spaulding, came very near entering death's door, but was finally brought too under the care of Dr. Ora S. Pease, of this city, who was instrumental in resuscitating several who were taken from the water," wrote Chester W. Robbins in the *Old Town Enterprise*.

Some people were not breathing when pulled from the water due to the water in their lungs. The laborious work of resuscitating victims was soon going on all over the station platform.

The accepted practice at the time for treating a drowning victim was rolling them over a barrel. Though barrels no longer have a place in the modern, box-based world, the large, wooden, keg-shaped items, filled with cargo mid-transit, were in abundance at Mount Desert Ferry that day. A description of this technique was provided in an article appearing in *Modern Swimming* magazine, titled "How to Resuscitate a Drowning Victim":

- First, be quick; lose no time; every second counts in the race with death.
- Second, loosen all clothing.
- Third, lift the body between you, with the head hanging down . . . grasp it by the upper arms with a good hold and seize the front part of the legs with the hands by passing the arms between them.

- Fourth, shake the body up and down two or three times so as to free the mouth and nostrils from slime and water.
- Fifth, place the victim upon his back.
- Sixth, draw the tongue well forward and tie it with your hand-kerchief so that it will not fall back and block the pharynx, thus choking the individual and making all your efforts useless.
- Begin artificial breathing, by taking hold of the forearms . . . and drawing them up and back of the head. Have your assistant place his hands upon the lower sides of the chest and . . . have him press the chest walls well in, releasing the pressure when the arms have reached their destination. . . . The arms should be moved with precision and regularity at the rate of from sixteen to eighteen times a minute.
- As soon as respiration is natural . . . give him access to all the fresh air possible. Do not talk or smoke around him.

A shipment of flour had been received at the Mount Desert Ferry freight depot the day before the accident. Capt. Henry N. Fairbanks, a guest at The Bluffs who had been on the wharf at the time of the accident, along with half a dozen other men, ran to the freight house and rolled out the barrels of flour, upon which the victims who were half-drowned were rolled until revived or declared dead.

Under the care of Captain Fairbanks and Dr. Pease, George Spaulding of Orono was one of many people saved from death this way. Mr. Spaulding, who weighed 240 pounds, was rolled by Captain Fairbanks and three other men under the supervision of Dr. Pease. They worked on Mr. Spaulding for more than an hour. "Spaulding was as near dead as he ever will be and get back again, and 30 minutes of work on him were required before a feeble groan suggested the rekindling of the dying spark. He had an immense amount of water inside, but at the end of an hour and a half he had revived sufficiently to say, 'O, for heaven's sake, let me alone,'" reported the *Boston Globe*.

Another man active in the resuscitation efforts that morning was William Miller, forty-five, of Bangor. Mr. Miller was a partner in the successful hardware firm of Rice and Miller, which had been in business in Bangor for 107 years. That hardware store would become part of Bangor history thirty-eight years later when members of the Brady Gang, who were on the FBI's Most Wanted List, tried to purchase guns there shortly before being shot to death in the street in Bangor.

Mr. Miller and his family, including his wife, Alice Bowler Miller, were passing their Sunday at The Bluffs when the accident occurred. Mr. Miller quickly joined in the lifesaving efforts, dragging five people out of the pen. One young woman that Mr. Miller brought out from under the wharf was nearly dead, and Mr. Miller saw at once that immediate action was necessary. The woman was Kate Fahey, who was employed as a domestic in the family of L. C. Tyler, of Tyler, Fogg & Company of Bangor.

Without waiting for a barrel to roll her on, Mr. Miller lifted Miss Fahey from the ground by her heels and held her in the air, allowing quantities of water to run out from her lungs. After a time, she regained consciousness and was taken to the hotel for further care. Miss Fahey's escape from death was described as one of the narrowest of the morning. Though surviving the water in her lungs, at The Bluffs attention was turned to the internal injuries she had sustained in the disaster.

Mr. Miller, along with Samuel R. Prentiss, who had been aboard the *Sappho* at the time of the disaster, succeeded in bringing at least five people back to life through the barrel-rolling technique.

When the 250 people fell into the water, the *Sappho* was both a blessing and a curse. Her positioning blocked any rescue by the small boats that were in the area. Also, because of her position at the slip of the wharf, she acted as a fourth wall to the pen, forcing those on the wharf and on the ship's decks to witness the hideous event.

The blessing of the ship's placement was in preventing any survivors or dead bodies from floating out to open water, likely never to be found. The *Sappho*'s placement also gave her a perfect position from which to conduct rescue efforts.

Anyone pulled from the pen by the *Sappho* is assumed to have been kept aboard the ship, regardless of their condition. There was simply no way back to shore. The gangplank for this slip had been ruined, and the *Sappho* could not be moved to the other slip without costing lives in the ongoing rescue effort.

After everyone had been removed from the water, living and dead, the *Sappho* left the slip and began her trip across Frenchman Bay. The *Sappho* was described as being full of passengers when it finally departed Mount Desert Ferry. On board, many of the people rescued from the water were taken to the ship's engine room, where the heat from the machinery would help warm them and dry their clothing.

Three of the survivors pulled from the water died on the way to Bar Harbor, where medical care awaited them: Miss Grace Sumner, one of the two children to die in the accident; Miss Elizabeth Ward; and Mrs. Lillian Derwent.

The injured at Mount Desert Ferry required further medical care. For those who survived the water uninjured, immediate care was needed to prevent potentially deadly side effects from the prolonged exposure to the fifty-eight-degree water and water in the lungs. Many survivors had further bodily injuries, and most were in a state of shock and hysteria from the events in which they had just been involved.

The staff of The Bluffs Hotel, the elegant coastal resort just one hundred yards away from the wharf, rose to the challenge that the disaster had created.

The Bluffs was being run that season by Peter Cuddy and George Bemis. Between them, they had several years of experience as hoteliers. Mr. Bemis had served, at different times, as the proprietor of The Bluffs at Mount Desert Ferry; the Millinocket Exchange and the Great Northern Hotel, both located in Millinocket; the Mount Kineo House at Moosehead Lake; and the Bangor House—all leading resort hotels in of their time.

On the wharf at the time of the accident was proprietor Peter Cuddy. Mr. Cuddy quickly sent all hotel staff currently on the wharf to return to the hotel for cots, beds, blankets, and sheets. He also gave directions to the staff for dispensing stimulants, assumed to mean hard alcohol, on a Sunday. Mr. Cuddy was among those credited with saving several lives through his generosity with the hotel's facilities.

This was the height of the summer season, and the handsome hotel was filled with guests, many of whom were at the wharf when the accident happened. This being The Bluffs' fourteenth year in service, and staffed by many of the self-reliant, dependable year-round residents of Hancock, the hotel's employees quickly sprang into action, along with the hotel's guests.

The lobby of The Bluffs became the triage center. The dining room became the emergency room. The hotel guests quickly and voluntarily gave up their rooms for use as hospital rooms for those who had been physically and mentally injured. One group of guests became a corps of nurses. Another group began collecting dry clothing for the wet, cold survivors.

Normally Sunday was a special day at The Bluffs, with its traditional Sunday dinner served in the early afternoon. People would make a day trip on the Maine Central Railroad just to partake of the meal. At the time that the gangplank broke, the staff inside The Bluffs was preparing for the famous dinner, a time of bustling activity inside the hot kitchen. The kitchen staff quickly transformed the busy space into a warming station and treatment facility.

Both the hot and cold food, in various states of preparation for the upcoming dinner, was moved aside to heat water for medical use and for hot drinks. The hotel's cooks began building extra hot fires in the hotel's kitchen. The hotel's chef went to work making hot drinks of coffee, pepper tea, ginger, and other ingredients to warm the insides of the chilled survivors. Soon the drenched survivors started coming through the kitchen doors to dry out and warm up. They had just undergone extreme physical exertion and mental trauma, and many were hysterical. The people at The Bluffs Hotel did all in their power to give aid and comfort to the survivors.

The staff and guests of The Bluffs had transformed the elegant resort hotel into a hospital in just a matter of minutes.

As survivors were still being picked out of the pen, an impromptu corps of amateur nurses drawn from the guests of the hotel was being organized by fellow hotel guest Susie Train Hand. The gruesomeness of that Sunday morning was ironic for Mrs. Hand, as this was the first day of her honeymoon.

Susie Train was the daughter of Capt. Charles J. Train, commander of the battleship *Massachusetts*. The *Massachusetts* had sailed into Bar Harbor on Thursday, ahead of the rest of the North Atlantic Squadron, allowing Captain Train to be at his daughter's wedding.

Miss Train had married Augustus Noble Hand of New York. Mr. Hand was a thirty-year-old private-practice lawyer in New York City, having graduated from Harvard five years previously. Mr. Hand would go on to serve as district judge of the US District Court for the Southern District of New York, and later was a US circuit judge of the US Court of Appeals for the Second Circuit. After their wedding ceremony in Bar Harbor on Saturday, Mr. and Mrs. Hand headed to The Bluffs, known for its quieter way of life compared to Bar Harbor, to start their honeymoon.

While Mrs. Hand was organizing the nurses and preparing for the injured, her new husband headed to the wharf to offer assistance there. Mr. Hand was described as being conspicuous as a lifesaver at the wharf. The Hands had also been among the first to throw open their apartments for the use of the injured. The newlyweds were described as being among the hardest of the workers among the guests of The Bluffs.

As The Bluffs whirled with the activity of preparation, those on staff who did not have an active hand in those preparations reported to the lobby to await the injured. They did not have long to wait. As soon as the survivors were plucked out of the water, those who could walk and did not need resuscitation or immediate first aid were directed, assisted, or carried to the hotel. Some just required a hot or a stiff drink, dry clothes, and the warmth of the kitchen fire to ward off the effects of the water's chill. Others were physically injured and required more involved medical care. Some just needed a private room to process all that they had just seen and experienced.

The *Boston Globe* described the survivors as being "exhausted from their struggles and nearly all the women suffered nervous collapse" immediately after being pulled from the water. Though that description fit a stereotype of the time, many men were also in a state of hysterics and shock.

"The frenzied shriek of the dying, the agonizing fear and terror on the faces of the drowning, going hopelessly to death with life and hope only a few feet away, the wailing of the wives or mothers who suddenly found loved ones, who but a few short minutes before were glowing with life and happiness and love for them, rigid in death, these are not sounds or sights that can be banished from memory by any human volition," wrote the *Bangor Daily Commercial.*

As the survivors started arriving at The Bluffs, Mrs. Hand went to work administering to the needs of the sufferers. Among those who benefited from Mrs. Hand's generosity were Miss Gertrude Veazie and Mrs. Lincoln G. Bragdon and her son, all from Bangor. Mrs. Bragdon and her son were said to be "half dead" when finally rescued from the water forty minutes after the breaking of the gangplank. Mr. Bragdon was described as being insane with grief, thinking his wife and son had drowned. Miss Veazie had been one of the last to leave the water, refusing to leave until her sister, whom Miss Veazie was helping keep above water, had been rescued. Mrs. Hand gave up her room to them, provided blankets, hot water bags, and medicine, and gave them every attention, for which they later expressed profound gratitude.

In nearly every room at one time in the afternoon were from one to three of the rescued people. Many just needed the warmth of the blankets and the beds of those rooms, and the seclusion they offered. The nurses went from room to room, offering whatever assistance required. They also provided food to the hungry. Nora Fairbanks, whose father was on the shore performing barrel resuscitations, cared for five half-drowned persons at one time. Mrs. James K. Chamberlain, whose first name was possibly Jane, spent the day caring for the injured, and during the night had three patients under her charge. The impromptu nursing corps was described as most efficient at rendering aid to the injured. All the guests willingly assisted in the work attending to the survivors.

Among those guests of The Bluffs not already mentioned who were especially energetic in caring for the victims of the disaster were Mrs. Abbie Fairbanks, Mrs. William L. Miller, Mrs. J. M. Oak, Mrs. E. C. Ryder, Mrs. Irene Stratton and her daughter, Ethel, Freeland H. Libbey, and Gen. and Mrs. Joseph S. Smith.

Mr. Cuddy reported having sixty-two injured people at the hotel at one time on Sunday. He reported fifteen of those were in such severe shock or so injured as to render them helpless. Many others, he stated, were in a dazed condition, but had not been in the water. "A young girl, address unknown, kept repeating a name. A man from Orono was in critical condition, with head injuries. A matron from Ellsworth was in severe hysterics," wrote a reporter at the scene.

As word of the disaster spread quickly around the town of Hancock, storeowners and residents started arriving at Mount Desert Ferry with food and supplies. Mr. Bemis and Mr. Cuddy estimated they fed three hundred people after the disaster and burned two cords of fireplace wood drying out the victims and their clothing.

The proprietors and guests of The Bluffs were described as indefatigable in their efforts to make all the sufferers comfortable. The rescued all spoke in high praise of the hotel's landlords and guests. The saving of many lives was credited to the efforts of The Bluffs. "[T]o the chef and to the guests at the hotel, the saving of a great many lives may be accredited," said Frederick Thompson of the Maine Press Association. "The water was intensely cold and everybody suffered from chills when they were taken out, and had it not been for the hot drinks, the warm beds and the splendid attention at the hotel, the death list would have been much larger."

One somewhat amusing scene did occur at The Bluffs during the morning. Chester W. Robbins did not leave the wharf until all the living had been rescued, long after the twelve other members of the Maine Press Association had been saved from the pen. Exhausted from his efforts, weakened by the prolonged immersion in the cold Maine water, Mr. Robbins made his way up the one-hundred-yard path to The Bluffs Hotel, perched on the small hill of land after which it had been named.

Mr. Robbins, the dedicated tour leader, needed to know if the members of his excursion, many of whom were personal friends, had all been rescued. Having stripped off his clothing during the rescue effort, Mr. Robbins walked into the lobby of the grand hotel clad only in a pair of wet underwear.

"He was the most noteworthy hero of the day, credited with saving all the way from eleven to 30 persons. It must have been nearly an hour after the disaster that he came up the hill to the hotel, where the half-drowned people were getting dried and thawed out. He had on nothing but the underclothes in which he had been in the water for a long time but showed no signs of exhaustion while checking on his party by the fireplace in the lobby of The Bluffs," wrote Maine Press Association survivor Arthur Forbes of the *Oxford Democrat*. "The only sign of excitement that he displayed was an intense joy that our party had all got out safely, it seemed to be all that was on his mind."

Besides the four doctors who were already at the scene of the accident, no additional medical help would arrive at Mount Desert Ferry for half an hour after the breaking of the gangplank, and then just one doctor. George Phillips, MD, of Ellsworth arrived at the disaster scene shortly after 11 a.m.

As the story goes, having received the telegraph in Ellsworth, presumably at his office there, Dr. Phillips was able to telephone ahead to the railroad station and ask them to hold the next train for him, which they did. Dr. Phillips then hurried to the station.

He arrived at Mount Desert Ferry at about the time that the majority of the living had been pulled out of the pen and others were starting to be rescued from under the wharf. The doctor was quickly immersed in the life-and-death struggle occurring on the shores of Mount Desert Ferry, providing direct medical care, and supervising and instructing the civilians who were also giving aid. Dr. Phillips was credited with saving many lives that Sunday morning.

Though the arrival of Dr. Phillips was greatly welcomed, it was not nearly enough help. Another hour would pass after his arrival before additional medical help reached Mount Desert Ferry.

The passenger steamship *Cimbria* had sailed from Bar Harbor with the four doctors and two nurses who had responded to Maine Central Railroad's urgent telephone call, hurrying to the wharf there to board the steamship. It would be the hurried nature in which the doctors and nurses arrived at the wharf and embarked on the *Cimbria*, combined with the *Sappho* not arriving in Bar Harbor at her regular time, that initially raised alarm at the Bar Harbor Public Landing that something had gone horribly wrong at Mount Desert Ferry.

By the time the *Cimbria* arrived at the scene of the disaster in Hancock, all the live survivors had been pulled out of the pen and from under the wharf. The doctors and nurses from Bar Harbor immediately joined in the medical effort, working with those already providing the lifesaving resuscitation efforts on the shore and helping with the other injuries and hysteria that now filled the elegant interior of The Bluffs Hotel.

On board the *Cimbria* were Dr. George R. Hagerty, thirty-three; Dr. Charles C. Morrison, forty-two; Dr. Elmer Morrison, thirty-six; and Dr. D. W. Bunker—all of Bar Harbor. The Misses Stewart, two nurses who were visiting Bar Harbor from Philadelphia, were also aboard. "After receiving the distress call from Mount Desert Ferry, the *Cimbria* was arrived in exceedingly quick time," according to the *Bar Harbor Record*, "reaching Mount Desert Ferry about 12 noon with doctors and surgeons. At once the doctors and nurses from Bar Harbor began to work upon those taken out of the water in whom the spark of life still lingered. They gave external application of heat, applying hot water bags, hot irons, etc. also hypodermics of strychnine and digitalis."

The saving of several lives was directly credited to the arrival of these medical professionals from Mount Desert Island.

At the beginning of the disaster, Maine Central Railroad general superintendent Morris McDonald had sent orders from Mount Desert Ferry to Bangor for a special train with every necessity for the care of the injured. In a short while that train was under way from Union Station in

Bangor, with nine very necessary doctors and an equally necessary nurse aboard.

Among the Bangor doctors were Drs. C. D. Edmunds, forty; W. C. Mason; Eugene B. Sanger, twenty-eight; E. A. McCullough; Daniel McCann, thirty-two; W. H. Simmons, fifty-one; J. K. Phillips; C. A. Gibson; and E. T. Nealley. The physicians were accompanied by Miss Roberta Logie, twenty-two, a nursing student at Eastern Maine General Hospital. Miss Logie was reported to have been of much assistance to the doctors whom she accompanied.

Waiting anxiously at the station in Ellsworth for the train from Bangor were three doctors and a nurse, all of whom had responded promptly to the urgent telegram requesting assistance from the Maine Central. Their haste was for naught, however. In order to save time, the emergency train from Bangor passed the station at Ellsworth without stopping, not realizing more doctors were waiting there. It would be half an hour before another train picked up the waiting physicians in Ellsworth and delivered them to Mount Desert Ferry.

The physicians on the Ellsworth train, when it finally did arrive, were:

- Dr. Daniel Brown of Ellsworth and Brockton, Massachusetts. At one time Dr. Brown co-owned two of the blocks in downtown Ellsworth: the Waverly Building and the Black Building. His father was the dean of the Hancock County Bar Association.

- Dr. Lewis Hodgkins of Ellsworth. Dr. Hodgkins was prominent in Ellsworth, both in his role as a physician and as a well-known businessman. A graduate of Bowdoin College, Dr. Hodgkins would practice medicine in Ellsworth for forty years and served as the city's mayor for three terms. He was well respected by his fellow Ellsworth physicians.

- Dr. Nathan C. King, forty-five, of Ellsworth, who served as the president of the Ellsworth Board of Trade in addition to actively practicing medicine.

The three doctors from Ellsworth were accompanied by Miss Harriet Rolfe, a graduate of the Eastern Maine General Hospital nurses' training program in Bangor, who boarded the train at Ellsworth thinking that she might be of service. Miss Rolf was described as having rendered valuable service at the scene of the disaster, some witnesses describing her efforts as heroic. All Sunday afternoon and evening she labored unceasingly taking care of the injured.

Miss Rolf's work that Sunday would come at a cost to her health. The Wednesday following the disaster, Miss Rolf suddenly took ill with congestion of the spine, caused by overexertion caring for the dead and dying at Mount Desert Ferry. "A new victim, indirectly, of the accident at Mt. Desert Ferry, was added to the list last Wednesday when Miss Harriet Rolf, of Bangor, a trained nurse who did such heroic work at the Ferry, was taken suddenly with congestion of the spine, at the home of Mr. and Mrs. I. L. Halman, where she was visiting," reported the *Ellsworth American*. "For several days her condition was critical, but she now seems to be steadily improving, the strain undoubtedly brought back a spinal trouble from which she had recently recovered."

The Freight House Morgue

*The scenes about the wharf and hotel were heart-rending. People were
hunting for lost friends; and about the freight shed, which was used as
a morgue, were the hysterical, almost crazed crowd of people.*
—CHARLES WILLIAMS, SURVIVOR

Prior to the building of the ferry and railroad terminal and all its associated facilities, Hancock was a small, quiet farming and fishing community. There were few homes, mostly land. Family names from the time of the disaster are still found in the area today.

The small point of land in Hancock that contains so much history is called McNeil Point, named after its former owner, William McNeil. McNeil Point would change hands over the years until it caught the eye of the Maine Central Railroad, which noticed its position on the coastline, bordered on two sides by open water, with breathtaking views of Frenchman Bay and Mount Desert Island and close proximity to Bar Harbor.

The town of Hancock is best known as the location where two German spies landed during World War II in a plot to hamper US war efforts. The two spies came ashore on November 29, 1944, at Crabtree Neck on Hancock Point, landed by a German submarine. The Germans had chosen the area in part because of how close the submarine was able to get to the Maine coast. The men walked five miles to US Route 1, hailed a taxicab that was returning from the naval base in neighboring Winter Harbor, and eventually made their way to New York, where they stayed for a month before being captured.

Some people in Maine, mostly from Bangor, had discovered the seclusion and scenery of Hancock long before the Maine Central Railroad. A handful of wealthy families from that city had built summer homes in the town before McNeil Point became Mount Desert Ferry. Along the shore, hidden among the trees, could be found the large, inviting structures, some still in use today. The places were large in comparison to a native Mainer's summer camp, but small in comparison to Bar Harbor's "cottages."

With the instant success of Mount Desert Ferry in 1884, the rural town of Hancock found itself the terminus of the Waukeag Line, the Maine Central Railroad's most important and profitable branch. The people of Hancock would find their lives being transformed as fast as the land on McNeil Point. "Where solitude once reigned supreme, there arose a bustling rail terminus serving Mount Desert Island," wrote Sanford Phippen, president of the Lois Johnson Historical Society of Hancock and a noted author. "The Ferry became a little 'city' all by itself."

Mount Desert Ferry was a place of beauty, both natural and man-made. The passenger facilities there had been designed for the upscale clientele who traveled on the Bar Harbor Express to Mount Desert Island to begin their summer season at their cottage or at one of the grand resort hotels that lined the island.

The railroad station was painted green on the outside. Inside, the station's main feature was its elaborate waiting room, which was large and beautifully decorated. The room featured a great open fireplace with a mantelpiece made of oak and large brass andirons. Black walnut armchairs and settees provided comfortable seating. Beautiful stained-glass windows provided light during the day, and at night elegant chandeliers lit the room.

Adding to the elegance and ambience of Mount Desert Ferry was The Bluffs Hotel, built just one hundred yards away from the railroad tracks, atop a small hill.

The Bluffs was a summer coastal resort built in 1885, one year after the Maine Central Railroad opened Mount Desert Ferry. The hotel was privately owned and operated, but because it sat on land leased from the Maine Central Railroad and was situated just one hundred yards from the ferry and train station, it was generally considered part of Mount Desert Ferry.

The Bluffs was a large, cedar-shingled Queen Anne–style building with over one hundred guest rooms when originally built. The building possessed a coordinated array of gable and dormer roof shapes, a surrounding stick-construction veranda, balconies, and a unifying end-wall octagonal tower with an open observation deck, the tower a common feature of many Maine coastal hotels of that time. "The view of the Mount Desert heights from the hotel windows and verandas is magnificent," wrote the *Bangor Daily News*.

The Bluffs Hotel was built by Bangor engineer and contractor Francis H. Clergue, originally from Canada. Mr. Clergue was the builder of the Summit House, a resort hotel that sat atop Cadillac Mountain, then known as Green Mountain, on Mount Desert Island. The Summit House, or the Hilltop House, as it was known, had been built five years before The Bluffs Hotel, in 1880. The Bluffs, along with its several cottages, overlooked the main ferry wharf and the waters of Frenchman Bay.

After its opening, The Bluffs quickly became a popular spot. The resort was touted as an ideal recreation and health resort. "Seashore and country combined" read one of The Bluffs' advertisements. "Send for booklet and special rates." Fred Johnson of Bangor was the first proprietor of the hotel.

The Bluffs was furnished with every amenity expected from a first-class resort hotel, including gas and running water, with hot and cold baths. Guests could summon hotel staff by use of an electric bell system. For communications, there was telegraph and telephone service, and a post office, with its own zip code.

"Of its several late nineteenth century hotels, The Bluffs was the largest and most impressive," wrote Bryant Franklin Tolkes in his book *Summer by the Seaside: The Architecture of New England Coastal Resort Hotels*.

"The Bluffs, Mt. Desert Ferry, Maine. Families, Tourists and Invalids will find The Bluffs one of the most beautiful spots on the coast of Maine to spend their vacation. Everyone delighted who has ever visited it," said an advertisement in the July 21, 1886, edition of the *Bangor Daily Whig and Courier*. "The house is new, the scenery unsurpassed, the dining room large and cheerful, and the table has the reputation of being the best east of Boston. Very low prices will be made to families of two, five or more. Gentlemen single, from $7 to $10 a week. For two gentlemen or two ladies occupying one room very low prices will be given."

The Bluffs took advantage of the rolling hills and fields of the immediate area of McNeil Point, the beauty of which was enhanced by the coastal setting and view of Mount Desert Island. A lawn was available for tennis and croquet. Open fields adjacent to the hotel, called The Groves, were ideal for expansive activities such as baseball. Swimming, boating, and fishing were popular with visitors of The Bluffs, with facilities provided for each activity.

Guests at the hotel were able to watch lively scenes played out daily. Trains and steamships, loaded with passengers and freight, were constantly coming and going, with as many as seven trips a day. Among the people being brought to the ferry on the trains were nationally and internationally prominent people headed to Mount Desert Island for the summer, their stories known from the daily newspapers. Guests could thrill at the sight of extravagant private railroad cars attached to the trains, and private boats arriving from Mount Desert Island to pick up guests. The Schieffelin family, regular summer colonists at Bar Harbor, purchased a special, well-appointed boat just to greet guests coming off the train at Mount Desert Ferry in the summer.

The clientele at The Bluffs was varied. The hotel catered to many of Bangor's new white-collar class, and also to the people of whom that class was in charge. While those two groups of Bangor's new society might briefly rub elbows at The Bluffs, it was their length of stay that set them apart. For the white-collar guests, who ran Bangor's industry, the stay at The Bluffs would be an extended one, from a weekend to the entire summer. For the blue-collar workers, who were providing the human labor essential to Bangor's industry, the visit was generally for the day, taking part in one of the many Sunday special excursions provided in cooperation between the coastal resorts and the Maine Central Railroad.

Some people chose to spend their extended summer holidays at The Bluffs in Hancock to avoid Bar Harbor's busier and more crowded way of summer life, opting for the quieter Mount Desert Ferry. The lively and social Bar Harbor was just an hour away by ferry if they so desired. Though Bar Harbor provided beautiful views, so did Mount Desert Ferry. And Bar Harbor could never provide a view of itself as could the coast of Hancock.

Once opened, the rooms, cottages, and facilities of The Bluffs often were booked many months in advance. There was always something going on at The Bluffs. Private dining rooms hosted special functions. The grounds were always in use by large groups. Every Saturday night there was a grand dance, accompanied by an orchestra.

Sunday dinner at the Bluffs was especially memorable. On Sundays, dinner was served from 12:30 p.m. to 2:00 p.m. People would plan their Sunday excursions around the time of the dinner. The menu was extensive, as listed in a story from the *Bangor Daily News*:

The Sunday Dinner:

Soup: Clam Chowder. Beef bouillon in cups. Queen olives. Sliced tomatoes. White onions. Dressed lettuce. Chilled cucumbers.

Fish: Boiled Penobscot salmon. Boiled: Ferris Ham—New beet greens. Roasts: Rib of Beef—Dish gravy, Sirloin of Beef—Brown gravy, Lamb—Brown sauce, Ribs of Pork—Apple Jelly.

Entrees: Italian fritters. Vanilla foam sauce. Baked macaroni au fromage rice.

Vegetables: New boiled potatoes. Mashed potatoes. Butter beets. Green peas. Sweet corn.

Relishes: Worcestershire sauce. Mixed pickles. French mustard. Tomato catsup.

Pastry and Dessert: Baked custard pudding. Chocolate ice cream. Perfection cake. Green apple pie. Strawberry shortcake. Whipped cream. Lemon meringue pie. Water crackers. American cheese. Milk. Coffee.

Mount Desert Ferry became part of the life not only of the people of Hancock, but of the entire region. The people of Bangor especially enjoyed the area. The willingness of the Maine Central Railroad to provide special fares to large groups of people to reach The Bluffs made the coastal resort hotel a popular location for the annual retreats of several service organizations and businesses in Bangor and the surrounding area.

Large community-service organizations flourished during this time in history. Statewide organizations had local chapters in most Maine towns. Participation in these groups offered an opportunity to provide assistance to the community and socialization among its members. For many of these organizations, and for many large employers in Bangor, it became tradition to spend their yearly summer retreat at The Bluffs. In 1887, two years after The Bluffs opened, the St. John's Episcopal Society of Bangor, the Universalist Sunday School of Bangor, and the Hammond Street Congregational Society and Sunday School were among the groups to use The Bluffs for their annual daylong retreat.

These excursions were large. Some organizations sold tickets to non-members as a fundraiser for their charitable work. One such excursion was the Annual Excursion and Field Day of the Maine's Knights of Columbus, hosted by the Pine Cone Council, Knights of Columbus, Bangor. The day of the event was July 4.

The excursion was open to all members of the state organization. A committee had been appointed to take charge of the event and was reported as "making every effort to make this the most notable event occurring at that famous resort this season," according to the *Bangor Daily News*. On the day of the excursion, the attendees from the upriver towns arrived in Bangor at 6:55 a.m., leaving at 7:30 a.m. They returned to Bangor by special train immediately after the completion of the excursion in the evening.

Events for the day included a baseball game between the St. Joseph Council and the Pine Cone Council of the Knights of Columbus, an amateur one-hundred-yard dash, a one-hundred-yard dash for boys under fifteen, a sack race, a potato race, and a hammer-throwing contest, among others. Generous prizes were awarded to the winner or winners of each event. Refreshments were served on the grounds of The Bluffs, and the hotel offered dinner for fifty cents per plate. Free dancing was provided in the hotel's music room after dinner, provided by a band.

"No excursion in recent years has created so much enthusiasm in and about Bangor as the Knights of Columbus annual field day and picnic at The Bluffs on July 4," wrote the *Bangor Daily News*. "The sports are many and varied. The great event of the day will be the hose race participated in by all the fast teams in this section. As the sport in itself is exciting and holds the interest of the spectators from start to finish, it becomes doubly so when the contestants are animated by an intense rivalry such as exists between the following teams that have entered . . . there will be free dancing in the ball room of the hotel, with music by Hick's Orchestra. There will be no lack of accommodations for all wishing to get dinner on the grounds as manager Cuddy says he has made ample preparations."

The Fourth of July holiday was always especially popular at The Bluffs. The Independence Day celebrations held there would draw revelers away from other places that had once been popular for the holiday, including Ellsworth.

"The fourth of July was an unusually quiet day in Ellsworth," wrote the *Bangor Daily News* the same year as the Knights of Columbus celebration at The Bluffs. "At midnight there was the usual ringing of bells, blowing of whistles and firing of cannons, and during the forenoon the small boys kept firecrackers whizzing about, but for the most part the streets were deserted and all the stores closed, with the exception of the apothecaries. Numerous persons went out of town to the celebration at the Bluffs, Mount Desert Ferry," wrote the *Bangor Daily News* in 1900.

The Bluffs was always the place to be.

The beauty and opulence of The Bluffs, its quiet splendor and air of gaiety, gave stark contrast to the grisly scene unfolding around the hotel on Sunday, August 6, 1899. "The scene on the bluff after the accident was horrifying. Hysterical people laughed and cried and shouted. Men and women were hunting about for missing friends and women and men too fainted away by the score. To add to the horror of it all, was the constant passing of people bearing the unconscious and dead persons," wrote the *Portland Daily Press*.

As the last of the survivors were taken from the water and the recovery of the dead bodies began, the immediate frantic nature of the scene on the shore of Mount Desert Ferry quieted—all the living had been rescued. "As the work of rescue progressed, and nearly all those who were yet alive were taken out, the excitement began to subside," wrote the *Boston Globe*.

The excitement was quickly replaced with chaos. The last of the survivors were being triaged at the wharf. The wharf, shore, and train yard were filled with barrel-rolling resuscitations and other improvised lifesaving medical care. The *Sappho* was hastily preparing to leave the wharf, to seek whatever medical care was available at Bar Harbor for her load of sick, injured, and dying. The departure of the *Sappho* further separated families and groups of friends, who had already been shuffled like a deck of cards in the rush when disembarking from the 8:25 train. "Separation at that moment meant heart breaking suspense," wrote the *Portland Daily Press*.

Many of the train's passengers had been forced by circumstance to ride aboard the *Sappho* to Bar Harbor simply because they had been rescued on that side of the penned-in area. There were no means of immediate communication. The survivors who remained at Mount Desert Ferry made their way around the shore and hotel, trying to find their loved ones, knowing that dead bodies remained in the pen. "The scenes about the wharf and hotel were heart-rending. People were hunting for lost friends; and about the freight shed, which was used as a morgue, were the hysterical, almost crazed crowd of people," said Charles Williams of the Maine Press Association.

Now that all the living had been rescued, the rescue effort became a recovery effort.

An underwater diver arrived at Mount Desert Ferry at the same time that the last of the survivors were being pulled out of the water. The diver went to work without delay.

In 1899, diving was still in its infancy. The study of decompression sickness had just begun, and its life-threatening effects still were not totally understood. The state-of-the-art diving technology was the metal bell suit. A diver would get into the iron suit and then have an iron bubble helmet placed over his head and attached to the suit. The helmet had a small glass area for viewing, and the suit provided the diver with the ability to use his arms and hands, though clumsily. Air lines attached to the headpiece from a machine on shore provided the diver's necessary oxygen.

Divers were dispatched from the North Atlantic Squadron at Bar Harbor, as was Herbert Sturgis of Standish, who was working on a US government project in East Sullivan, eight miles away. They would arrive at Mount Desert Ferry throughout the morning and early afternoon to aid in the search for bodies.

Among the divers who served at Mount Desert Ferry that day and the following morning were Herbert Sturgis of Standish, Sam Crocker of Old Town, and Mr. N. T. Watson of Boston.

As the recovery effort began, an enormous crowd stood on the wharf and the shore watching the operation unfold, many waiting with anxiety for a glimpse of a missing loved one from among the dead.

Bodies were recovered from the main pen area before moving to the area under the wharf. When a diver found a body, he brought it to a small platform that had been made from the wreckage of the gangplank. From there the body was lifted to the wharf and taken to the nearby freight shed. "Body after body was taken out of the horrible trap, each being received with groans and cries as the eyes of bereaved relatives rested upon some beloved face," reported the *Bangor Daily Commercial*.

Ten bodies had been taken from the pen shortly after the recovery effort began. By 1:00 p.m., two hours after the accident, seventeen bodies had been recovered and were laid out on the floor in the Maine Central Railroad freight house. The three additional victims had been taken out alive and placed on the *Sappho* but died on the trip across Frenchman Bay.

"[S]eventeen bodies told the horrible story of the harvest of death," wrote the *Ellsworth American*.

The Maine Central Railroad freight house had turned into a makeshift morgue, the bodies recovered from the water being taken there as fast as they were pulled out of the water.

As the bodies were brought to the freight shed, doctors made one last attempt to bring back life where there was none. A few people were saved this way. Those who could not be brought back to life were laid to one side in the freight house and "tenderly covered with a sheet, to await identification," according to the *Bangor Daily Commercial*.

"Mt. Desert ferry was a sad looking place this afternoon," wrote the *Boston Globe*. "In the freight house lying on the floor and covered with cloths and blankets were the bodies of 17 victims."

All afternoon sad-faced men, women, and children who were missing loved ones sought admission to the temporary morgue to gaze upon the faces of the dead, to see if they could discern a friend or relation. "The scene here as the identification proceeded was a heartrending one, piteous in the extreme. Husbands or wives, brothers or sisters, entered tremblingly, fearing lest they should find what they sought. A low moan or sudden shriek would tell that their quest had been only too successful, and to those who were parted from no dear ones, the sight of those pallid faces with the dank hair sticking to the marble forehead, the foam flecked lips and glassy eyes, was no pleasant spectacle," wrote the *Bangor Daily Commercial*.

The men of the Maine Central did everything possible to assist the injured and to aid in the identification of the dead—two of whom worked for the railroad, a third being the wife of one of those two rail workers, and a fourth being the wife of a worker who went in the water but survived.

The body of Maine Central Railroad assistant baggage master George Bennett was identified by means of a railroad pass in one of his pockets, and that of Frank Sweetser, the head of the railroad's lost freight division in Portland, by a set of keys in his pocket.

The identification of the dead was reported to be slow in many instances, but by nightfall all but two of the bodies at the freight house had been identified by friends or relatives. "It was a gruesome sight and a most pitiful scene as identifications were made," wrote the *Portland Daily Press.*

After all the bodies in the freight house that could be identified had been, the coroner of Ellsworth, Dr. Dorpheus L. Fields, gave the necessary permission to have them moved. The bodies were made ready to be loaded into the caskets that were expected by train from Bangor that evening, while family members waited at The Bluffs to accompany the body of their loved one back to their home, from which they had left so merrily that morning.

Though it was known the next day that all the dead had been found, on Sunday afternoon many more were feared to be dead. Because many train passengers had been forced to sail to Bar Harbor aboard the *Sappho*, the list of missing people at Mount Desert Ferry was long. There was concern that the lowering tide had carried away some bodies, raising the troubling possibility that some victims might never be found. "There are yet many persons missing and the death list may yet be swelled to 30," wrote the *Portland Daily Press.*

The search for bodies continued all afternoon. None were recovered, but divers did find satchels, pocketbooks, articles of wearing apparel, and other personal effects, which were collected on the wharf.

For the rest of the day on the shore of Mount Desert Ferry, the anxious eyes of the crowd scanned the boats arriving from Bar Harbor for familiar faces, and gradually friends were united. With each reunion, names were taken off the list of missing, and by the following morning officials realized that all twenty of the dead at Mount Desert Ferry had been recovered on Sunday afternoon.

By 3:00 p.m. on Sunday, with the low tide exposing the floor of the cove, it was generally agreed by railroad and county officials, including the Hancock County coroner, that all the bodies that could be recovered had been. With no more bodies expected to be recovered that day, and with the identification process as complete as it could be, the county coroner began compiling an official list of the dead. "Given the circumstances, the confusion, the shock, the list, naturally contained some errors," wrote the *Portland Daily Press*.

The original list of deceased, telegraphed to newspapers across the country Sunday evening, contained the following incorrect names: Mrs. William Muzzey, Brewer, and Edward M. Fahey, Bangor. Louise Bridges's name was included on the list of deceased along with that of her brother, Irving Bridges, of Ellsworth and Hancock, respectively. Irving Bridges had died in the disaster, but all of his sisters, including Louise, and the rest of the party had survived, though were badly injured.

As word of the disaster was slowly making its way across the state, other people were reported to have been drowned in the disaster who had actually survived. "Many false reports have been received here of persons being drowned who have afterward turned up all right, and great distress has thereby been occasioned," wrote the *Portland Daily Press*.

Mr. Herbert A. Whitmore, twenty-five, of Bangor was a clerk for the financial firm of Blake, Barrows and Brown. Mr. Whitmore had been reported as missing after the disaster and could not be located Sunday night. Mr. Whitmore was found alive Monday morning, confined to his bed in his Bangor home. Mr. Whitmore had been in the water for some time before being rescued, and was sore and lame from his injuries.

With the list of deceased compiled and circulating across the state and the country, there were still two bodies on the floor of the freight house, unable to be identified by anyone at Mount Desert Ferry. Both were female. One was younger, and one was older and described as large and stout.

The first unidentified body was initially identified as Miss Louise Bartlett of Orrington. Louise Bartlett was the daughter of Alden B. Bartlett, a beloved resident of Orrington. Miss Bartlett had gone to Mount Desert Ferry that day and was in the middle of the gangplank when it broke. Finding herself falling, Miss Bartlett shut her mouth tightly and went down into the utter darkness of the water. Upon reaching the surface, a man helped her grasp a board. Miss Bartlett held on to the board until she was rescued. She was severely bruised and lost her *portemonnaie*, or wallet, containing quite a sum of money. She spoke in the highest terms of the kindness of the proprietors of The Bluffs, saying they showed her every attention.

Ultimately the body would be correctly identified as Miss Blanche Lewis, nineteen, of Hamden. Miss Lewis was identified by her brother-in-law in one of the undertakers' parlors in Bangor early Monday morning, after the bodies arrived from Mount Desert Ferry.

The second unidentified body ultimately was found to be Mrs. Margaret Mower, sixty-seven, who was a Mainer living in San Francisco, and who had been in the state visiting family.

That unidentified body was sent on the funeral train to Bangor Sunday night. After arrival, the woman was misidentified by an unknown source at the Finnegan undertaker shop as Mrs. G. W. Wyler, a book agent of 24 Dwight Street in Boston. Mrs. Wyler had been engaged in canvassing Maine for books for a Boston firm at the time of the accident. The confusion with the identification appears to have come from the fact that both women were from Boston. "A report was circulated that Mrs. G. W. Wyler, a book agent of Dwight Street, Boston, was numbered among the victims, but on investigation she was found alive and well," reported the *Boston Globe*.

When that identification was found to be a mistake, the body was then incorrectly identified as Mrs. John O'Donahue, of Bangor, the mother of a well-known Bangor police officer. After that misidentification was cleared up, the body was next identified as a Mrs. Sleeper of Bangor. This identification was also a mistake. Ultimately, Mrs. Mower's identification was made by H. G. Mower, of Dexter.

The Bar Harbor Public Landing was crowded with people even before the accident at Mount Desert Ferry. All of Bar Harbor, especially the wharf, had been extraordinarily busy the entire weekend with the impending arrival of the North Atlantic Squadron. People had been assembling at the town's wharf all morning. Many in the crowd were there to greet friends and family expected on the *Sappho* from the 8:25 train. Others were waiting to be ferried to the train at Mount Desert Ferry for their trip home.

After the breaking of the gangplank in Mount Desert Ferry, the first that was heard of the disaster was through the telegraph messages and telephone calls made by officials of the Maine Central Railroad to the towns of Bar Harbor, Ellsworth, and Bangor, requesting physicians to be sent immediately to the area. Inside the ferry terminal at the Bar Harbor wharf, railroad officials were making frantic phone calls to the doctors that were known to be in Bar Harbor that weekend.

On the wharf the large, unsuspecting crowd started to grow anxious as the scheduled arrival time of the *Sappho* came and went. The crowd's concern increased with the arrival at the wharf of the island's available doctors and a few nurses, who hurriedly embarked on the *Cimbria* carrying medical supplies.

The sight of the doctors and nurses confirmed the concerns of the five thousand people now assembled on the wharf—there had been some sort of accident at Mount Desert Ferry. Joy and merriment turned to fear and anxiety. Word started to spread around the small town of Bar Harbor, and soon the crowd at the wharf started swelling with even more people, all waiting for further news or hoping to find their loved ones when the *Sappho* eventually did arrive. "At Bar Harbor the greatest alarm and excitement prevailed for several hours, as only meagre particulars reached here concerning the accident," wrote the *Bar Harbor Record*. "News had run through Bar Harbor like wildfire and people were worried about relatives and loved ones expected on the *Sappho* from the 8:25 train. Both the summer people and year-round residents of Bar Harbor were tremendously excited. A crowd estimated to be as high as 5,000 people waited at the wharf at Bar Harbor."

Never had the *Sappho* been so anxiously awaited at the Bar Harbor Public Landing. "The news of the accident soon spread, and consternation was on every one's face. A few women became hysterical, and the large crowd could only wait with blanched faces and heavy hearts until definite news was received," wrote the *Boston Globe*.

When finally the *Sappho* did arrive in Bar Harbor, approximately an hour after her normally scheduled time, the crowd on the wharf could see that the ferry was not nearly as packed as it should have been. On board the *Sappho* were the passengers from the train who had made their way aboard the ship before the breaking of the gangplank, as well as the passengers who had been pulled out of the water by the rescuers on the *Sappho*. Many of those passengers still required medical care, blocked from obtaining more immediate help at Mount Desert Ferry because of the broken gangplank.

Among the survivors aboard the *Sappho* were two women and a girl, all three having been pulled out of the water alive but in bad shape. By the time the *Sappho* had reached Bar Harbor, two of them had already died: Miss Grace Sumner, fifteen, and Miss Elizabeth Ward, nineteen, both of Bangor.

The third person, Mrs. Lillian Derwent, was met by four doctors at the wharf in Bar Harbor, all summer residents who appear to have stayed behind in Bar Harbor to take care of the survivors brought aboard the *Sappho*. The doctors immediately went to work on Mrs. Derwent, who was reported to have arrived in Bar Harbor "with life almost extinct." They worked on her for two hours before pronouncing her dead.

The arrival of the *Sappho* with the injured confirmed the rumors circulating among the crowd at the wharf that there had been an accident at Mount Desert Ferry, and the three dead bodies unloaded on the wharf proved that the accident had been deadly. If there were three victims on the wharf at Bar Harbor, how many more were on the wharf in Hancock? The sight of the three bodies must have caused particular concern among the thousands of people at the Bar Harbor wharf who did not find their loved ones aboard that first trip of the *Sappho*, of whom there were many.

With the arrival of the *Sappho*, the spirit of festivity that had prevailed all week in anticipation of the arrival of the North Atlantic Squadron in Bar Harbor instantly evaporated. "The arrival of the *Sappho* somewhat allayed the excitement, as definite news was brought concerning the accident. The affair cast a terrible gloom over everybody, and there was little pleasure seeking or sightseeing today," reported the *Boston Globe*.

Many survivors arriving in Bar Harbor were still in a state of injury. The four doctors who had remained at Bar Harbor assisted them, and Maine Central Railroad officials provided what support they could. Still, because of the confusion of the afternoon, some of the injured arriving on the *Sappho* were lost in the crowd. Among them was Ludella Fogg, of Bangor.

Mr. Fogg was about twenty-one years old and was described as a young man of quiet disposition who worked on his family's farm. He had been on the gangplank when it broke. Ludella Fogg went underwater, and it was some time before he came to the surface, as he made no use of his legs for fear of kicking the people that he could feel underneath him. Mr. Fogg was rescued by means of a ladder that had been lowered from the *Sappho*, the lowest rung of which he could just reach with one finger. During the ordeal he swallowed much water.

Mr. Fogg had been separated from his aunt, with whom he had been traveling. The two had traveled to Bar Harbor aboard the *Sappho* immediately after the disaster without finding each other among the crowd on the ship. Arriving in Bar Harbor, Mrs. Fogg immediately set out to find her nephew, not knowing if he was alive or dead. Soon Mrs. Fogg found Ludella lying on the side of Bar Harbor's Shore Path, not far from the wharf where the *Sappho* had just landed.

Mrs. Fogg took her nephew home to Union Street in Bangor on the next train from Mount Desert Ferry, still dressed in his wet clothing. The following day Ludella Fogg was reported as being sick from the ordeal at his Bangor home. Mr. Fogg had lost his watch and some money in the disaster, and his hat.

The five thousand people at the wharf in Bar Harbor soon began clamoring to get across to Mount Desert Ferry in an attempt to find missing loved ones. The *Sappho* would arrive back at Mount Desert Ferry filled to capacity. By now all of the living had been plucked out of the water, as had most of the dead. The arriving passengers of the *Sappho* looked sharply for a glimpse of their loved ones among the still-crowded shore and hotel. Those who did not find the person they were looking for were directed to the freight shed on the wharf to look at the seventeen dead bodies there.

The arrival of the *Sappho* back at Mount Desert Ferry did not immediately reunite all parties. With no means of immediate communications, as well as the size of the crowds in both Hancock and Bar Harbor, and the confusion of the emergency, members of various parties were shuffled from location to location, until the number of people at the ferry dwindled with each reunification.

After the initial phone calls for medical assistance, news that there had been a deadly disaster at Mount Desert Ferry started to spread from Ellsworth and Bangor across the state. All that was known was the gangplank had broken, there were many injured and dead, and doctors were needed.

The news was met with anxiety across the state. Because of the interlocking network of railroad tracks and railroad companies, people from all over Maine had been on the excursion train. "The news spread rapidly through the different towns of the state, and the greatest anxiety was felt all day until a telegram or the return of the excursionists brought the news," reported the *Boston Globe*. "Eastern Maine will long remember the visit of the North Atlantic squadron to Bar Harbor."

In Waterville, "there was considerable excitement in this city when the news of the accident came but it soon quieted down when it was learned that all from here were safe. A lady whose whole family had gone on the excursion had hysterics and was obliged to take to her bed," wrote the *Waterville Mail*.

As soon as news reached the various newspapers throughout the state, reporters spent the afternoon and evening at their local railroad station, waiting for a chance to interview survivors or witnesses traveling home from Mount Desert Ferry. US marshal Hudson B. Saunders, whose home was in Ellsworth, traveled to Portland by rail on the day of the disaster, leaving Ellsworth Sunday evening. To the *Portland Daily Express*, he described the excitement of the great crowds at all the stations along the Maine Central Railroad line as "most intense." He said the crowd at Brewer was especially large, and that in Bangor the anxiety and excitement among the people at Union Station "amounted almost to wildness."

The news hit hard in Ellsworth, as many of its citizens had been aboard the train. People rushed to the Ellsworth train station, some to board whichever train might next go to Mount Desert Ferry, while others went to the telegraph and telephone offices in the city to seek further news. They could find out little, however, and it was a long time before any definite news was received, despite the close proximity of Ellsworth to Hancock.

"Ellsworth was horrified Sunday forenoon when the news of the terrible accident at Mt. Desert Ferry reached here," wrote the *Bangor Daily Commercial*. "All day long the town has been in a state of excitement as news came from Mt. Desert Ferry. So many Ellsworth people were among the passengers who fell at the slip that the deepest anxiety has been felt."

As word of the disaster spread through the city of Bangor, people immediately started forming crowds at that city's railroad station and newspaper offices. Soon those places were besieged by anxious loved ones, reporters, and the curious.

Evidence of the deadliness of the disaster could be found in the phone calls made to the undertakers of Bangor by Maine Central Railroad officials, informing them that all twenty bodies recovered Sunday would be brought to that city for preparation and then transportation to their various homes throughout the state. The crowds at Bangor's Union Station would stay late into the night, and were still assembled at midnight, awaiting the funeral train with the victims' bodies.

"The accident has cast a gloom over the city and people await anxiously for further details of this the most fearful catastrophe that this county has ever seen," wrote the *Bangor Daily Commercial*.

It was a little after two o'clock Sunday afternoon when the *Portland Daily Press* first heard about the disaster that had occurred three hours previously. A man came into the newspaper's offices at 97 Exchange Street that afternoon, carrying a telegram he had received from his son, Edmund Phinney Greenough. Edmund had telegraphed his father to inform him of his safety from the disaster. "This was the first news received in Portland of the accident outside of the railroad offices," wrote the *Portland Daily Press*.

The reporters of the paper were soon on the telephone and telegraph, trying to obtain an account of the accident. They quickly telegraphed Bar Harbor for particulars. Within half an hour the newspaper had posted a special news bulletin on the board in front of their office at 97 Exchange Street. There had been fifty-three people from Portland aboard the 8:25 special-excursion train, causing great concern in the city. Soon a crowd was assembled both in front of the newspaper and at the train station in Portland.

"The news of the great disaster was early received here and the first report was that the excursionists from Portland were in the water, and there was great excitement," wrote the *Boston Globe*.

Through the rest of the afternoon and into the night, the *Portland Daily Press* continued to post bulletins on the board as fast as stories were telegraphed into the office. The newspaper's bulletin board was surrounded by people from half past two in the afternoon until late Sunday night. Many of the people who read the bulletins had friends on the train, and to these people the story of the accident was of more than ordinary interest. "There has been no such excitement here since the loss of the Maine," wrote the *Portland Daily Press*.

Edmund Phinney Greenough, who had sent the telegram that had alerted the city of Portland to the disaster at Mount Desert Ferry, had been thrown into the water with the breaking of the gangplank.

Edmund Greenough, thirty, had been traveling with his friend and coworker, Frank Sweetser, both employees of the Maine Central Railroad in Portland. Mr. Greenough served as a clerk with the railroad, and until recently Mr. Sweetser had also been a clerk but had just been promoted to head of the railroad's lost freight division. Both had been on the 8:25 train.

FRANK SWEETSER

Frank Sweetser of Portland was thirty-one years old when he stepped foot on the gangplank at the Mount Desert Ferry wharf. He was born in Pownal, Maine, the son of Edwin Sweetser, of Pownal, and Phinelia H. True Sweetser, of Yarmouth. Frank Sweetser's father died when he was only two years old. Frank's mother would be remarried, to Col. E. C. Milliken, a Maine state pension agent.

Frank Sweetser was described as being exemplary of character and possessing sterling business qualities. He was quite popular in the lively city of Portland and had a wide circle of friends. He had been educated in the public schools of Portland, and after graduation took a business course at Shaw's College in Portland. He would go on to work at a few different places in Portland, including as a clerk at F. A. Blackstone, a plumbing company, and as a clerk at the firm of Edwards and Walker, a sporting goods store. For the five years previous to the disaster, Mr. Sweetser had been a clerk in the general freight office of the Maine Central Railroad, before his recent promotion to division head.

Frank Sweetser served for many years as a church sexton at the West End Congregational Church, where he was charged with the care of the buildings and the performance of various duties to prepare for church services. Frank took an active interest in church matters. He was also a member of the Bramhall Lodge, Knights of Pythias, and was a member of the Railroad Relief Association. Frank Sweetser was described as being one of the most popular employees of the Maine Central Railroad.

On the day before the disaster, the two Portland men had traveled from Portland to Bangor on the noon train of their employer. Their ultimate destination was Bar Harbor, to see the North Atlantic Squadron. When they left Portland, however, they were uncertain as to whether they would go directly through to Bar Harbor Saturday night or spend the night in Bangor and catch the 8:25 a.m. train Sunday morning. Their decision to stay in Bangor for the night would prove to be a fateful one.

Upon arriving at Mount Desert Ferry on Sunday, Edmund said the train's passengers made a rush to get to the first boat, and that he and Mr. Sweetser went along with the rest of the crowd. Approaching the entrance to the gangplank, the two were separated in the wave of people attempting to enter all at once, but Edmund could still see Frank, who was ahead of him. Both were on the gangplank when it unexpectedly broke, and Mr. Greenough estimated that Frank Sweetser was then near the center. Those nearest the center were the first to go in, and were the ones most likely to have the rest of the unfortunate people fall on top of them. The two men found themselves in the water, separated from each other.

"The first I felt of anything wrong was a sinking sensation and then I struck the water, going down, and it seemed as though I would never reach bottom," Mr. Goodenough told the *Portland Daily Press*. "About this time, I felt that I must get a breath of air and took a little short gasp and did not get any water in my mouth. Then I opened my eyes to find that I was on top of the water."

Someone held a plank down to Edmund, which he grabbed hold of. Still dazed by the accident, Edmund looked around the pen for Frank and to see what he could do for others. "Then I realized the magnitude of the accident. Some of the men acted like madmen, while most of them did everything they could to help those who were not able to help themselves," said Edmund.

Edmund Greenough appears to have been part of the rescue operation in which those on the wharf or the *Sappho* offered objects to those in the water to cling to, keeping them above water until one of the ropes could be brought to them, with which they would be dragged to safety. Edmund waited his turn as Chester W. Robbins, editor of the *Old Town Enterprise*, united each waiting person with the rescue rope.

"A large woman was hanging to a rope then another lady was pushed to the rope by a gentleman, who I did not know. He was a blessing to a great many of the people who would surely have been drowned if it had not been for his heroic efforts. After he helped the women to the rope and turned to help another, a large able-bodied fellow grabbed hold of the two women, who were holding on and attempted to climb up over them to the top of the pier."

Edmund did not know how that situation turned out, however, for suddenly he was swept away from the relative safety of his grasp of the plank, through a hole and into the darkness under the wharf. "I was swept under the wharf when I let go of the plank and grabbed a log and climbed on it nearly exhausted. I managed, however, to help one or two ladies on to the log, one of whom was almost crazy with fright. She was the only one I heard make any outcry. After about everyone had been taken out that was afloat, we were rescued."

Mr. Greenough heaped praises on the people he watched act as heroes in the disaster. "The people, and especially the men belonging to the steamer, did wonders and how it was that more were not drowned I cannot understand," Edmund told his hometown newspaper.

While Mr. Greenough was heaping praise upon others, many in the crowd noticed Edmund Greenough's own bravery. The *Boston Globe* praised Mr. Greenough's heroics:

> *There were some in the panic-stricken crowd, however, who did not lose their presence of mind . . . three men, Capt. Dickson, commander of the Sappho, Fred Sanborn of Portland, conductor in charge of the excursion train, and E. P. Greenough of Portland, a clerk in the freight office were among the bravest of the rescuers. These men, the latter of whom was among those who were pitched into the water, kept their heads under the most trying circumstances, and the two former calmly directed the work of rescue and by almost superhuman work themselves rescued 60 people.*
>
> *Greenough refused to leave the water until everyone else alive had been taken out, and he saved several persons by holding them from sinking until a rope or board could be reached to them. When he was taken from the water almost exhausted a mighty cheer went up for the hero.*

After Edmund's rescue, despite his prolonged exposure in the frigid water, he immediately set out to find his friend and coworker Frank Sweetser. Edmund thought he had briefly seen Frank in the pen after the breaking of the gangplank. While Edmund had been in the water holding the plank and waiting for rescue, he saw a man being pulled out of the water whose clothing matched Frank's. "Just before I went under the wharf, I saw one of the rescuing party take a man out of the water and I supposed it was Frank Sweetser as I didn't see his face, only saw his blue trousers and tan shoes."

Edmund could not find his friend among the chaos and the swarm of humanity at the Mount Desert Ferry wharf at that moment. He decided to take the next trip aboard the *Sappho* across Frenchman Bay, hoping Frank had been on the first boatload of people taken to Bar Harbor.

The task of trying to find one person in the crowd on shore at Mount Desert Ferry, on the *Sappho*, or on the wharf at Bar Harbor was difficult. Many of the passengers were men in their thirties, as were Edmund and Frank. With no success at finding Frank in Bar Harbor, Edmund took the next boat back to Mount Desert Ferry. By then relief efforts appear to have taken shape in Bar Harbor, as Edmund Greenough was able to secure a set of dry clothes and a piece of luggage in which to carry his wet ones. "On my way over I went down into the engine room and got partially dry. I got a change of clothing in Bar Harbor and put my clothes which I wore during the accident in a grip which I borrowed, for I had lost mine overboard."

The scene back at Mount Desert Ferry had settled down, though confusion over the fate of many passengers still loomed. The process of identifying the seventeen bodies housed in the freight shed on the wharf, which was described as slow, had just begun.

By now at least four hours had passed since the accident. Frank did not seem to be in Bar Harbor, he did not appear to be on the *Sappho* during Edmund's two trips, and he was not in The Bluffs. Edmund started making inquiries of the people on the shore of Mount Desert Ferry about his friend Frank. Though Frank Sweetser was a Maine Central Railroad employee, he worked out of Portland, so he was not known to the Maine Central men in Hancock.

In Edmund's confusion and growing despair, he turned to Morris McDonald, general superintendent of the Maine Central Railroad. Edmund gave Superintendent McDonald a description of Frank Sweetser, whereupon Mr. McDonald gave Edmund the news that Frank Sweetser had drowned in the disaster at Mount Desert Ferry. "This gave me a greater shock than going through the catastrophe of the forenoon," said Edmund Greenough.

Edmund was taken to the freight shed and shown Frank's body. Though Frank Sweetser had been tentatively identified by a set of keys he carried in his pocket, it was Edmund Greenough who made the official identification. "I think, however, that Frank was hit by a plank or kicked by someone, for he had a bruise on his head which in all probability stunned him and caused him to drown," said Edmund. "He was in good health, strong as a lion and could swim like a fish, so you see he was able to help himself, unless he had been hit with a plank or something else."

With Frank's identification having been made, late Sunday afternoon Frank Sweetser's family in Portland received a telegram from A. A. White, agent of the Maine Central Railroad from Bangor who was at Bar Harbor that day. The telegram informed them of Frank Sweetser's drowning at Mount Desert Ferry.

"His sudden death was a terrible shock to the family who were completely prostrated when the sad intelligence was received," reported the *Portland Daily Press*. "He was a general favorite and was a young man of much promise.

Edmund took charge of Frank's body and awaited the midnight funeral train, which would be the trip back home for both men. "I never witnessed nor desire to see such a terrible affair again."

The News Spreads

The returning trains brought stories of the saddest description of the deaths of these people on what was to have been a day of happiness for them and of heroic rescues and noble deaths. All of them had stories to tell of what they saw and heard.

—PORTLAND DAILY PRESS

The exact running times of trains to and from Mount Desert Ferry is unknown subsequent to the 8:25 special-excursion train. Whether the regularly running trains were canceled in light of the disaster is also unknown, though one news report did indicate that subsequent excursionists went through Mount Desert Ferry later that day.

The next documented train to arrive at Mount Desert Ferry from Bangor, aside from those with the physicians and nurses, was at 2:30 p.m. One of its passengers was Donald Snow of Bangor. Donald's father, James H. Snow, was a grocer in the city who had embarked on the excursion train that morning. When his son Donald heard about the accident, he took the next train to Mount Desert Ferry, not knowing if his father was dead or alive. Donald would arrive at The Bluffs to find his father badly bruised but stable. The elder Mr. Snow told his son how, in the water, he had supported a woman for ten minutes or more but could not recall whether she was saved.

Donald took his father home to Bangor on the same train, which left Mount Desert Ferry at 3:30 p.m., an hour after its arrival. Aboard the train were thirty-three people who had been rescued from the water, several of them having been revived after being rolled on the flour barrels.

Herbert Anderson, a news agent for the Maine Central Railroad, told of one woman returning home on the train who had gone under the water twice, was rescued in an unconscious condition, and had been revived after half an hour's work on the barrels. The woman's husband, who had helped rescue and revive the woman, was on the train with her, and Mr. Anderson said they were a thankful couple.

As news was spreading from mouth to mouth and town to town across the state, crowds started assembling at the state's numerous train stations. As the first trains out of Mount Desert Ferry started arriving in Ellsworth and Bangor, many of those who had experienced or witnessed the event excitedly told their stories to the reporters waiting at all the stops. "The returning trains brought stories of the saddest description of the deaths of these people on what was to have been a day of happiness for them and of heroic rescues and noble deaths," wrote the *Portland Daily Press*. "All of them had stories to tell of what they saw and heard."

Members of the Maine Press Association were among the first to tell their tales. Most of them left Mount Desert Ferry Sunday evening by train. At Ellsworth many continued on their trip home, while a handful spent the night in the city as guests of Mr. and Mrs. R. M. Campbell of the *Ellsworth Enterprise*, the only two of the Maine Press Association excursion who did not fall into the water.

Arthur E. Forbes, of Paris, Maine, editor of the *Oxford Democrat*, was standing in the sunshine allowing his clothes to dry when interviewed for the *Bangor Daily Commercial*. "The train was crowded coming down with just standing room and hardly that and when the Ferry was reached there naturally was a great rush to get aboard the boat," said Mr. Forbes. "The people were pushing forward hurriedly on to the slip which was crowded, when with no warning came the crackling of planks and then a struggling mass of humanity in the water. I was in the middle of the mess and it seemed to me that I was under water ten minutes. Then boards were shoved down and I caught hold of one and then was all right being shortly after hauled up to safety. It appeared to me that some of the people lost consciousness very quickly."

Horace E. Bowditch was a noted druggist in Augusta and photographer for the *Kennebec Journal.* He said that after the people on the dock realized what was happening, they began the work of rescue by lowering ropes and everything portable. Mr. Bowditch said he was fortunate in securing a hold on a piling, where he clung, with three women clinging to his back. "I cannot swim a stroke," said Mr. Bowditch.

After fifteen minutes Mr. Bowditch and the three women were offered a rope. With the assistance of another man, Mr. Bowditch sent the women up by means of the rope and then went up himself.

Mr. Bowditch was not shy with his praise of the heroics he witnessed that day. He told how Bangor and Aroostook conductor Charles Parsons saved a woman's life by catching her by the hair as she was going down under the water for the last time. Mr. Bowditch also described how Charles Haskell, editor of the *Pittsfield Advertiser*, saved the wife of Jesse Ogler, editor of the *Camden Herald*. He said the men on the wharf and the *Sappho* in general did a good job saving the women. "The greater number of those drowned were men, and I believe it was on account of the heroic work they did in saving the women," Mr. Bowditch told reporters.

Mr. Bowditch, along with many others, would heap praise on Chester W. Robbins of the *Old Town Enterprise* for his heroic actions that day. "I saw Chester Robbins, the editor of the Old Town Enterprise and the manager of our excursion, save live women by towing them to piles to which they could cling. He then went up on the wharf and removed his clothing and came back and rescued six more women to any certain knowledge, and there were other just such cases."

Horace Bowditch had taken pictures along the way during the Maine Press Association's weeklong excursion, and lost in the fall from the gangplank had been a number of glass plates that contained his undeveloped photographs. "The accident at Mt. Desert Ferry has been instrumental in establishing the fact that a photographer's 'dry plate' will live through a salt-water bath. Mr. H. E. Bowditch, of Augusta, had his camera with him when he went into the water. The plates had been exposed and he was very anxious not to lose the pictures, which were of members of the press excursion party. The plates were recovered, and upon being placed in a developing preparation some fairly good negatives were obtained," wrote the *Portland Daily Press* on Saturday, August 12, 1899.

Unfortunately, there is no further record of the photographs.

Charles Williams was a newspaper printer and member of the Maine Press Association. Mr. Williams told reporters:

> *The first thing I heard was a crack, followed by another crack, and the planks beneath my feet seemed to go out from under me. It was a gradual settling at first. Some of the crowd attempted to get off the slip. There was no crying out or shouting, no panic.*
>
> *Suddenly the slip broke in two and I dropped with the rest of the crowd about 15 feet into the cold water. I went down, down, down, and began to kick to get to the surface. I was pretty well frightened too. When I got to the top of the water all that I could see around me was a sea of faces, some of them distorted, with fear, but the most of them only looking surprised.*
>
> *Of course, the first thought that entered our minds was for the safety of the ladies of our party and this was followed by a desire to help all that we could. I think that every one of us, men and women, remained perfectly cool, not losing our heads in the least and I attribute the air of safety to this entirely.*
>
> *It was the coolest, bravest crowd I ever saw. The men around me were helping the women keep above water and all the excitement seemed to be on the wharf. The men on the wharf were using boards, ladders, pieces of rope, settees, and everything movable in the work of rescue.*
>
> *Suddenly someone from the wharf pushed down a long board to us [Williams and Frederick Thompson, fellow member of the Maine Press Association]. He made a grab at this and was yanked out of the water and onto the wharf. As soon as we were out of the water and found that our party was in no immediate danger we began to look about. The first thing I saw was Mr. Robbins of the Old Town Enterprise, clinging to a piling and dragging people out from beneath the*

wharf and assisting in passing them up to the people above. He saved eight or ten people in this matter.

From the wharf Mr. Williams and the other rescued members of the Maine Press Association were hustled through the crowd toward The Bluffs. Mr. Williams said he was pushed into the hotel's laundry room, where his clothes were dried.

"He showed evidence of having been in the water a long time; but was not injured," wrote the *Portland Daily Press*. "He had lost his baggage and hat and had to borrow one to get home with."

"One of the most lucid accounts of the calamity was that given by J. H. Ogler, editor of the Camden Herald. Mr. Ogler had been on the summer excursion of the Maine Press association and with 19 other members of the association, had left the larger party and taken the morning train at Ellsworth with the intention of visiting Bar Harbor," wrote the *Bangor Daily Commercial*.

Mr. Ogler told the reporter:

Upon arrival at the Ferry everybody rushed for the slip, being anxious to get to Bar Harbor as quickly as possible. As our party, with the exception of Mr. and Mrs. Campbell, who were still on the wharf, reached the middle of the slip I felt a gradual cracking and settling of the slip and then very suddenly found myself in the water.

At first, I kept above water placing one arm about Mrs. Ogler and treading water to keep above the surface. The mass of people seemed to go under us. I was suddenly seized by someone beneath and drawn under water. As I went, I loosened my grasp upon my wife in order that she should not be drawn down too. I struggled and got free and again rose above the surface, then got hold of a piling where I remained for some little time and had a chance to view the scene around me. Of course, the people who were underneath fought desperately to rise and the scene was an appalling one. She had a very narrow escape and had sunk once when she was caught by Charles

Haskell of Pittsfield, who held her until somebody reached down from the wharf and got hold of her hand.

Those who were ashore struck me as remarkably cool, considering the circumstances. The mass of people on the wharf above were panic-stricken and seemed far more frantic than those in the water. Everything possible, however, was done to save the unfortunates in the water. First boards were let down and these supported many, although they were not effective in assisting them out. This was done by means of ropes and ladders, the latter especially being very effective. I got out by means of a ladder and at last found Mrs. Ogler in safety.

There was concern for Mr. Ogler's physical condition after his rescue, and he received extra care at The Bluffs, but was able to leave Mount Desert Ferry on the evening train.

Frederick Thompson of the *Portland Courier and Telegram* lived in the Woodfords section of that city. Mr. Thompson's mother accompanied him on the trip that Sunday.

Mr. Thompson told how he plunged into the water somewhere in the middle of the dense mass of struggling people, being pushed under the water and touching bottom. Mr. Thompson then began to rise and finally came to the surface. He had hardly gotten his head above water before someone hit his straw hat, pushing it down over his eyes. This he tore off and then instinctively began to tread water. After clearing his eyes, he looked around to see what chances he had for getting out of the hole, but the idea of escape looked hopeless. On the sides of the pen were nothing but smooth planks, with very little chance to seize anything for support, and all around, packed in like sardines, were men, women, and children struggling, crying, and doing everything possible to get out of the awful place.

Suddenly, someone from above pushed a deck chair down to Mr. Thompson, and he started to climb up the back of this. Before he could climb to safety, however, another man also started climbing the deck chair, which could not hold both their weight. Mr. Thompson was thrown back into the water.

This time he did not go down so far under the water, and soon arose to the surface and began to tread water again. Mr. Thompson had entirely given up hope of being rescued when out of nowhere appeared a rope in front of him, thrown from the *Sappho*. Mr. Thompson grabbed the rope and clung to it. There was a young girl near him, and he managed to get hold of her and pull her to the rope, and both were drawn to the steamer, hoisted from the water, and laid on deck. Here someone picked Mr. Thompson up and carried him inside the steamer, where he was given hot drinks and other stimulants. Mr. Thompson said that after a period of time he was again able to function.

Mr. Thompson said that those people thrown in the water were unusually calm and that they acted nobly. There had been considerable noise and crying, but it appeared to him to be coming mostly from the wharf. The men did all in their power to save the lives of the women, and many men drowned in their efforts, Mr. Thompson told reporters that planks, boards, ropes, and so on were thrown to them, and afterward life preservers from the steamers, and people were yanked from the hole with surprising rapidity. He said the railroad men did all that was possible to rescue the drowning and relieve the distress of all involved.

Mrs. Frederick H. Thompson, mother of Frederick Thompson, whose first name possibly was Lillie, was rescued after being stranded under the wharf.

It was not just the members of the Maine Press Association who were telling the story of what they had witnessed that afternoon. Charles Adams of Bangor worked in the lumbering business, in management. He was treasurer of the Penobscot Lumbering Association, auditor for the Home for Aged Men in Bangor, director for the Stillwater Log Driving Company, secretary and treasurer of the Mattawamkeag Log Driving Company, and director of the Penobscot Valley Development Company. He was also community minded, serving as treasurer to the committee helping to restore the clock in Bangor's Universalist Church tower.

Mr. Adams told reporters he thought the gangplank was only about six feet from the water of the high tide, and as the wharf was planked on both sides, practically closing it in like a box, the only opening left was at the bottom where the two broken ends of the gangplank parted. After the first plunge downward of those who were in the middle of the gang-plank, the ends of the slip floated together and partly closed up, pinning scores of people in the trap thus formed.

He would never forget the look on the faces of the people below as they turned their gaze toward those on the wharf, Mr. Adams told report-ers. "The situation was something terrible and was fearfully impressive."

Peter H. Peterson, sixty, and his wife, Mary, fifty-four, of War-ren Street in Bangor, immigrants from Sweden, along with their seventeen-year-old son Albert, were among those who went down with the gangplank. Peter Peterson was a gardener for private families in Bangor, and his son Albert was an electrician. Mrs. Peterson, who was described as a large woman, was sinking under the water when her son, who was described as a slightly built boy, came to her assistance and kept his mother's head above water. The son was able to get his mother to some posts beneath the pier, to which they clung until seen from above. A rope was sent down to them, and they were rescued, as was Mr. Peterson.

George Mattox, a young boy from Bangor, had persuaded another Bangor boy, Howard Gillie, described as a small-built deaf lad, to join him on the excursion train in Bangor, without the permission of Gillie's mother, who did not know her son had left the city. Both boys went into the water, and Mattox was quickly saved. Mattox gazed into the mass of horror from the safety of the wharf and was able to single out his friend among the struggling crowd in the pen. Mattox felt responsible for Gillie running away to Bar Harbor that day. With Mattox's conscience getting the best of him, he jumped back into the frigid, dangerous water and, after a hard fight, brought Gillie safely to the wharf, and eventually back to his mother in Bangor.

Mr. and Mrs. P. O'Leary of Pickering Square in Bangor were thrown, along with their little girl, into the water. After a desperate struggle, they succeeded in reaching the wharf in safety, though they were described as perfectly exhausted.

Mr. Fred B. Tuck, a carpenter from Harlow Street in Bangor, along with his fiancée, Miss Lena Smith, of Exeter, were in the center of the gangplank when it broke that Sunday morning. Being at the center, several more passengers soon fell in on top of them. Though the water was sixteen feet deep, both Tuck and Smith touched the bottom immediately after being thrown in.

They were "surrounded by a seething mass of legs and arms of the struggling crowds above them," they told the *Bangor Daily Commercial.* Despite trying to get above water, they both were held down by the scores of people who had fallen in after them.

Miss Smith had the presence of mind to place her hand over her mouth against the water before going under, and she desperately fought to get to the surface, preserving the last breath inside her. She quickly found that she was held down by a person in the water whom she later described as being one of the people who ultimately perished in the disaster. After escaping that person's grasp, Lena said she rose to the surface like a cork. Fred and Lena would come up out of the water about fifteen feet from the point where they went under. They were pulled out of the water by one of the rescuers.

Mr. Tuck escaped without any serious injury, though he was having difficulty breathing, was sore and lame, and was suffering from "nervous shock." Miss Smith's chest, arms, and legs were severely bruised from the blows of those with whom she had fought to sustain her own life.

Fred and Lena returned to Bangor that evening on the train and were placed under the care of Dr. A. C. Gibson of Bangor. The morning after the disaster, Miss Smith was in a state of high fever and great excitement, having passed a restless night as the result of the exposure and "tension on her nervous system." Ultimately Miss Smith would recover, and five months later, at midnight on Sunday, January 1, 1900, the couple hoped to wash away that year's tragedy with their New Year's wedding. The marriage of Fred B. Tuck and Lena F. Smith was celebrated at St. John's Episcopal church in Bangor. Their ceremony was one of three New Year's weddings performed in Bangor that morning.

Patrick Leonard of 125 Warren Street in Bangor had taken his wife and two sons on the excursion train to see the warships. All four of them were on the end of the gangplank when it crashed into the water.

Though he was watching his wife drowning before his eyes, Mr. Leonard kept his head. He grabbed his wife's hand and was able to place one son on each shoulder. Together the party moved away from the struggling mass in the water.

Mr. Leonard was able to keep his wife above water, but he knew that he could not get his entire family out of the water at once, so he made a difficult decision. Mr. Leonard left his two sons in the water as he aided his wife to safety on the dock. He then grabbed one end of a rope and jumped back in the water to save his two boys. "Leonard's act was one of the bravest of the day and had he not been equally cool headed some of his family would doubtless have been drowned," said the *Bangor Daily Commercial*.

The Leonard family was able to return to their home in Bangor on the train that evening. Mrs. Leonard was described as being extremely bruised, suffering from severe shock, and very ill.

Walker B. Smith was a shoe-factory employee from Bangor who had decided to spend his Sunday off from work by visiting Mount Desert Island. "I was the last one out from under the wharf and it seemed as if I was in the water fully two hours although it probably was not more than 20 minutes. I supported myself by clinging to a plank until they threw a life preserver to me. I was pretty weak when I got out."

Mr. William H. Savage, twenty-eight, of Waterville worked for the New England Telephone and Telegraph Company. He, along with his wife, Lottie, twenty-four, and two children, daughter Gladys, five, and one-year-old son, Carl, were thrown into the water that Sunday morning. "Mr. W. H. Savage of this city tells the following story of the sad accident at Mount Desert Ferry Sunday," reported the *Waterville Mail*:

My wife and I and two children started for Bar Harbor on the early train Sunday morning. We got into Bangor in time to catch the first train for Bar Harbor and arrived at the Ferry with the first of the excursionists. When we got off the train, I told my wife that as there was such a crowd, we had better stay back a little till there was less of a jam. We kept working along toward the gangway, however, and just before we got to it, I heard the cracking and snapping of breaking timbers, and right ahead of us a section of the crowd, 42 feet by 10 feet, dropped out of sight and about 250 people were struggling in the water below.

It was terrible. Women screamed and cried and for a time the crowd was nearly frantic. The officers of the boat and the cooler ones on the wharf began the work of rescue. Boats were launched and ropes and life preservers thrown to those in the water. Not many of us were able to help much and it was pitiful to watch the struggles of the drowning. One would get a hold on a pile and start to draw himself up when he would be clutched by several others in their desperate fight for life and be pulled back into the water. I saw hundreds of pieces of cloth that had been torn from men's clothing and women's dresses.

The work done by some of the rescuers was fine. A newspaper man from Old Town [Chester W. Robbins, editor of the Old Town Enterprise] did noble work. He fell into the water with the rest but got out taking two or three with him, and then stripping off his outside clothing went back into the water and saved eight or ten women who probably would have been drowned had it not been for him. When I left, I counted 22 bodies that had been taken from the water.

Albert Hartshorn, thirty-four, was a painter for the Maine Central Railroad in Waterville:

I was among the first to go on board the boat and just after my feet had left the gangplank it broke in two near the middle letting the people who were on it into the water. The crowd that had gone on the boat ahead of me crowded to the side and there I was, looking over the side of the boat, unable to do a thing to help, watching that struggling mass of people, drowning, it seemed at the time, like rats in a cage. I saw people with their heads and shoulders out of water standing on the bodies of those who had been forced below the surface. I wouldn't go through it again for $10,000.

In Portland, Mr. H. W. Robb told his story to a reporter from the *Portland Daily Press* after emerging from the first train arriving there from Mount Desert Ferry:

Mr. H. W. Robb, the proprietor of the Chase House on Congress Street in Portland, said that Harry Lancy of Pittsfield grabbed the steamer when the slip broke and got on board. Lancy caught a woman by the shoulders just as she was sliding down into the terrible death trap. In the desperate struggle for life, a man already in the water grabbed the woman's feet, and another man had ahold of that man's legs. With all the added weight, Lancy was having trouble keeping hold of the imperiled woman. To the fortune of the woman, a small group of men came along the deck to help Mr. Lancy, and together they pulled her on to the steamer, along with the man holding her legs. The second man lost hold of the first man's legs and fell back into the water. Mr. Lancy told Mr. Robb that he had never seen so much bravery displayed in his life as he did that morning.

Mr. Harry Colpitts told the *Portland Daily Press* that one man was pulled up out of the water, and around his foot was entangled the hair of a woman who had probably been trampled beneath the feet of the crowd. He said there were only two children in the crowd that fell into the water, babies in their mothers' arms, and it was reported that they were drowned, although their bodies had not been recovered. Colpitts said that four women were pulled out of the water onto the deck of the steamer; three of them died before help could reach them. "The fourth was strangled by her false teeth."

Obviously, many parts of Mr. Colpitts's story had been exaggerated by the time he reached Portland.

At the time of the disaster at Mount Desert Ferry, Maine Central Railroad president Franklin Wilson was, coincidentally, close at hand, the Wilson family spending that Sunday in their cottage in Bar Harbor. After receiving word of the disaster, Mr. Wilson chose to stay in Bar Harbor and direct emergency operations from there. Several people plucked from the water at Mount Desert Ferry had been taken to Bar Harbor aboard the *Sappho*, and arrangements had to be made for their medical care and whatever else they might need. There would also be the three dead bodies to take care of. "Mr. Wilson saw that every case was given good care," wrote the *Boston Globe*.

He spent part of that Sunday writing individual letters to the Maine Central Railroad's board of directors regarding the accident. He also talked to the reporters who eventually arrived at his cottage. Mr. Wilson did not travel to the scene of the accident until embarking on the last steamboat ferry that left Bar Harbor Sunday night.

President Wilson was visited at his cottage by two reporters Sunday afternoon. The cause of the accident was not known at the time, and because of a lack of communications, he had very few details of the accident. There had not yet been a chance to examine the gangplank, which had been rebuilt just two months earlier and was supposed to be able to handle any weight placed upon it. The accident was inexplicable. The only event out of the ordinary that morning had been the enormous crowd and the rush for the gangplank.

Mr. Wilson was first visited by a reporter from the *Bar Harbor Record*. "There is nothing for me to say except that the affair was terrible and deplorable. I attribute the cause of the accident to the undue strain placed upon the beams by the great crowd. Everything will be done for the injured, but until I have heard from the various heads of the company, I can say nothing," Mr. Wilson told the reporter.

The next visit to President Wilson's cottage would be from the *Boston Globe*. Mr. Wilson told that reporter, Mr. J. Taylor, that the slip could not have been weak, as great weights had many times been taken across it without any signs of its giving way. "I know that certainly enough timber was sent down to build a strong slip," Wilson told the reporter. "There is nothing that I can say. It is a terribly sad affair, and I, of course, cannot tell who or what is to be blamed. I am just writing to one of my directors telling him of the accident. Of course, I cannot tell what will be done in regard to damages, losses, et cetera, until later developments take place."

By the time Sunday afternoon turned into evening, the chaos at Mount Desert Ferry had calmed. Reuniting the missing had been ongoing throughout the afternoon, the list of missing passengers had dwindled down until it was empty, and the survivors able to travel had been leaving on subsequent trains.

Maine Central Railroad superintendent Morris McDonald of Portland and division superintendent A. A. White of Bangor had been at the scene of the accident all day. Their time was spent caring for the bodies, aiding anxious inquirers searching for friends, and sending word to the families of those drowned. "This terrible catastrophe is the source of much sorrow to the officers of the Maine Central, irrespective of all financial issues," wrote the *Bangor Daily Commercial.* "They are very sorry to have so dreadful a happening blot their very clean record as to loss of life."

Many of the fortunate passengers of the 8:25 train who had not gone in the water returned home on the first trains out of Mount Desert Ferry, not caring to continue their excursion. The spreading news of the morning's horror had cast a shadow of gloom over the otherwise merry day and the arrival of the North Atlantic Squadron. Passengers for later excursion trains that day would arrive at their respective railroad stations and hear the news of the disaster. Some of them would opt to return home, while others would choose to continue their train trip. Some had family and friends involved in the disaster, whom they wanted to check on personally.

"The accident has caused a profound sensation in this part of Maine and will keep many visitors away during the stay of the warships," wrote the *Bar Harbor Record.*

The accident quickly was finding many armchair quarterbacks sharing their opinions of what ought to have been done during the disaster. "The accident developed the usual corps of faultfinders," wrote the *Boston Globe.* "Had Capt. Dixon moved the *Sappho* away from her berth, said these, more people would have been saved, as rowboats could have been utilized, but good judges of the action of current are of the opinion that had Capt. Dixon moved away from the wharf, the loss of life would have been much greater. The boat, lying as she did across the entrance to the slip, prevented those in the water from being carried away from the piling, to which a great many clung until rescued."

Moving the *Sappho* during the crisis could have killed more people than it might have saved. People were clinging to the sides of the ship immediately after the accident. The ship and its crew almost immediately became a major source of rescue, with many desperate people being pulled to safety over her sides with ropes and deck chairs. The placement of the *Sappho* prevented any survivors or victims from floating out to open water, where they could have been lost forever.

People were also starting to grow curious about the cause of the gangplank's structural failure. The Maine Central Railroad officials who were at the scene of the accident were at a loss to account for the accident. Some people started theorizing, incorrectly, that the gangplank had been built too thin for its purpose. A quick glance at the boards of the gangplank visible in the pen dispelled that theory.

The gangplank was examined that day as much as it could be with both ends still poking down in the water and in use by the divers. For the train passengers who would arrive at Mount Desert Ferry after the accident, the broken gangplank became an attraction. "The slip was surrounded all day by a curious crowd," wrote the *Portland Daily Press*.

Railroad president Wilson would arrive from Bar Harbor that night and inspect the broken gangplank in the daylight the following morning. The *Portland Daily Press* wrote:

There is a great deal of speculation as to the cause of the break in the ferry slip to which the disaster was due. The structure was nearly new and it is claimed should have been capable of withstanding the weight of as many persons as its dimensions would permit to get upon it. The material of which it was made apparently was well-seasoned and sound, and its appearance after the accident seemed to indicate that its substantial construction had been carried to the breaking point. Several persons who witnessed the accident are inclined to the belief that the slip would have sustained the weight of the crowd upon it, had they moved in an orderly manner, but some were running, while there was almost a continuous line of people who in an attempt to get on board the ferry jumped over the rail which guarded the opening in the pier into which the slip swung which, it is pointed out must have added greatly to the strain.

"The inquest is to begin at once."

Also looking over the broken gangplank Sunday were the Hancock County officials who would be responsible for conducting the coroner's inquest into the disaster. The officials had been arriving all afternoon, and the inquest officially began that evening, though no official proceedings would be held until the following morning.

John E. Bunker, Esq., county attorney for Hancock County, was one of the first to arrive, from Bar Harbor. He immediately undertook the task of obtaining identification of the bodies, and it was largely through his efforts that the victims' names became so quickly known. Mr. Bunker would remain on the scene to render whatever assistance was possible.

Coroner Dorpheus L. Fields, fifty-five, of Ellsworth was at the scene of the accident early in the afternoon and took charge of the remains and of valuables found on the bodies and personal effects taken from the water by the divers.

The two men were joined by Hancock County sheriff L. F. Hooper. The three county officials consulted with two officials of the Maine Central Railroad, the general superintendent Morris McDonald and the division superintendent A. A. White. They were joined by Charles Drummey, thirty-four, a lawyer enlisted by county attorney Bunker to help with the inquest.

Before the night was over, Coroner Fields had impaneled a jury of six Hancock County men for the coroner's inquest. As the *Boston Globe* reported it, "[C]oroner D. L. Fields of Ellsworth . . . had rounded up six intelligent-looking inhabitants to act as jury."

After the selection of the jury, the coroner's investigation began that evening. The jury, along with the county and railroad officials, walked to the freight house and viewed the remains of the deceased. They examined as best they could the broken gangplank, still in use by the divers. The inquest was then adjourned until eight o'clock the following morning.

After receiving care at The Bluffs, many of the survivors were able to ride back to their homes on the next few trains that left Mount Desert Ferry during the afternoon and evening. Fifteen of them were too ill to be moved Sunday, however, and remained at The Bluffs overnight:

Miss Mary Sweeney, Bangor, spine injury, kidneys affected, pneumonia, in very serious condition.

Miss Mary Shorten, twenty-three, Bangor, prostration.

Miss Lillian Danielson, Brewer, nervous prostration.

Miss Nora McNamara, twenty-three, back and chest injury.

Mrs. George W. Wyler, Bangor, shock. Mrs. Wyler had been in a party that included Mrs. Delia Oakes, who died in the disaster.

George Southard, forty, East Hampden, shock.

Eugene Dudley, Bangor, shock.

Charles Flynt, of the Maine Press Association, exact diagnosis not given.

Mr. George Spaulding, Orono, not expected to recover.

When pulled from the water, Mrs. Herbert Dunning was suffering injuries to her neck and spine. It was not known if she would survive the night.

Mrs. James Dunning spent the night at The Bluffs, though her relationship to Mrs. Herbert Dunning is unknown. Whether she stayed the night because of a medical condition or simply to stay with Mrs. Herbert Dunning is also not known.

Mrs. George H. Brooks was listed as suffering from shock, with her heart being affected by the trauma. She was in the most precarious condition Sunday night of any of the injured from Ellsworth. She and her husband, the popular minister of the First Congregational Church of Ellsworth, had gone into the water when the gangplank broke and were carried under the wharf.

Mrs. Brooks had a longstanding heart condition, and this was aggravated by the shock of having been unexpectedly thrown into a life-or-death struggle in the water. Mrs. Brooks's life was saved by another woman who had also plunged in. That woman, whose name is not known, held Mrs. Brooks above the water and got her to a place under the pier where she could hold on until help came.

Mrs. Brooks was one of the last people taken from the water that day. She estimated having been in for an hour before she was rescued. Her husband refused offers of rescue for himself until his wife was rescued. A news report read: "S. R. Prentiss, of Bangor, cut a rope from the *Sappho* and threw it to the struggling people. 'An old man,' says Mr. Prentiss, 'stood on the precarious footing afforded by the submerged end of the slip. As I threw down the rope, he seized it, and either tied it around others or handed it over to them to be pulled out. I called to him to come up himself, that he would be drowned, but back came the cool and unexpected answer; 'Oh, I'm in no hurry; I'll come up by and by.'"

That man was Reverend Brooks. He, too, was reported to have been one of the last people rescued from the water that day, refusing to leave until his wife had been saved. When taken from the water, the bruised and ailing Mrs. Brooks was taken to The Bluffs in serious condition, described as hovering between life and death.

Besides Charles Flynt, two other members of the Maine Press Association excursion spent the night at The Bluffs.

Mr. Fred Thompson and his mother, Mrs. F. H. Thompson, of Portland, both had gone into the water during the accident. Mrs. Thompson was suffering with slight weakness. Mr. Thompson was also weak and suffering with quite a heavy cold as a result of being chilled through. Overall, however, on Monday they were described as doing quite nicely. Their overnight stay at The Bluffs may have been more out of convenience than necessity.

"The rescued ones can't be too thankful to the managers of The Bluffs for they were untiring in their attentions to all of us," said Mrs. Thompson. "The guests should also have great praise."

Fifty to sixty people received treatment at The Bluffs. Fifteen doctors worked tirelessly there Sunday afternoon and evening. Dr. McNally, who had been on the excursion train but who had been spared going into the water, stayed overnight Sunday with the fifteen survivors who remained at The Bluffs. Dr. McNally's labors were spoken of in the highest terms by all who were there.

At six o'clock Sunday evening, a train arrived at Mount Desert Ferry from Bangor with caskets for the dead. At some point a decision had been made to take all the bodies to Bangor, where they could be handled by the numerous undertakers of that city. Because Bangor was a major hub for the Maine Central Railroad, this would also make shipment of the bodies home to various locations throughout eastern and central Maine easier.

During the next four hours at Mount Desert Ferry, the seventeen bodies were loaded into the coffins, moved from the freight shed, and loaded on a special train that had been arranged by the railroad. At ten o'clock Sunday night, the train left Mount Desert Ferry with seventeen of the twenty bodies of the dead aboard, traveling back along the tracks that only twelve hours before had brought them to Mount Desert Ferry as part of a singing, joyful crowd. The excursion train had become the funeral train. "A sadder load never left Mt. Desert Ferry, which is little accustomed to scenes of grief and trouble," reported the *Boston Globe*.

In Bangor, the train was received at Union Station by an enormous crowd. "The scene at Bangor . . . when the funeral train arrived was one never to be forgotten. Hundreds of people packed the station and friends searching out the bodies of those whom they knew among the dead, required the entire Bangor police force to keep them in order," reported the *Portland Daily Press*.

All seventeen bodies on the funeral train would be drawn by carriages to various area undertaking parlors, where they were prepared for shipping. Two bodies remained unidentified, one a young woman, one an older woman. After several cases of mistaken identity, the two females were at last correctly identified. When the undertakers' preparations had been completed, the seventeen bodies would be forwarded to their next destination, by horse and carriage in the case of the people of Bangor, and by train for the other Maine victims who lived farther away. The bodies of the three women who died on the *Sappho* would arrive at another time.

The body of Frank Sweetser of Portland was one of those on the funeral train. The plan had been to transfer his body to the train that left Bangor after midnight and arrived in Portland at 4:20 a.m. Monday morning. The funeral train did not arrive in Bangor from Mount Desert

Ferry in time for the departure of the Portland train, however. Edmund Greenough remained with friends in Bangor so that he could accompany home his friend Frank Sweetser the following morning. They would arrive in Portland on Monday at noon.

The Inquest

*[A] death trap for twenty souls, and untold suffering for scores of
innocent victims . . . to think of this, the worst of all, the result of one
man's careless negligence.*

—Old Town Enterprise

The sun arose Monday morning to a busy scene at Mount Desert Ferry.
Officials of the Maine Central Railroad were on the wharf, doing their
best to inspect the gangplank and determine the cause of the seemingly
unexplainable accident. They were not allowed to pull the gangplank out
of the water because it was necessary for the ongoing work of the divers,
who were looking for any bodies that might have been missed the day
before. Inside The Bluffs, fourteen of the fifteen survivors who had been
too ill to move home the night before were made ready for the special
train that was being sent from Bangor for them. Meanwhile, in one of
the hotel's cottages, the proceedings of the coroner's inquest were about
to open.

Late Sunday night a train had been sent from Bangor, which carried
Maine Central Railroad chief engineer Theodore Dunn, who was in
charge of bridges and buildings. The construction of the gangplank fell
under his department's responsibility.

Mr. Dunn and other railroad officials were on the wharf Monday
morning, inspecting the damage from the day before. Railroad president
Wilson had arrived from his summer cottage in Bar Harbor the night
before and was now also inspecting the broken gangplank.

The official coroner's inquest was due to begin in a few hours, and so far the officials of the railroad had only quickly examined the gangplank the day before, while it was still hanging in the water and being used as a platform for the divers. That examination had told them how the accident happened. Railroad officials needed a closer look at the gangplank to know for sure why the accident had occurred.

After that morning's two divers had used the broken gangplank to get in the water, the two broken pieces were pulled out and laid on the wharf for inspection. Chief engineer Dunn made an official examination and took measurements of the fatal gangplank, and then began an inspection of the immediate vicinity.

During the previous day's quick examination, it appeared that the only support of the gangway had been the five timbers that ran its length underneath. When the wreck was removed Monday, however, it was seen that the cause of the accident, apparently, was the pulling out of three one-inch iron rods that held the support timbers in place. Apparently, the bolts that secured the metal frame to the wooden gangplank had pulled through the ten-inch stringer piece, causing the three iron support rods to fall away, throwing all the strain of the weight of two hundred people on the wooden girders. The only question now was why the bolts had pulled through the wood in the first place.

After the Maine Central Railroad officials had seen all that they needed to see, part of the broken gangplank would be lowered back into the water for the use of the two divers, still engaged in their search under the wharf. At 9:30 a.m., before railroad officials removed the gangplank for inspection, the two divers got into their armor to look for bodies, which were not expected to be found, and to search for personal effects.

One diver had to come back to the surface twice within the first hour to remedy a leak in his diving armor's headpiece. The diver from Boston explored under the wharf in the direction of the set of the current and did not come to the surface for an hour and twenty minutes.

"A night of anxiety was followed by a day full of effort to determine if any other lives had been sacrificed and happily the suspense was not long. When daylight came, the waters under the wharf at the Ferry were carefully inspected and as the tide receded men wandered about in the mud in search for traces of other victims. Divers were also at work in deep places, but the fears that the death list was greater than indicated last night were not realized," wrote the *Portland Daily Press*.

Throughout the morning the pile of personal effects recovered by the divers grew in size outside the freight house on the wharf. The items included clothing, consisting primarily of women's jackets, capes, and other outer garments, and a large number of parasols. There were also many bags and satchels, "most of which were filled with lunch for a day's outing."

"At the Ferry Monday morning there remained many reminders of the catastrophe of the day before. All bodies had been removed to houses or to undertaking rooms in Bangor, but a pile of unclaimed hats, umbrellas, satchels and wearing apparel, but above all the broken gangplank told the sad story of the day before," wrote the *Ellsworth American*.

Eventually two trunks full of unclaimed clothing were taken to the office of the baggage master at the Maine Central Railroad offices in Bangor.

Among all the activity Monday morning at Mount Desert Ferry was the constant arrival of onlookers. "Spectators are still coming here to look at the scene of the accident," wrote the *Portland Daily Press*.

Inside The Bluffs, preparations were being made to take home the injured.

Already claim adjusters representing Maine Central Railroad had arrived at Mount Desert Ferry, there presumably to start the legal claims process against the railroad on behalf of the injured.

The train out of Bangor the night before that had carried chief engineer Dunn also carried Maine Central Railroad claim agent John S. Heald and claim agent F. M. Grover, of the Boston and Maine Railroad. Mr. Grover happened to be in Bangor on Sunday with a party of railroad men and was pressed into service by the Maine Central Railroad for the unusual mass casualty situation.

John Heald, who also served as the director of the Eastern Maine State Fair, was well known in Bangor. "No man who comes to Bangor is better known than he. He knows his business and saves thousands of dollars for the road which he represents every year," wrote the *Bangor Daily News.*

At the time of the disaster, the law computed the worth of a life at five thousand dollars. Injuries were assessed individually. The Maine Central Railroad was facing one hundred thousand dollars in damages just for the loss of life, the equivalent of over three million dollars in 2020.

"Everywhere this morning the physicians and those interested in the railroad company's affairs were busy attending to the injured who were quartered near the Ferry," wrote the *Bangor Daily Commercial.*

As the doctors and adjusters were speaking to the survivors, they were also being prepared for their trip home. All but one of the survivors had recovered sufficiently to be released. The majority of them had needed but little medical attention overnight, aside from Mr. George Southard and two patients with pneumonia.

A special train had been arranged by the Maine Central Railroad, which included a sleeping car for the injured. Those still disabled from their injuries were carried on cots from The Bluffs and placed in berths that had been made up specially for them. The train was accompanied by a number of nurses who had spent the night at the hotel caring for the injured.

The train left Mount Desert Ferry at 11:30 a.m. under the charge of Dr. McNally of Bangor. Arriving in Bangor, the injured were returned home in the Bangor police ambulance and by horse-drawn carriages. The labors of Dr. McNally, who spent Sunday night at The Bluffs caring for the sick and injured, were spoken of in the highest terms by all who were there.

The only survivor to remain at The Bluffs was Mrs. Herbert Dunning of Bangor. Mrs. Dunning was suffering from a neck and spine injury, and her condition was considered critical enough that it was thought not advisable to move her on Monday. Whether she would survive or not was still unknown on Monday morning. "The condition of Mrs. Herbert Dunning, the only injured one remaining at the Bluffs on Monday, was stated to be very serious on Tuesday morning. She passed a very bad night Monday and some of those ministering to her wants are fearful that she will not recover. Others held out more hope for her," wrote the *Bangor Daily Commercial.*

Immediately after the departure of the injured on the 11:30 special train, Hancock County coroner D. L. Fields of Ellsworth went about Mount Desert Ferry and rounded up witnesses for the inquest, which originally had been scheduled to begin at 8 a.m.

The Maine Central Railroad had much at stake with the verdict of the inquest, both financially and in the court of public opinion. The railroads served the public good, and a good reputation was important. A reputation for safety and honesty was critical.

The exact cause of the accident was still in question. At first it had been assumed that the rush for the gangplank by the out-of-control crowd, an unusual circumstance, had caused the break. Maine Central officials, however, were saying the new gangplank should have been strong enough to handle any strain of weight normally put upon it.

A preliminary look at the visible parts of the gangplank while its ends were hanging in the water made it obvious that at least one of the five support timbers that ran the length of the structure had broken and the others had come apart. What was not visible was the metal structure that also ran the length of the gangplank, under the timber, which gave support to the wood. This had fallen unnoticed into the water at the beginning of the disaster, silently under the roar of the excited, singing crowd that had been pushing for the *Sappho*. It had fallen because the bolts had come out. But why had the bolts come out?

Another question of importance to the railroad was, if the railroad was at fault for the accident, what percent of the fault was the railroad's, and what percent was played by factors such as the pushing crowd. What percent of the deaths had been caused by people throwing objects into the pen during the initial rescue effort? With the structured laws regarding railroad accidents and apportionment of blame, the answers would translate into real dollars and cents.

A third question was raised during the first day of inquest testimony as to whether Maine Central officials had been negligent in their duties that Sunday morning in controlling the crowd as it disembarked from the train.

Editorials across Maine newspapers seemed to blame the actions of the crowd on Sunday morning for the accident, refusing to believe the newly constructed gangplank could be at fault. "Of the accident at Mt. Desert Ferry little can be said except in expressions of sorrow for the fate of the victims. An official investigation will probably reveal more clearly the causes of the accident and may determine the responsibility. Before such investigation, any expressions of opinion must necessarily be founded on an imperfect understanding of facts," wrote the *Portland Daily Press*. "When the train arrived there was a rush for the *Sappho* and the immense new slip which measured 42 feet long and 10 or 12 feet wide was soon crowded and creaking under the heavy load imposed upon it. This alone is what caused the accident and it was certainly no fault of the Maine Central for the slip was of new planks three inches in thickness. All were supported by five large stringers and would have held any ordinary crowd."

The implication of the editorial in the *Bangor Daily Commercial* and the *Daily Reporter Journal* of Gardiner seemed to be that the fault of the accident was that of the crowd, not considering at all the possibility that the newly constructed gangplank could have been to blame. "There can be no discussion as to how the accident occurred. A look at the slip explains that fully. The slip is about 35 feet long and 10 feet across. Beneath the flooring are five large wooden stringers, 14 inches by 3, and in addition are three iron tresses. The iron must have given way first and then the stringers, although there could not have been more than a fraction of a second between. The slip was a new one, constructed and placed but about six weeks ago, the one previously in use being regarded as becoming unsafe," wrote the *Bangor Daily Commercial*.

"The disaster is one not due to any carelessness. The stage that gave way was a new one and was supposed to be strong enough to sustain any crowd that could be put upon it, but, as it proved, it was not," wrote the *Daily Reporter Journal* of Gardiner.

The *Waterville Mail* called for punishment if negligence was to be proved during the upcoming inquest. "Whether or not human negligence is the cause of the accident remains to be seen. There seems to be some difference of opinion on the subject at present. If such proves to be the fact, no censure can be too great for the guilty ones."

Other newspapers pleaded for mercy for the railroad company even if the fault was found to be theirs. "The rarity of such disasters in Maine gives this one all the more emphasis and prominence. It is not easy to place the blame, and judgement must not be harsh on the railroad company," wrote the *Kennebec Journal*.

In general, the Maine Central Railroad's safety record was considered quite good. No matter how safely the Maine Central operated, though, accidents in the railroad industry were inevitable, much like automobile accidents today. "The Maine Central has been exceptionally fortunate hitherto in the matter of accidents," wrote the *Portland Daily Press* the day after the disaster.

Because of the large number of fatalities in the Mount Desert Ferry disaster, the deadliest accident in Maine history at the time, 1899 automatically became the railroad's worst year in terms of fatalities. Only one other year, 1871, had even been close.

The year 1871 had been a bad one for the Maine Central Railroad, in operation for fifteen years at the time. In the summer of 1871, in Bangor, an evening train approaching the city broke through an overpass bridge in Hampden that still runs over a public road. Four passenger cars and one baggage car broke through and landed on the road below. A passenger and a brakeman were killed, and several passengers were injured. At one point after the accident, a crowd of ten thousand people had assembled at the accident scene to witness the spectacle of the wreckage.

The same summer, two miles outside Freeport, the axle of a railroad car broke, and the baggage car and five passenger cars were thrown off the tracks. The baggage master and brakeman were killed.

Luck was running heavily against the Maine Central Railroad that summer, for the very next day at Farmingdale, the Augusta and Gardiner train collided with a special train returning from the state Democratic convention. An engineer and fireman were killed. Also that summer, two freight trains collided at Vassalboro, injuring several passengers.

"On the whole 1871 was a terrible year for the road," wrote the *Portland Daily Press*.

There were other accidents involving the Maine Central Railroad. On April 18, 1886, about one mile from Mount Desert Ferry, one of the wheels of the five-car noon freight train broke, throwing the train from the tracks. Four cars were piled up in such a mass that a wrecking train was summoned from Bangor and worked until after midnight clearing the tracks. No one was injured.

Just a year before the Mount Desert Ferry disaster, on January 29, 1898, near Orono, a Maine Central Railroad passenger train left the rails and four passengers were killed and more than thirty injured, more or less seriously. This was the worst accident of the rail line until the disaster at Mount Desert Ferry. The town of Hancock would hold that unfortunate record for twenty years, until in 1919 a train accident in the town of Onawa, Maine, killed twenty-three people and injured fifty, again the deadliest accident in Maine history at the time.

One railroad mishap at Mount Desert Ferry that cost no lives but did cost the railroad money occurred in 1915. A train conductor arrived at Mount Desert Ferry to find a number of luxury Maxwell Roadster automobiles on the dock, awaiting transport to Sullivan and Sorrento to their new owners. Intrigued, the train crew was looking over the cars and Mr. Marston, the conductor, playfully seized the crank handle of one of them and gave it a turn. The car had been inadvertently left in gear, and it started to move. It bounced down the pier and rolled into Frenchman Bay. It was later recovered, at great expense, by Maine Central Railroad.

While the coroner's inquest was preparing to open in Mount Desert Ferry Monday morning, in Portland the president of the Maine Central Railroad was telling the railroad's side of the story.

Company president Franklin Wilson had arrived at Mount Desert Ferry late the night before by ferry from his summer home in Bar Harbor. Early Monday morning he and other railroad company officials had inspected the gangplank after removing it from the water. The gangplank was new, having been constructed just two months before. By now the officials had surmised that the accident had been caused by structural failure. They may or may not have known the reason for that failure, which would officially be brought out later that day during inquest testimony.

After inspecting the gangplank, President Wilson would head by train from Mount Desert Ferry to the Maine Central Railroad offices in Portland. There, surrounded by railroad general manager George F. Evans, and W. G. Davis, one of the company's directors, Wilson welcomed a reporter from the *Portland Daily Press*. "President Wilson talked in an earnest and feeling manner about the great calamity which happened on his road," said the reporter.

Mr. Wilson was asked if he had any theory as to what most contributed to the disaster. "In a most thoughtful manner he said in substance, that when it was known that the warships were to be at Bar Harbor, the Maine Central Railroad made every arrangement to accommodate the large crowds along its line, which it knew would most likely avail themselves of the excursion rates. Careful instructions were sent to all the employees of the road to do everything in their power for the comfort of the visitors and ample accommodations in the way of steamers were provided to take the crowds from the cars on arrival at the ferry. The trains moved with the greatest regularity and everything seemed to be going along like clockwork, and it was not until the early excursionists left the cars and began to cross the slip at Mt. Desert Ferry that any trouble began."

"At this spot things took a most serious turn," President Wilson told the reporter. "They acted like a set of crazy people."

Mr. Wilson told the reporter that he thought there was no necessity for the crowd's behavior because the Maine Central had all the water transportation that was required for the train's passengers, and a good deal more. He said the *Sappho* was at the slip, and this boat could easily take on board 1,200 passengers. He said that besides the *Sappho* there was the *Sebenoa*, capable of accommodating 400 passengers, and if these two boats had not been sufficient, another one was on call on the Bar Harbor side of Frenchman Bay.

Mr. Wilson also disputed the number of passengers of the 8:25 train. He said that as a matter of statistics, the early excursion train from

Bangor and places along the line had 968 persons aboard, not the 1,300 as was claimed by the train's passengers and other witnesses. Wilson's statement is assumed to be based on the number of tickets sold for the 8:25 train. In the crowded confusion of Sunday morning, the exact number of passengers on the train may never be known.

President Wilson said that the officers of the *Sappho*, when they saw how the crowd was pushing, did everything in their power to check it. The ship's mate and the crew tried to reason with the people and resorted almost to force to keep them back. General superintendent Morris McDonald had been directed the day before to be on hand at Mount Desert Ferry and to take a general supervision of matters because of the large crowd expected on Sunday with the arrival of the warships. He was on the spot at the time, said Mr. Wilson. Fearing trouble, Mr. McDonald did the best he could to avert it.

President Wilson said that despite all efforts on the part of the employees of the railroad to persuade the crowd to move in an orderly way, the train passengers surged on the slip and began to board the *Sappho* with the wildest kind of a rush. He estimated that two hundred people were packed together on the gangplank like sardines, and it was likely that even with this number everything would have gone well had not a most singular movement on the part of the crowd taken place. Mr. Wilson said that just before the slip broke, "for some unaccountable reason" the people nearest the boat and at the farthest end of the gangplank were seen by bystanders to push backward. The greater portion of the crowd, however, who were at the other end of the slip, spreading out beyond the center of it, continued to surge forward and thus created a very unequal strain. He said the result was a pressure on a certain spot in the slip, which doubled it up like a jackknife.

What President Wilson was describing as the cause of the accident seemed instead to be the immediate result of the accident. People on the gangplank had just a split-second warning that the gangplank was breaking beneath their feet, and there had been a very brief attempt by those at the point of the break to escape, while those on the wharf continued to try to push more passengers on the gangplank. This was the movement Wilson seemed to be describing.

Being asked about the strength and other details of the gangplank, President Wilson said the railroad company's officers had always considered it strong enough to hold all the people that could get on it at any one time. In fact, he said, it had been renovated not more than two months ago with new timber. When he was at Mount Desert Ferry, Wilson told the reporter, he had carefully inspected the work and believed that it was as good and sound as any to be found.

Despite the inspection of the gangplank Monday morning, Maine Central officials still were not sure what caused the bolts to pull out of the metal support brace, putting all the weight on the boards and thus causing the breaking of the wood. The only thing out of the ordinary that day had been the movements of the unruly crowd. This seemed a likely explanation of the accident's cause. It would not be until the inquest testimony Monday afternoon by the man who did the actual construction of the gangplank that the truth would be known.

At the end of the interview, Mr. Wilson made a statement on behalf of the Maine Central Railroad:

> *We feel that we have done everything in our power to care for the safety of our passengers, and since the accident nothing has been left undone by us to relieve the suffering. No pecuniary loss is weighing with us, it is the great calamity that has occurred on one of our lines to travel that gives us the most anxiety. We have spent a great deal of time and money to ensure the greatest safety of the traveling public and we feel that we have done it to the last degree. We know one thing that at the time of the accident all the employees of the road, trainmen, boatmen, etc., did everything in their power to save life and to make the loss of life and injuries to passengers as small as possible.*

Preparation for the coroner's inquest had begun just hours after the disaster with the arrival of Hancock County officials Sunday afternoon. By the end of Sunday night, Coroner Fields had impaneled the coroner's jury for the inquest into the disaster. The inquest jury consisted of five Hancock men: William F. Grant, S. C. Moore, James Butler, George W. Googins, and Nelson Stewart; and one man from Ellsworth: Henry Eppes.

The inquest was held on the grounds of The Bluffs, in the cottage of Mr. B. C. Addition, who had donated his summer home for the proceedings. The inquest was scheduled to begin at eight o'clock Monday morning, but the opening was delayed. Coroner Fields was still busy completing arrangements for the proceedings.

The first matter that needed to be settled before the inquest could proceed was by whom it would be conducted. John Bunker Jr., county attorney for Hancock County, had arrived at Mount Desert Ferry the day before. On Monday he planned to conduct the witness examinations. Accompanying Mr. Bunker to the inquest was a second coroner to assist with the proceedings.

Coroner Fields, who had also arrived at Mount Desert Ferry shortly after the disaster, said he had been on the scene of the disaster for twenty hours and assured Mr. Bunker that he would see the matter through.

Another major delay was caused by the lack of a stenographer to take down the inquest testimony. Hancock County officials had sent to Bangor for the services of a stenographer, but due to the high demand for that profession, one could not be had on short notice.

There was also a need for witnesses at the inquest. Late Monday morning, inside Mr. Addition's summer cottage, Coroner Fields officially opened the hearing into the deaths of the twenty victims of the disaster at Mount Desert Ferry. Before the beginning of the inquest, Coroner Fields had already solicited one witness, Capt. H. N. Fairbanks, a well-respected citizen of Bangor who was a guest at The Bluffs along with his family. The Fairbanks family were already on the wharf, waiting to board the *Sappho*, at the time the gangplank broke. More witnesses, however, would be needed. The inquest went into recess while Coroner Fields and Captain Fairbanks went to The Bluffs to find more witnesses.

Dr. Fields appears to have specifically waited until the train with the injured who had spent the night at The Bluffs had left Mount Desert Ferry before beginning his search. This may have been out of deference to their injuries. Perhaps he wanted less emotionally involved witnesses, as none of the witnesses who did eventually testify had gone into the water. Perhaps the timing was simply a coincidence. After fifteen minutes of scouring The Bluffs for witnesses. Dr. Fields and Captain Fairbanks returned to the cottage with a list of ten witness names: Mrs. John M. Oak, Mrs. W. L. Miller, Mrs. A. C. Higgins, Mrs. J. S. Smith, Miss Ethel Stratton, Miss Ryder, Miss Miller, Mrs. Herbert Dunning, Mrs. Abbie Fairbanks, and Miss Nora Fairbanks.

Mrs. Herbert Dunning, who was the only disaster survivor left at The Bluffs late Monday morning, was solicited to be a witness, though inquest officials thought she would not be able to render testimony on account of her physical condition and general weakness.

Out of that list, only three of the guests at The Bluffs testified at the inquest, as well as Captain Fairbanks.

The proceedings of the coroner's inquest were delayed until almost noon. They appear to have been unorganized and at times confusing. The cause of the accident, however, was fairly come to, with science- and fact-based evidence.

Dr. Fields reopened the proceedings and swore in the witnesses. There was a brief discussion as to whether the court should hear evidence without a stenographer to record it. The sentiment of the men of the jury was that testimony be taken in longhand. County attorney Bunker was given the job. Not knowing shorthand, Mr. Bunker had to write everything longhand, with the witnesses speaking slowly so that he could keep up with them. At the conclusion of their testimony, the witnesses would sign Mr. Bunker's written recording of that testimony.

For an unknown reason, legal counsel for the Maine Central Railroad was not in attendance at the inquest.

The first witness to testify was Capt. Henry N. Fairbanks of Bangor, who had been vacationing at The Bluffs with his wife, Abbie, and his daughter, Nora, when the disaster occurred.

Captain Fairbanks was one of Bangor's most prominent businessmen and a member of many military and social orders in that city. He was a noted US Army veteran with a distinguished career that included being wounded in the Civil War. He also served as a director for the European and North American Railroad and had been a member of the Maine legislature. A kind and generous man, Captain Fairbanks was known for his unusually gifted business acumen and charitable work. Henry Fairbanks was described as one of those citizens who made Bangor a better place for having lived in it.

Dr. Fields began the questioning, and Captain Fairbanks told his story. "I was standing on the wharf at about 10:20 a.m., awaiting the arrival of the train," he testified.

He stood beside the gangway near the outer end of the wharf, he said, watching the people going aboard and speaking to those he knew. He said it was an orderly crowd, no unusual pushing, but it was the size of the crowd that he noticed, all bent in the same direction and anxious to board the boat.

Captain Fairbanks said that a few people may have jumped over the chains at the side of the wharf to reach the ship quickly, but that there was no roughness. He said that an instant before the crash he heard a slight noise above the rush of feet, which he now believed was caused by the bolts pulling through the wooden headpiece of the gangway. Then, testified Captain Fairbanks, followed the crash of the breaking timbers and the fatal plunge.

I should judge that perhaps two hundred had gone into the boat when there was a noise followed so closely with a crash that the two were scarcely distinguishable. The slip broke in two about three feet at my right and let the mass down into the water. My first move was to seize a settee and with aid it was put over lengthwise. Next, myself and others took hold and moved one of the gangplanks around to the head of the slip, and that was lowered down to the people who were in the water. To the best of my judgement, after having counted the planks in the slip [46 in number], I estimated five persons on each plank, that would be 230 persons on the slip.

Asked by the coroner if there were any washers between the nuts and the timbers on the rods at the outer headpiece, Mr. Fairbanks said he could not say. He had looked at the headpiece, but the rod heads were covered by a cap of two-inch plank spiked on.

In reply to a question from one of the jurors, touching on the quality of the headpiece, Captain Fairbanks said he was of the opinion that it was very good spruce. The iron truss was also, in his opinion, a substantial one, and the stringers appeared at the broken parts to be free from rot. The lumber was of the size usually used in such construction, testified Captain Fairbanks.

County attorney Bunker then began his questioning, to which Captain Fairbanks gave the following answers:

I found five stringers had given away; four had broken and one had parted where it was nailed together. Later examination developed the fact that the bolts had pulled through the timber on the outside of the slip, which let the truss down into the water; and it is my impression that the first noise heard was when the bolts pulled through the timber. I should say that the head timber was such as would ordinarily be used in such construction. I did not measure it as it was in the water. I should think the iron trusses were in good order. I examined them casually. The stringers were of spruce and seemed to be of the usual strength for such lumber, without any appearance of decomposition.

Coroner Fields asked, "Have you noticed any change in the condition of that slip since last night?"

Captain Fairbanks replied, "The part of the slip next to the wharf had been removed to give the diver an opportunity to do his work, either by cutting away or sawing. The stringers were cut or sawed away and the planking had been taken up."

Mr. Addition, at whose cottage the inquest was being held but who himself was simply a spectator to the proceedings, suddenly interjected. "Put that down," he instructed the county attorney, who was recording the testimony by hand as quickly as he could.

Mr. Addition's command to the county attorney took the court by surprise. County attorney Bunker asked Mr. Addition who he represented. Mr. Addition replied that he represented a group of people affected by the tragedy and also acted as a citizen who wanted to see fair play. "I represent the friends of eight or ten of those who lost their lives in the slip yesterday," Mr. Addition told the court.

Charles B. Drummey, Esq., the young lawyer from Ellsworth who had been enlisted by Hancock County officials to help with the questioning, said that the participation in the proceedings by a spectator, even one who said he represented friends of the victims, was irregular.

"There was not much argument," reported the *Boston Globe*, who had a reporter in attendance.

Bennington A. Addition, fifty-six, of Bangor, was a Civil War veteran. He was described by the *Boston Globe* as having "distinguished himself by his efficient work of rescue" during the disaster the previous day. Mr. Addition had been spending Sunday with his family at his rented summer cottage at Mount Desert Ferry and was on the wharf when the gangplank broke. He at once put a boat in the water and tried to get under the slip but was blocked by the *Sappho*, already in the middle of rescue operations. Despite that, Mr. Addition was able to save several persons from the water. After the rescue, Mr. Addition threw open his cottage for use by the rescued, and during the day cared for four people, including Mr. and Mrs. Lysander Palmer, Elmer Nichols, and Miss Ida Edminster, all of Bangor.

The county attorney was advised that Coroner Fields had solicited Mr. Addition to assist in the hearing. Mr. Addition's original request of the court was obeyed.

"How was that, Mr. Fairbanks?" asked the county attorney of the witness.

"I said that part of the stringers were sawed or cut away." Captain Fairbanks went on to say that the broken ends of the gangplank had been removed from the stringers before he looked at the wreckage.

The *Boston Globe* put Captain Fairbanks's remark into context. They pointed out that the cutting had been done between eight and nine o'clock that morning and had been witnessed by everybody on the busy wharf at the time. The ragged ends were in the way of the divers and had been sawed off by the Maine Central Railroad workmen engaged in converting the outer half of the wrecked slip into a float from which the divers could work. The ends easily could have been thrown into the water, but instead were placed on the wharf so that all who cared to might examine them.

"Had the Maine Central Road desired to conceal anything it might easily have done so by clearing away the wreck during the night and sending out of town the employee under whose supervision the slip was made. But the company did not. It courted the keenest inquiry, and did nothing to balk a complete investigation," wrote the *Boston Globe*.

Mr. Addition was also allowed to question the witness. Reporters noted that all of Mr. Addition's questions were designed to bring replies showing faulty construction in the wrecked slip.

"Were not there stringers of unequal thickness, and shaky and gnarly?" Mr. Addition asked Captain Fairbanks.

"I should say the thickness was about the same, but the width of the stringers varied. I did not see any gnarls," replied Fairbanks.

At the end of Captain Fairbanks's testimony, C. B. Drummey sought to take care of the technicalities of the proceedings. He asked the captain how, in his opinion, the dead met their death.

"By being drowned," replied Captain Fairbanks.

"When?"

"Between 10:00 and 11:00 a.m., August 6, 1899, in consequence of the breaking of the slip."

"And where?"

"At Mount Desert Ferry."

Captain Fairbanks concluded his testimony at one o'clock in the afternoon, and the court then adjourned to The Bluffs for dinner. Inquest officials returned to the cottage shortly after two o'clock, and after having been there a few minutes, then went down to the wharf at the suggestion of county attorney Bunker. Mr. Bunker, the coroner, and the jury got down on their knees on the wharf and gave the timbers of the gangplank a closer examination than the brief look the night before. The court returned to the cottage at 2:43 p.m. Before the inquest officially went back into session, Mr. Addition produced a short piece of stringer from the broken gangplank for the inspection of the men of the inquest in his cottage.

"The piece of stringer was of one of the broken stringers, a three by 12 piece, which, during the dinner hour, had been nosed, tasted, whittled and otherwise studied by the jury. It was a piece of tree that had grown quickly, the rings were not compact, and the wood looked brittle," wrote the *Bangor Daily Commercial*.

The issue was whether the gangplank had been constructed of spruce, as contended by the Maine Central Railroad, or instead had been made with the weaker wood conifer, commonly referred to as fir. One of the Hancock men on the jury advanced the opinion that the lumber was not spruce but fir instead.

"That's no spruce," said the juror. "That's a sort of outcast in the lumber market, and pretty mean stuff anyhow. Darn me if that don't set me thinking; it smells like spruce, and it don't; it's fir, that's what it is. Look at that knot," and he pointed at a little round whirlpool of grain. A juror with a long, sharp nose put his nostrils close to one end of it and sniffed three or four times of the broken piece of wood.

"That's what, fir."

Captain Fairbanks, described by the *Boston Globe* during the exchange as "a grave-looking man with sandy side whiskers," sniffed at the wood, as did one of the reporters covering the inquest. Captain Fairbanks and Mr. J. N. Taylor, reporter for the *Boston Globe*, said they felt satisfied that they had seen enough Maine lumber to be able to recognize spruce when they saw it, and they declared they were looking at spruce at that moment. After further discussion and some whittling of the wood in question, the disputing critics agreed that the wood must be white or Norway spruce, supporting the railroad's contention that they used quality wood in the construction of the gangplank.

"That there stuff is white spruce. It has bark something like a Norway pine and it whittles easy; some call it pumpkin spruce," wrote the *Boston Globe*.

The matter was settled.

Captain Fairbank's wife, Abbie, and daughter Nora, who were with him at the time of the disaster, testified substantially to the same effect as did

Captain Fairbanks regarding the events of the accident, except that they did not hear any noise before the breaking of the gangplank as he had.

Both Mrs. Fairbanks and her daughter contradicted previous public statements by Maine Central Railroad, both testifying that no efforts were made by anyone associated with the railroad to keep the crowd back from the gangway.

All three of the witnesses believed that all the dead were drowned, not crushed in the fall or by planks being thrown in for their rescue, an important point in the legal apportionment of blame.

Mrs. Abbie A. Fairbanks told the court her story:

I was at the accident. At about 10:25 I was leaning against the chain which extends along the side of the slip, when I heard the train coming down the track. Almost before it came to a stop a throng of people seemed to rush upon the wharf, going at once to the prow of the boat and to the slip. I was frightened then for fear of the torrent of people which came pouring down on the rush. Harder and harder they crowded onto the slip until all at once it seemed as if there was a moment of suspense and then a long, creaking crash and a splash and scream and they were under. For a moment all seemed unable to know what to do, and then all hands set to work in their different ways of trying to help the distressed. Then I turned from the scene.

In reply to additional questions from the county attorney, Mrs. Fairbanks testified:

I was impressed with the feeling that the slip dropped slowly at first; that is why I was frightened for the people on the slip. I remarked to someone that they would never get through without an accident. Mrs. Billings was the only one of the dead whom I recognized. As far as I could see there were no precautions taken by the officers of the boat to prevent the people from rushing onto the slip. People around me were asking, "Where are the officers, I do not see any officers." It seemed as though there were none there to look after the crowd. I knew nothing

of the weakness of the structure but was led to make the remark about
fearing an accident by the way the crowd rushed upon the slip.

Miss Nora L. Fairbanks of Bangor then gave her testimony. In addition to having witnessed the accident, Miss Fairbanks had also given up her room at the hotel for the use of the injured and had worked all day and evening on Sunday nursing the injured back to health. She testified as follows:

I was at the wharf when the accident occurred. The 10:15 train
arrived crowded with people; all made a rush for the boat. Some
climbed over the side of the railing of the boat and were pushed under
the chain where I was standing, but that was soon stopped. Next came
the crash. All were thrown down into the water. I did not notice the
slip dropping slowly. I heard one loud crash. In my opinion the death
of the people whose bodies I saw were caused by drowning. Mrs. Bill-
ings was the only person taken from the water whom I knew. I do not
know whether she was dead when taken from the water.

Miss Fairbanks was then questioned by Mr. Addition. "Did you see any of the employees of the railroad or officers of the boat preventing this mass of people crowding onto this slip?"

"I did not."

"How far were you standing from the slip when it went down?"

"I was standing a foot away from the slip."

Miss Ethel M. Stratton of Bangor was the fourth witness of the day. A student at Smith College, Miss Stratton had also been a guest at The Bluffs Hotel the day the accident happened.

"I was present at the accident. I was on the wharf when the 10:15 train came in. The train was crowded and the wharf was soon thronged. I think about 200 people had gone down into the boat, when I heard an awful crash and saw the slip go into the water with all the people. The water seemed to rush right in on top of them, I turned back. That is all I saw."

Miss Stratton corroborated the other witness statements that Maine Central officials had done nothing to try to control the crowd. "Many climbed over the bow of the boat and others tried to push by the chain on the sides of the slip and were prevented only by the bystanders," testified Miss Stratton.

The next person to give their story was William Witham, of Lisbon Falls, who would turn out to be the inquest's most important witness.

William Witham, forty-nine, was the Maine Central Railroad foreman of bridges, headquartered out of Bangor, who had charge of the construction of the gangplank. He also had actively participated in the gangplank's construction just two months earlier. It was the newness of the gangplank that caused many people to never suspect it as the culprit in the disaster. "His words bore heavy weight," wrote the *Bangor Daily Commercial*.

At the inquest, Mr. Witham was first asked questions by county attorney Bunker.

Mr. Witham testified that his orders for the building of the gangplank came from Mr. Powers, superintendent of the Bridge and Building Department of the Maine Central Railroad. The material for the gangway was not ordered by Mr. Witham himself, he testified, but had been landed on the wharf at Mount Desert Ferry that summer for his use.

The new gangway was thirty-seven and a half feet long and ten feet wide. There were five support beams running the length of the gangway. These timbers were reinforced by three one-inch truss rods set in a hard pine cross timber at the hinge of the pier and a spruce timber at the outer end. These rods were placed through holes made with a chisel, not auger, and were fastened on the outside by two-and-a-half-inch bolts, screwed flush with the timber.

Mr. Witham said he was not an expert on quality of timber but thought the material provided was in good condition. He said the gangplank should have been strong enough to bear all strain that could be put upon it.

Below is the testimony of William Witham. Some testimony is a summation by the newspaper reporters of the words used by Mr.

Witham. Testimony in quotation marks are direct quotes. The questioning was begun by county attorney Bunker.

Q: Are you the foreman of the construction of the slip that was broken yesterday?

A: I am, sir.

Q: State when the slip was built and if in your opinion it was thoroughly constructed.

A: Completed June 4th, this year. I think it was thoroughly constructed as far as the workmanship. I constructed the slip as near my orders as I understood.

Q: How long and how wide is the slip, and how supported and constructed?

A: Slip 37 feet, six inches long, 10 feet wide. Inner end, or head of slip, was an 8 x 12 hard pine timber, about one foot longer on each end than the length of the slip, the ends resting on the caps of the piling of the wharf, thereby forming the hinge, the ends being rounded on the underside. The outer ends were supported by a beam under the slip, about four foot from the outer end, suspended by a gallows flare and chains over pulleys. Was constructed of four stringers, 8 x 12 and a double tenant, one end fitting into the hard pine timber at the head of the slip, the other ends fitting in to the head piece, 6 x 12, spruce. The center of the slip was further supported by three brass rods running the head timbers under two truss breams, 4 x 12, dividing the slip into about three equal spaces and covered with two inch plank put in between the stringers, set edgewise, for the purpose of stiffening the center of the covering, in reference to running heavy truck loads of lumber. The rods were 1 & 1/8 inches in diameter, of iron, and the ends upset to 1 & 2/8 inches, where the threads were. Nuts, I should think, were about 2 & ½ inches in diameter.

Q: Were the head timbers countersunk to let the nuts in flush with the outer side of the timbers?

A: The timber at the head of the slip and the other one were cut in but very little; not flush. The plank covering the outside timber was cut to let the nuts in.

Q: How big an auger were the holes bored with?

A: About 1 & 3/8 inches; I know we had to drive the bolts through the holes.

Q: What kind of lumber was used in the stringers?

A: I thought it was spruce.

Q: How many persons, if they were crowded on, would it hold, do you think?

A: Have no idea.

Q: How far were the nuts turned on the threads of the truss rods?

A: The nuts were flush. To let the nuts into the head timber we cut with mallet and chisel. I have seen the ends today.

At the end of Mr. Witham's testimony, Mr. Addition whispered across the round table to the inquest officials, after which the county attorney asked this critical question: "Should there not have been iron plates or washers between the nuts and the head piece to prevent the truss rods from pulling through?"

"I think the circumstances now show that there should have been," replied William A. Witham, the man who constructed the gangplank at Mount Desert Ferry.

Coroner Fields then asked, "What, in your opinion, was the direct cause of the accident?"

"My opinion is that the nuts drew through the timber, and as they did so, the slip kept settling, and the final collapse came at one instant," replied Mr. Witham.

Mr. Addition then started asking questions of Mr. Witham directly. "Why didn't you put some washers onto the nuts?" asked Mr. Addition.

"Because I had none," came Mr. Witham's "steady reply," as described by reporters in attendance. "That was one reason; another was that I did not think washers were needed."

The cause of the accident had been revealed. The cause had not been the disorderly crowd that rushed the gangplank from the still-moving train. The cause of the accident was the lack of a handful of simple metal washers. They had not been landed with the supplies to build the gangplank, and the man who built the gangplank, when he discovered the oversight, said he thought them unnecessary anyway.

Mr. Addition continued with his questions.

Q: Who gave you orders to construct the slip?

A: Mr. P. M. Watson, superintendent of bridges and buildings, Maine Central Railroad.

Q: Did he give you orders as to the size of the timber to be used in it?

A: I had nothing to do with the ordering of the timber.

Q: Where did you find the timber when you did the work?

A: On the wharf.

The mention of lumber gave Mr. Addition an opening for a lead in a new direction. Mr. Addition handed the witness the piece of wood that the out-of-session court had examined and argued over earlier during the lunch break.

"Is the grain in that piece of stringer firm or is it soft and shaky?" asked Mr. Addition.

"It looks like soft spruce," replied Mr. Witham. The witness then sat the piece of wood down.

"Are you acquainted with the different kinds of lumber?" asked Mr. Addition.

"No, I could not state it according to the grading at the mill."

Mr. Addition then voiced an aside, remarking loudly enough to be heard by those in the audience, about things having gone to a pretty state when a builder would make the confession that he did not know the quality of lumber.

Mr. Addition was misconstruing what the witness had just said. Mr. Witham distinctly stated that he did not know the mill grading of lumber, but that he could distinguish between good and inferior stock. Mr. Addition's anger toward the witness and the Maine Central Railroad seemed obvious, and understandable.

Mr. Witham's testimony ended at five o'clock on Monday afternoon.

Hugh Chapman of Bangor, attorney for the Maine Central Railroad, arrived late in the afternoon, after Mr. Witham's testimony had been taken. After looking over the testimony, in which the actions of the Maine Central Railroad were directly implicated as the cause of the accident, Mr. Chapman told the court that he had nothing to offer.

A difference of facts had arisen during the first day of testimony. Maine Central Railroad officials had said publicly that railroad officials on the wharf at Mount Desert Ferry had attempted to control the crowd, while the testimony offered from witnesses on Monday contradicted that statement. The jury requested statements from the officers of the *Sappho* and other Maine Central employees in regard to whether or not any effort was made on the part of the railroad to prevent the mad rush to the gangplank. The inquest was adjourned for the evening so that inquest officials could search for witnesses who could testify to that effect.

"The opening of the coroner's inquest into yesterday's frightful accident at Mt. Desert Ferry when 20 persons lost their lives and a score or more were badly hurt, has brought to the surface, as it were, an especially keen interest in the accident's cause," wrote the *Portland Daily Express*. "But interest does not lessen in the least the feeling of horror and sadness which spread over the entire community when the news of the disaster first went forward."

By Tuesday morning life at Mount Desert Ferry was returning to normal. "Save the vacant place from which the broken slip has been removed, there is little to remind one of the accident," wrote the *Bangor Daily Commercial*.

At 8:15 a.m. the inquest had reassembled at the cottage of Mr. Addition. There were no spectators at the inquest this morning. County attorney Bunker was not present. Mr. Drummey assisted the inquest jurors on behalf of the county in questioning the witnesses.

Hannibal E. Hamlin, forty, an attorney from Ellsworth, was in attendance Tuesday morning, representing the Maine Central Railroad. Mr. Hamlin's name had clout. He was the son of former US vice president Hannibal Hamlin of Maine, who had served under former president Abraham Lincoln during Lincoln's first term in office. The junior Hamlin had grown up in Bangor and was a graduate of Colby College and the Boston University School of Law. He was both a lawyer and a Maine legislator, as well as a future Maine attorney general.

The fault of the accident, the lack of simple washers in the construction of the gangplank, seemed to have been established the day before. There was little the Maine Central Railroad could do on Tuesday other than nurse its public relations black eye. Mr. Hamlin asked no questions of the witnesses, nor did he object to questions asked by anyone else.

Tuesday's testimony focused on what part the Maine Central Railroad officials played in trying to control the crowd on the morning of the disaster. Specifically, questions were asked regarding whether general superintendent Morris McDonald had been on the wharf at the time of the train's arrival, as had been contended by the railroad

Just two witnesses were examined that morning, both Maine Central Railroad employees. Ivory L. Wardwell, station agent at Mount Desert Ferry, and William W. Jellison, the station's baggage master, both took the stand.

"Their testimony added practically nothing new to that previously presented," commented the *Portland Daily Press*.

Mr. Wardwell was the first to be examined. He testified that he had placed safety chains along both sides of the gangplank so that the crowd could enter it only at the ends. Mr. Wardwell said this was a precaution to keep the crowd from rushing the gangplank. When asked about what he observed during the accident, Mr. Wardwell stated that he could not state whether any precautions were taken to keep the crowd in check. Mr. Wardwell was asked about the location of Mr. McDonald at the time the train arrived at the wharf Sunday morning.

"I do not know whether Superintendent McDonald of the Maine Central was on the wharf at the time of the breaking of the slip," replied Mr. Wardwell.

Mr. Wardwell was then asked about the construction of the slip. He said he had carefully inspected the wood to be used in the construction of the gangplank, and that it looked like old-growth spruce without sap. He said he had never looked closely at the gangplank once it was completed.

I had examined the timbers of the slip when the slip was built. I called the stringers old growth spruce, in which there was no sap. The lumber was apparently all right, and in my opinion was suited for the purpose to which it was put. I certainly thought the slip of sufficient strength to hold any excursion traffic which would come to it. I had carefully handled the lumber over before it was put into use. I found it perfectly sound. I was on the wharf every minute while the frame of the slip was being put together. I did not examine the inside construction, for I did not happen to be on the spot to see the inside construction.

William Jellison, the next witness, testified that he had received no instructions from supervisors about taking care that the excursionists did not meet with an accident at the ferry. He could not tell whether any officials of the railroad company were taking care of the people at the gangplank, he testified, as his duties with the baggage kept him away from the gangplank when the accident occurred.

Mr. Jellison was also asked about the construction of the gangplank. He said he certainly thought that the slip was strong enough to hold all the persons who could get on it. He said he had never given the timber of the slip a particular examination and did not know whether it was a plate or washers on the outer end of the slip where the truss rods were fastened to it. "I had not thought it any part of my duties to examine the slip," said Mr. Jellison.

The two new witnesses both testified that the tremendous crowd rushed upon the wharf with fearful force in spite of considerations of good judgment.

Mr. Jellison would be the final inquest witness. Upon completion of his testimony, county officials declared the proceedings closed. The jury's attention now turned to determining its verdict, which seemed to be arrived at with little difficulty.

As was legal form and tradition, the names of the dead of the disaster at Mount Desert Ferry were read aloud before the reading of the verdict:

George H. Bennett, of Bangor, age 35

Mrs. G. H. Bennett, of Bangor, age unknown

Mrs. A. H. Billings, of Bangor, age 68

Irving Bridges, of Hancock, age 28

Albert Colson, of Levant, age 40

Clifford Cushman, of Corinth, age 25

Mrs. George Derwent, of Bangor, age 23

Charles W. Downes, of Ellsworth, age 13 or 14

Mrs. Hollis B. Estey, of Ellsworth, age 31

Ora M. Lank, of Danforth, age 28

Miss Blanche Lewis, of Hampden, age 19

Melvin McCard, of Corinth, age 31

Margaret Mower, of San Francisco, age 67

Joseph Murphy, of Old Town, age 30

Mrs. William Murray, of Brewer, age 23

Mrs. Alonzo P. Oakes, of Bangor, age 35

Mrs. Charles Stover, of Ellsworth, age 47

Miss Grace Sumner, of Bangor, age 15

F. E. Sweetser, of Portland, age 31

Miss Elizabeth Ward, of Bangor, age 19

"All came to their death by drowning near the slip of the Maine Central Railroad company's wharf at Mt. Desert Ferry, town of Hancock, Hancock County, State of Maine, on Sunday, the 6th day of August, A.D. 1899, at about 10:40 in the forenoon, and further say that said drowning was caused by the breaking of the slip in said wharf, which said slip was imperfectly and defectively constructed."

Editorial writers from the state's newspapers were overall mum on the verdict. The Maine Central Railroad was defended by the *Bangor Daily Commercial*:

> *Admitting the fact of the law of accidents; of their unknown occurrence, and of their taking place even when every possible precaution is made against them; and also taking into account the high condition of the Maine Central physically and in its administration, there comes this fact: That no one can suffer in consequence of so terrible a calamity as that of Sunday, as does the management at the road, and that none can deplore it more than they. They are for the people of Maine, devoted to all our interests, and deriving its business for our people it is the first object of the management to give the state a good service. If the people of Maine could realize their feelings in the face of so great*

a calamity as this, they would surely be led to stay their criticism and to give them the fullest sympathy and helpfulness in the great strain to which they must be subjected.

The only real criticism in the wake of the verdict came from Chester W. Robbins, the editor of the *Old Town Enterprise*. Mr. Robbins had been saved from the water that Sunday, only to stay in safety long enough to gather his wits before jumping back in. Of any newspaper editor in Maine, Mr. Robbins certainly had earned the right to criticize the railroad. He chose to lay the blame where it was due—at the feet of Maine Central Railroad employee William Witham.

It is extremely unfortunate that the MCRR should suffer so much loss from recent serious accidents. We recall the Orono accident of last year, the claims for all of which have not as yet been settled, and to think of this, the worst of all, the result of one man's careless negligence, to allow those rods, too short for washers if he had them, so short even that the head pieces were cut away to reach them, in putting on the nuts—a sham—a sham—and covered over—a death trap for twenty souls, and untold suffering for scores of innocent victims.

The Mourning

The terrible catastrophe at Mt. Desert Ferry Sunday, when a merry excursion party suddenly became the saddest of funerals, has cast a gloom over all of Maine.

—Ellsworth American

The cause of the accident having been established and the verdict being announced at Mount Desert Ferry on Tuesday morning would be little comfort for the people of Ellsworth and Bangor, who spent that day burying their dead.

Since the news of the disaster had first been heard in Ellsworth two days previously, the city had been in mourning. "In Ellsworth four homes are made desolate—four useful lives have been snuffed out as a candle, and the homes which they brightened are dark. There are others there who are not yet without the shadow of death, and the prayers of a community are with them that they may recover. . . . It is needless to say that the sympathy of the whole community is with the families from which loved ones have been snatched away," wrote the *Ellsworth American*.

George Lowell, sixty-two, who was suffering from a fractured rib and bruises, was said to be not recovering as quickly as hoped.

Carrie S. Pomeroy was the mother of one of the two children to die in the disaster, teenager Charles W. Downes. Mrs. Pomeroy had gone into the water with her son when the gangplank broke. She was described as suffering from shock and bruises.

Shortly after the disaster, the postponement of the annual Castine excursion of the Ellsworth chapter of the Rebekahs was announced, which had been scheduled for just a few days after the disaster. One member of the organization had been lost in the disaster, Mrs. Bertha Estey, and several other members of the social service group had been thrown in the water, including Mrs. Estey's parents, who had watched their only daughter drown. Miss Louise Bridges and Mrs. Melvin Davis, who lost their brother, Irving Bridges, were also part of the Rebekahs, as were Julia Billington and Maud Raymond, all still severely injured.

Mrs. Davis was in serious condition suffering from pneumonia. Miss Billington was described to be suffering from hysteria. Miss Raymond, who was first reported drowned, was unconscious when taken from the water. She was at home suffering from pneumonia and an injury to the spine.

As was routine, the death notices for Ellsworth's dead ran in the next edition of the *Ellsworth American*:

DIED:

BRIDGES—Drowned at Mt. Desert Ferry, Aug 6, Irving Bridges, of North Hancock, aged 31 years, 3 months.

DOWNES—Drowned at Mt. Desert Ferry, Aug 6, Charles W. Downes, of Ellsworth, aged 12 [actually 13 or 14] years.

ESTEY—Drowned at Mt. Desert Ferry, Aug 6, Mrs. Hollis B. Estey, of Ellsworth, aged 31 years.

STOVER—Drowned at Mt. Desert Ferry, Aug 6, Mrs. Charles E. Stover, of Ellsworth, aged 47 years.

On Tuesday, at about the same time the verdict was being announced at Mount Desert Ferry, the first two funerals in Ellsworth were being held. At 10:00 a.m. Charles Downes, the youngest victim of the disaster, was eulogized by Rev. J. P. Simonton of Ellsworth before being buried in the Woodbine Cemetery in that city. Separately was held the funeral of Irving Bridges, with the Rev. C. S. McLearn officiating.

Services for thirty-one-year-old newlywed Bertha Estey were held in the Estey home in Ellsworth Tuesday afternoon. Rev. Simonton, having conducted the service for young Charles Downes just a few hours earlier, also officiated for Mrs. Estey.

"Funeral services at the home yesterday afternoon were attended by a host of sorrowing friends," wrote the *Ellsworth American*. "Death, when it takes one of ripened years, is sad, but when a young wife is cut down it is still more sad."

At 3:00 p.m. was held the funeral of Addie Stover, forty-seven, who left behind a husband and three children. Her funeral was held on Grant Street, with the Rev. J. M. Adams officiating.

Wrote the *Ellsworth American*:

Ellsworth is plunged into deepest mourning. When four bodies were carried to their last resting place, was one of the saddest days in the history of Ellsworth,"

The terrible catastrophe at Mt. Desert Ferry Sunday, when a merry excursion party suddenly became the saddest of funerals, has cast a gloom over all of Maine, and particularly over this section. In Ellsworth, where four dead were buried, and where others are still hovering within the shadow, there is sadness in all hearts.

The story of that dreadful scene has been told and retold, and the horror of it has not been lessened by the telling. In the minds of all who witnessed the accident, the picture will ever be fresh in their memory, nor will any who visited the place within a few hours after the accident ever forget the heartrending scenes of that fatal day.

The story of the catastrophe is the story of an instantaneous transition from merriment to mourning, the story of frightful death and noble heroism. And what is perhaps remarkable is that no one of the hundreds of people who witnessed or participated in that terrible death struggle, tells of a single instance of cowardly self-preservation at the sacrifice of others, but only of noble effort to rescue others at personal risk.

The same heart-wrenching scenes were playing out at the same time in Bangor as members of that community made their final goodbyes.

In Bangor the mourning had begun the day before, with the burial of Miss Elizabeth A. Ward, nineteen years old. Amid a congregation of one thousand people in St. Mary's Church in Bangor, Elizabeth Ward was accorded the rites of the Catholic church before being borne to Mount Pleasant Cemetery for interment.

On Tuesday morning Bangor's churches were opened for funeral services, and clergymen from every denomination were called upon to perform the last duties to the dead. The ceremonies in Bangor that day were described as impressive. The demand for flowers had practically emptied the stock of the local florists, who, since the disaster, had been sending out of the city for roses and other floral offerings.

On Tuesday morning Mrs. A. H. Billings, sixty-eight, and Mrs. Margaret Mower, sixty-seven, two childhood friends who now as widows had been passing a merry summer Sunday together, lay side by side in a double funeral at the Universalist Church in Bangor.

In separate funerals that day were laid to rest Miss Grace Sumner, fifteen, Mrs. George H. Derwent, twenty-three, and Mrs. Alonzo P. Oakes, thirty-five. Joseph Murphy Sr., thirty, who left behind a six-month-old child, was laid to rest in Old Town the same day.

"Bangor was a city of mourning today," wrote the *Boston Globe*. "All over the city hundreds of people are sorrowing for friends or relatives lost in the frightful accident at Mount Desert Ferry on Sunday."

The funeral of Frank Sweetser, the popular Maine Central Railroad employee from Portland who had been traveling with his friend, Edmund Greenough, was conducted in Portland on Wednesday. At 2:30 p.m. the services were begun privately, with prayers being said at the home of Mr. Sweetser's mother and stepfather, Col. and Mrs. E. C. Milliken. At 3:00 p.m. the public service for Mr. Sweetser was held at the West End Congregational Church in Portland.

The church was crowded to the very doors, and a great many who attended the services were obliged to stand during the exercises. Nearly all of the employees of the Maine Central Railroad were present, as well as a delegation from Bramhall Lodge, Knights of Pythias, and many friends and acquaintances of the young man. The floral tributes were very elaborate, almost hiding the altar and casket from view. Among them was a magnificent floral arrangement from the clerk of the auditor's department of the Maine Central and other floral designs from railroad president Wilson, general passenger agent Mr. Boothby, and other railroad officials. Music was furnished by a quartet composed of Messrs. Davie, Tracey, Evans, and Mitchell. Addresses were delivered by Rev. Mr. Philip Dunbar and Rev. Mr. Charles Garland, both of whom were friends of the deceased. After the service Mr. Sweetser was buried at the Evergreen Cemetery in Portland.

THE DEAD OF THE DISASTER AT MOUNT DESERT FERRY

ELLSWORTH

Irving Bridges

Irving Bridges, thirty-one, was the only resident of Hancock to die in the disaster at Mount Desert Ferry. At the time of the disaster, Irving Bridges was a farmer, with a farm on Hancock Road. Though he lived in Hancock, Mr. Bridges had many friends in Ellsworth and spent much time there. "Irving Bridges, though really a resident of Hancock, has always been closely identified with Ellsworth, and is thus considered one of its people," wrote the *Portland Daily Press*.

Mr. Bridges was the son of Phoebe Bridges of Hancock, and the late James Bridges, both originally from Penobscot. Irving was one of nine children, with five brothers: Lytton, Wadsworth, George, Isaac, Sydney; and three sisters: Cora Reynolds, Mabel Davis, and Luella, known as Louise.

Mr. Bridges was a widower, having lost his wife Anna four years before the disaster. The couple had no children. Irving Bridges was one of the few people at Mount Desert Ferry who was not going to Bar Harbor to see the North Atlantic Squadron. Instead, he was traveling to spend the Sunday with his fiancée.

Mr. Bridges was as well known in Bar Harbor as he was in Ellsworth. He met his betrothed, Miss Marshall of Bar Harbor, while he was employed for Mr. Fremont Smith, a prominent Mount Desert Island resident for whom Mr. Bridges worked for several years. Mr. Bridges and Miss Marshall planned to be married in the fall.

Irving Bridges was accompanied to Mount Desert Ferry on Sunday morning by two of his sisters, Miss Louise Bridges and Mrs. Mabel Davis, as well as Mrs. Davis's sister-in-law, Ettie Davis. Many members of the Bridges family were involved in the Rebekahs, a service organization, and two members of the organization were also traveling with the Bridges party, Miss Maud Raymond, and Julia Billington of Ellsworth, as well as others.

The entire Bridges party went into the water when the gangplank broke. Louise Bridges found herself under the water but was able to get her head back to the air. She found herself near a piling, to which she clung until rescued, all the while watching the struggle for life playing out around her. After being rescued, Louise Bridges was listed as being in a serious medical condition, suffering from nervous shock. Irving's sister Mabel Davis found herself pulled underwater several times by the struggling mass above her. Mrs. Davis was described as being injured and badly bruised.

Miss Ettie Davis, Mabel's sister-in-law, had a very narrow escape from death in the water and was reported to be almost totally exhausted after her hard struggle for life. She was listed as suffering from severe nervous shock and hysteria. Family friend Maud Raymond was badly injured in the disaster, and at first was mistakenly added to the list of deceased. "Miss Maud Raymond, who was first reported drowned, was unconscious when taken from the water. She is now suffering from pneumonia and injury to the spine," wrote the *Ellsworth American*.

Irving Bridges was killed in the disaster. He is buried next to his wife, Anna, at the Woodbine Cemetery in Ellsworth.

His family would file a claim against the Maine Central Railroad and would receive three thousand dollars, which was divided among the remaining family. Two years after Irving Bridges's death, a son was born in Hancock to Isaac and Carrie Bridges, Irving's brother and sister-in-law. The child was named Irving Bridges.

Mrs. Bertha Curtis Estey

Bertha Estey was born and died in Hancock, Maine.

Bertha B. Curtis, thirty-one, was the only child of Mr. and Mrs. A. W. Curtis of Ellsworth. Bertha Curtis married Hollis B. Estey, from Trescott, three years before the disaster. Together Mr. and Mrs. Estey operated an Ellsworth steam laundry.

Bertha Estey was described as having a pleasing personality and many friends. She was a member of Nokomis Rebekah Lodge, as were the sisters of fellow victim Irving Bridges.

In the disaster, both Mr. and Mrs. Estey had been thrown into the water when the gangplank broke, as were Bertha Estey's parents. Mr. Estey was able to support his wife, putting and keeping his arm around her. Bertha Estey was a victim of a well-intentioned person on the wharf who threw a plank wildly into the pen. The plank separated Bertha and Hollis Estey, and Bertha sank beneath the water.

"The news of her death in the arms of her husband in sight of her father and mother was the cause of general sorrow," wrote the *Boston Globe*.

Mrs. Estey is buried in the Woodbine Cemetery in Ellsworth. On March 3, 1901, Bertha Curtis Estey was born in Ellsworth to Scott Estey, a farmer, and Mary E. Morrison Estey, believed to be Bertha's namesake.

Charles William Downes

Willie Downes of Ellsworth was the youngest victim of the disaster.

Charles William Downes was born in Ellsworth in 1885, the son of Alphonso and Carrie A. (Jordan) Downes. Willie's father was born in Cherryfield, Maine, and was a laborer at the time of the disaster. His mother was born in Ellsworth. At the time of Willie's death, the couple apparently had been divorced, as Willie's mother was listed as being married to Mr. Nelson Pomeroy of Hancock.

Willie's age was listed variously as eleven, thirteen, and fifteen at the time of the accident. In a sad twist of fate for Willie's family, he was at first reported in the newspapers as having been rescued.

Willie Downes was described as a bright, good-natured little fellow whom everybody liked. He was known to be a constant ray of joy to his grandfather, William Jordan, of Ellsworth.

Mrs. Charles "Addie M." Stover

Addie M. Tripp Stover, forty-seven, was a native of Ellsworth and had lived there all her life. She was married to Charles Stover, who worked in the lumbering business in Jonesboro, sixty miles away. The couple had three children, Cassie, Maude, and Fred. Addie Stover was a beloved member of the Ellsworth community. She was described as retiring by nature, but it was said that her lovable qualities were admired by her friends and bound them to her.

Mrs. Stover's family originally thought her to be safe from the disaster. It was not until five o'clock Sunday evening that her body was identified by friends "who could not be mistaken as to her identity," wrote the *Boston Globe*.

Addie Stover is buried in the Woodbine Cemetery, Ellsworth.

"Her deserved popularity manifests itself in expressions of sorrow one hears on every side," said the *Boston Globe*.

BANGOR

Ellen Elizabeth Horn Billings

Ellen Billings, sixty-eight, had been an upper-end hairdresser in Bangor at a time when the upper-end women of the city had the time and money to spend on what was considered by many as an extravagance.

Ellen Horn was born on April 16, 1931, in Ripley, Maine. In 1853 she married Albert Holland Billings from Albion, a Civil War veteran working as a traveling salesman.

Ellen and Albert Billings, both raised in the country, moved to the city of Bangor to raise their family. They had four children: Annie, born in 1854; Charles, born in 1858; John, born in 1863; and William, born in 1865. Their first son, Charles, would die in 1863, at age five; and their youngest child, William, would die two years later, in 1865, shortly after birth.

Mr. A. H. Billings worked as a sales agent for Colton's maps, traveling door to door with samples of maps of the United States and North America, both large and small scale, "including the new division of Territories," according to the *Bangor Daily Whig and Courier*. Colton's had a good reputation as mapmakers at a time when maps were necessary for the growing country. The maps were all finely engraved, considered very accurate, and priced moderately. "[O]ur citizens will do well to embrace the opportunity of obtaining the latest editions," wrote the *Bangor Whig and Courier*.

Albert Billings was also active in Republican politics in Penobscot County.

Ellen Billings was professionally known in the Bangor area as Mrs. A. H. Billings. She was an award-winning hairdresser with a wealthy following.

With the advent of electricity, a skillful hairdresser was in great demand. Many new hairstyling inventions arrived along with the use of electrical current, as well as many new techniques and beauty treatments.

From an advertisement in the *Bangor Daily Whig and Courier*:

ARTISTIC HAIR WORK!

Mrs. A. H. Billings

Desires to call the attention of the ladies of Bangor and vicinity to her large and elegant assortment of Fall and winter styles in hair goods.

Elegant Front Pieces and coiffures from one dollar upwards.

Handsome switches in all shades.

All work guaranteed. Mrs. Billings' goods sold only in her own rooms. Up two flights—over Fairbanks' Insurance Office.

Room 12, Rines' Block, 21 Main St.

"Come to Mrs. A. H. Billings' and have your bangs curled with Specht's Curlet. Wind and perspiration have no effect. Without a rival in the world. We also use Electrine when desired. 21 Main St., Bangor, ME," read an ad in the *Bangor Daily Whig and Courier* in December 1892.

The proof of the success of Ellen and Albert Billings is shown in the success of their son, John A. Billings, who qualified for the practice of dentistry and opened an office in Rockland, Massachusetts, after apprenticing in the office of Dr. D. W. Maxfield of Bangor.

Albert Billings died in 1896, three years before the Mount Desert Ferry disaster. The year her husband died, Mrs. A. H. Billings was awarded first place for display hair work for ladies' headwear at Norumbega Hall in Bangor at the Eastern Maine State Fair.

A week before losing her life at the disaster at Mount Desert Ferry, Ellen Billings, along with another victim of the ferry disaster, Mrs. Margaret Mower, of California, were in Old Town, paying a call on Mrs. Hartwell Lancaster.

Mrs. A. H. Billings was sixty-eight when she was killed in the disaster at Mount Desert Ferry. Her business rooms had been located above the insurance company of Capt. Henry N. Fairbanks, who had been a guest at The Bluffs and had been on the wharf at the time of the disaster. Two of the inquest witnesses, Captain Fairbanks's wife, Abbie, and their daughter Nora, recognized Mrs. Billings when she was pulled out of the water.

After the double funeral with Mrs. Margaret Mower, Ellen Horn Billings was buried in the Elmwood Cemetery, Dexter, Maine.

Mrs. Margaret Mower

Mrs. Margaret Mower, sixty-seven, was traveling with Bangor hairstylist Mrs. A. H. Billings on Sunday.

Margaret Mower and Ellen Billings appear to have been childhood friends from the Dexter area. Marriage and family took both away from there as young women, Mrs. Billings to Bangor and Mrs. Mower to California.

Mrs. Mower was visiting the East Coast that summer from San Francisco. She was the widow of Amos Mower, who also had family in Dexter. She had a sister in Oakland, California, a son in Santa Cruz, New Mexico, a daughter visiting France at the time of the disaster, and a daughter in Boston. Mrs. Mower's visit to her daughter in Boston was the occasion that led her back to her home state of Maine, and to Mount Desert Ferry.

Ellen Billings and Margaret Mower, two country girls from rural Maine who had grown up, raised families, and in general had been successful at life, were now two widows passing a joyful Sunday afternoon traveling to Bar Harbor to visit the warships of the North Atlantic Squadron.

G. R. Collier of Boston and William Vance of Providence, Rhode Island, were two men who fell into the water after the breaking of the gangplank. After coming to the surface, they swam to the wharf end of the broken gangplank and grabbed wooden boards for use in rescue. The two men said the first person they saved was Mrs. Mower. They said she was alive when taken from the water but died almost instantly upon reaching the wharf. Mr. Collier said he thought her heart just gave out.

Because Mrs. Mower had lived away from Maine for so long, she was not well known by those at Mount Desert Ferry, as had been Mrs. Billings. This led to the misidentification of Margaret Mower's body after it had been removed from the water. Mrs. Mower and Mrs. Billings must have been traveling in a party by themselves, as there was no one to identify Mrs. Mower's body at the freight house. Initially Mrs. Mower was identified as Mrs. O'Donahue of Bangor, mother of a Bangor police officer. It was not until Monday morning, after she had been taken to Finnegan's undertaking rooms in Bangor, that she would be correctly identified by H. G. Mower, of Dexter, a relative of Mrs. Mower. George L. Adell, of Boston, Mrs. Mower's son-in-law, was notified of her death and took charge of the body.

After the double funeral in Bangor for Margaret Mower and Ellen Billings on Tuesday, Mrs. Mower was buried in Bangor.

Lillian Sleeper Derwent

Lillian Sleeper Derwent, twenty-three, was a young woman who lived in Bangor with her husband, George, a news agent who was newly employed on the Maine Central Railroad trains running out of Bangor. Lillian and George were newlyweds, having been married only eleven months at the time of the disaster. Lillian was described as a handsome young woman who was a great favorite among her acquaintances and beloved by her friends.

Mr. and Mrs. Derwent fell into the water with the breaking of the gangplank and found themselves in a desperate situation. Lillian Derwent's head slipped under the water twice. George was able to grab hold of a rope with one hand and his wife with the other, holding her up in safety from a last plunge under the cold water.

During the initial phase of the rescue, the efforts of the panicked rescuers had caused more harm than good. In an effort to aid with rescue, someone with good intentions threw a plank from the wharf, hitting Mrs. Derwent directly in the head. As Lillian lost consciousness, George was no longer able to support her weight and she started slipping from her husband's desperate grasp. She went under the water again, this time not to be seen by her husband until she was recovered an hour later.

Miss Grace Rena Sumner

Miss Grace Rena Sumner of 228 York Street in Bangor was just a teenager when she died in the disaster at Mount Desert Ferry, just two weeks shy of turning sixteen. Miss Sumner was the daughter of Charles Edgar and Margaret Daneley Sumner, both of whom were born in Ireland. The couple had a second child, Louis J. Sumner.

Grace Sumner, who was described as a young woman of unusual ability for business skills, was a recent graduate of Shaw's Business College and was to have taken a position as a stenographer the day after the disaster. She was also a well-known singer in the Bangor area.

Joseph Cobb, a survivor of the disaster, said that after the breaking of the gangplank, as he fought his way to safety through the struggling crowd in the water, he tried to save a young girl at the same time. He reported that the girl was near the *Sappho*, and just as he got close to her, she was pulled down under the water from behind by another struggling passenger. Grace Sumner was believed to be that girl.

Miss Sumner ultimately was pulled out of the water and placed on the *Sappho*. She was one of the three women who died aboard the ship on the race across Frenchman Bay.

Grace Rena Sumner is buried at Mt. Hope Cemetery in Bangor.

Miss Elizabeth (Lizzie) Ward

Miss Lizzie Ward of Bangor was nineteen years old when she died in the disaster. She was the daughter of Andrew and Mary Conroy of Bangor. Her father, now deceased, had been born in Portland, her mother in Ireland. Lizzie Ward lived in the rear of 44 May Street in Bangor with her mother. She was described as having many friends and having been a great favorite of all her associates. She was single, and her occupation is listed as "Domestic" on her record of death.

Miss Ward, like Miss Sumner, was one of the people taken out of the water and placed directly on the *Sappho*. She died on the way to Bar Harbor.

Mr. and Mrs. George Bennett

Mr. and Mrs. George Bennett of Bangor were, and still are, a bit of a mystery couple.

George Bennett was an assistant baggage master at the Exchange Street Station of the Maine Central Railroad in Bangor. He was accompanied to Mount Desert Ferry that Sunday by his wife.

Little is known about Mr. and Mrs. Bennett. They were in their thirties and lived at 27 Pleasant Street. Mr. Bennett worked the night shift at the railroad station, so he was not readily known to his fellow railroad employees. So little was known about the Bennetts that Mr. Bennett, even though he was a railroad employee, had to be identified by means of the railroad pass in his pocket rather than by being recognized by anyone else at Mount Desert Ferry. This would also indicate that Mr. and Mrs. Bennett were on the excursion train alone.

While Mr. George Bennett was identified by the railroad pass, one of three unidentified bodies in the freight shed that afternoon was presumptively identified as Mrs. Bennett. That presumption proved to be correct.

Despite a thorough search through historical records, Mrs. Bennett's first name remains unknown. All that is known about her is that she was born in England.

The bodies of Mr. and Mrs. Bennett were taken to a local undertaker in the city of Bangor, where they had lived for the past two to four years. Maine Central Railroad division superintendent A. A. White spent Monday morning trying to reach friends or family of the Bennetts, thought to be in Massachusetts, to notify them of the deaths and to make arrangements for the two bodies.

"Their bodies are at Abel Hunt's rooms, where they will remain until orders are received in regard to their disposition," wrote the *Bangor Daily Commercial* on Monday, the day after the disaster.

The bodies waited for a time at Hunt's for arrangements to be made, but no relatives of the Bennetts could be found. The remains were then taken to Mt. Hope Cemetery. Final orders regarding the bodies of Mr. and Mrs. Bennett would not be received for over a month. In late September someone from the Bennett family did contact Bangor city officials, and Mr. and Mrs. George U. Bennett were then buried in pauper's graves at the Bangor City Cemetery on September 25, 1899, almost two months after the disaster.

Other Maine Towns

Mrs. William Murray

Minerva Susan Murray was twenty-three years old at the time of the disaster. She was born in Tabusintac, Northumberland County, New Brunswick, Canada, the daughter of Robert Fayle, a house carpenter, and Honora Robertson. She was married to William Murray of Brewer, where she resided with her husband.

Minerva Murray is buried in the Oak Hill Cemetery in Brewer, under a large stone.

Miss Blanche Lewis

Miss Blanche Lewis of Hampden was nineteen years old at the time of the disaster. She was engaged to be married.

Miss Lewis is buried in the Locust Grove Cemetery in Hampden, in the Joseph B. Lewis lot.

Joseph Murphy

Joseph Murphy Sr., thirty, of Old Town, had become a first-time father just six months before dying at Mount Desert Ferry.

Born in 1869, Joseph Murphy Sr. was the son of John Murphy, of Old Town, and Hannah Roscoe Murphy, who had been born in Ireland. He had two brothers, Thomas and John Murphy, of Old Town, and one sister, Mrs. James Cavanaugh, of Auburn. Joseph Murphy was described as a very capable young man. Throughout his life, Joseph had been engaged in various kinds of business, at one point serving as a telegraph operator for the Maine Central Railroad. He was described as being popular, was well known in Bangor, and was a member of the Old Town Council of Knights of Columbus.

For the past few years, Mr. Murphy had been in business for himself as a merchant in Old Town. Six months before the disaster at Mount Desert Ferry, on February 4, 1899, Joseph and his wife, Mabel Grace

Crane Murphy, welcomed their first child to the world, Joseph Murphy Jr.

Joseph Murphy Sr. is buried in Old Town.

Clifford Cushman

Clifford Cushman, twenty-five, was from South Corinth, Maine.

Mr. Cushman was accompanied on the train to Mount Desert Ferry by relatives, including his cousin Loring Fitz.

When the gangplank broke, Mr. Cushman went into the water, while his cousin Loring, who had not yet reached the gangplank, remained safely on the wharf. From that vantage point, Loring watched the struggle in the water. He said the crash of the gangplank came as unexpectedly to those on the wharf as to those on the gangplank. There was no premonition, no warning, just a sudden grinding noise and then chaos.

"He says the scene was indeed a dreadful one, and the sight of people drowning right before his eyes was one which it will be difficult to efface from his memory for a long time to come," reported the *Bangor Daily News*.

Melvin McCard

Melvin McCard, listed as being from both East Exeter and Corinth, was a single farmer, lumberman, and Maine Guide. He was thirty-one years old at the time of the disaster. He was the son of Thomas McCard, who was born in Exeter, and Joanna Shaw.

Melvin McCard is buried in the Tibbetts Cemetery in Exeter Center, Maine, under a very large, impressive stone.

Ora M. Lank

Ora M. Lank, twenty-eight, was from Danforth, Maine. His father was born in Nova Scotia and served on a tugboat in Maine. His mother was a Maine native and a homemaker. He was the youngest of seven children, which also included James, Emily, Henry, Ella, Elias, and Stuart. Ora Lank had been living in Brewer for some time before the disaster.

Mr. Lank is buried in the James W. Lank Lot in Maple Cemetery on Maple Street in Danforth.

Albert Colson

Albert Colson, forty, of Levant, Maine, perished in the disaster at Mount Desert Ferry. Little is known about him. In the newspapers of the time, his name appears only in the list of deceased. The State of Maine has no records regarding Mr. Colson.

Frank Sweetser and Delia Oakes

The stories of Frank Sweetser and Delia Oakes are told separately different parts of the book.

The Aftermath

They will be glad to see this factory, which employs a large number of hands, once more in operation, and also to learn that Miss Danielson has so far recovered from the effects of the injuries which she received in the Mt. Desert Ferry disaster of August 6, last, as to be able to once again take an active part in business affairs.
—BANGOR DAILY NEWS, *APRIL 11, 1900*

Throughout Sunday afternoon news of the disaster had spread from town to town, and then state to state. Monday morning the disaster at Mount Desert Ferry was the front-page headline spread across almost every newspaper in America. The *Boston Globe,* which had a reporter at the disaster site, provided extensive coverage. "DEATH IN HASTE," read the *Boston Globe* front page. "Mt. Desert Ferry Slip Failed The Impatient Crowd."

At a time when photographs were almost nonexistent, the *Boston Globe* commissioned a sketch artist to provide pencil drawings of the females who died in the disaster. The newspaper also featured a drawing of The Bluffs—"The Hotel That Was Turned Into A Hospital," as well as a drawing of the boat and train landing at the wharf. The series of drawings was titled "Sketches at scene of mt desert ferry accident."

Newspapers from the East Coast to the West ran large, sometimes sensational headlines and story leads, though it was hard to further sensationalize such an already sensational event. The name Bar Harbor was guaranteed to draw instant attention to any newspaper, and because of that, or perhaps because many newspapers from outside the area considered the geography of Bar Harbor to cover everything in Maine north of Portland and south of Canada, many stories incorrectly identified the site of the accident as Bar Harbor, instead of the less known neighboring town of Hancock.

New York Journal: "Nice Sort of Death Trap."

Reading Times, Reading, Pennsylvania: "A Horror At Bar Harbor."

Daily New Era, Lancaster, Pennsylvania: "Sunday's Death Harvest."

Sandusky Star-Journal, Sandusky, Ohio: "Scores of people are dumped into the swirling water."

Middletown Daily Argus, Middletown, New York: "The Bar Harbor Horror."

York Daily, York, Pennsylvania: "Many persons thrown into watery graves."

Fitchburg Sentinel, Fitchburg, Massachusetts: "A Score Killed . . . Victims penned in frightfully small space."

The Courier, Waterloo, Iowa: "Bay at Bar Harbor Searched but no victims found."

Spokesman-Review, Spokane, Washington: "A Horror up in Maine. Strangling beings clutched each other."

Star-Gazette, Elmira, New York: "Drowned like rats in a trap."

"Twenty Pleasure Seekers go down to watery graves," was the headline in the *Buffalo Review* out of New York. "But the day, which began with such joyful anticipations, ended in gloom and weeping, and will go down in the history as the most sorrowful Sabbath in the annals of this far-famed summer resort."

Coverage of the disaster was naturally extensive across Maine. Few areas in the state had been spared from the concern for loved ones or acquaintances when the news first broke Sunday afternoon.

The front page of the *Portland Daily Press* featured an artist's rendering of the layout of the wharf at Mount Desert Ferry. The illustration was directly underneath the list of names of the dead, which was in the center of the front page. The illustration emphasized how much of a role was played by the layout of the wharf at Mount Desert Ferry, with the unfortunate 250 people being boxed in on all sides.

Editors of Maine's newspapers expressed their sorrow and their opinions. "It was the worst accident remembered in the history of the state and especially in the career of the Maine Central Road, under whose auspices so many excursionists had been brought here," wrote the *Portland Daily Press.*

"The catastrophe was frightful in the extreme, for it came when scores of persons, young and old, were penned into a trap, to escape from which they fought with desperation against great odds," wrote the *Waterville Mail.* "The awful scene at the Mt. Desert Ferry on Sunday was relieved by the display of heroism shown by brave souls who disregarded their own safety in order to lend a saving hand to others. It would be impossible to conceive of such an accident among Americans where similar heroic rescues were not likely to be made. Swift action in case of emergency is a quality possessed by the average American to a marked degree and it was just this quality that prevented the dire catastrophe at the Ferry from being much worse."

In Bangor, a large city by Maine standards but still a small community, almost everyone had been affected by the tragedy in some way. Many homes had been touched directly by the disaster—some now with an empty place, others with members hovering between life and death. For those not impacted directly, many had been at the train station late Sunday night for the arrival of the funeral train carrying the dead bodies. The caskets had been walked slowly through the city in horse-drawn carriages to the undertakers throughout Bangor. The people of Bangor watched again on Monday as many of the bodies were carried back to the train station for the last trip home.

The people of Bangor were intimately involved. The sorrow of the disaster lingered long there. Wrote the *Bangor Daily Commercial*:

> *By the breaking of the slip at Mt. Desert Ferry more than a score of lives were lost and countless families plunged into mourning for the loss of a beloved friend or relative.*
>
> *Like a bolt from the blue sky fell the blow, terrible in its suddenness, awful in its horrors, most bitter in its results, which are confined to no one section but reach with all encircling arms over Maine's whole expanse, few sections having escaped the loss of some lives.*
>
> *The catastrophe came without warning and in a few short minutes, lips that just before were uttering some merry jest were silent in death, and over the whole throng of pleasure seekers was cast a gloom that will not be dissipated for months to come, either night or day, for to many of the spectators of the dreadful scenes of death's awful harvest at Mt. Desert Ferry on this beautiful Sabbath morning, the terrible visions will continue to appear both in their sleeping and waking hours.*

The *Portland Daily Press* also could not pass up an opportunity to do a little boasting, though with bad timing. "The Portland Daily Press was the first paper in Portland to give to the public an account of the disaster at Mt. Desert Ferry and was the only paper in the city to bulletin the news as fast as it was received," wrote the paper, adding a little dig, "as usual."

A bit of a rivalry between the larger city of Bangor and the smaller city of Ellsworth was hinted at by a sentence written in the *Ellsworth American* shortly after the disaster: "The blow fell more heavily upon her [Ellsworth] than upon Bangor, for in smaller cities and towns the feeling of kinship among the neighbors is closer than in larger cities."

Contributing to the national attention being given to the event in Hancock, Maine, was another horrible, gruesome disaster that occurred on the same day in the nearby New England state of Connecticut. The two news stories seemed made for each other, and the headlines from both tragedies were together spread across the nation's newspapers for the next few days.

In the Connecticut tragedy, the disaster was a trolley car that went off the rails and over the side of a high bridge, sending fifty singing, joyful passengers to their deaths in the muc below. The *Portland Daily Press* ran the following story on Monday:

Nearly Forty Killed. Distressing Electric Car Accident. Over a Tres-
tle at Bridgeport, Connecticut. A fall of forty feet to death. Passengers
were singing when crash came.

   The most frightful catastrophe recorded in Connecticut for nearly
half a century occurred shortly before four o'clock this afternoon on the
Stratford extension of the Shelton Street Railway company when a
loaded car went off the trestle over Peck's Mill Pond at Oronoque,
about six miles north of Bridgeport, and sunk in the flats forty feet
below.

   The car was approaching a trestle that was 410 feet long, made
of iron with stone foundations and was not protected by any guard
rails. South of the trestle is quite an incline on which the car ran down
at a very fast rate of speed. After it ran on to the trestle for about ten
feet, the trucks left the rails and then the car continued on the ties for
about 75 feet when it went off the trestle and dropped into the pond
below, overturning completely and upending. When the car struck, the
motor, which weighted four tons, and the heavy trucks, crushed into it,
instantly killing many of the passengers.

   A few people survived, mainly a lucky few who jumped just at
the right time.

The two gruesome stories were placed side by side on the front page of the *Portland Daily Press*, one headlined "Mt. Desert Horror," the other labeled "Trolley Car Disaster."

The *Boston Globe* combined the death totals from both of Sunday's disasters for their screeching headline Monday:

50 DEAD

21 Excursionists Drowned in Mt Desert Ferry dock

29 victims of trolley car accident near Bridgeport

Awful Struggles in the Ferry Slip—Car Plunges 50 feet into ravine.

Though the disaster in Connecticut did not have the golden name of Bar Harbor to help draw attention, other similarities to the disaster at Mount Desert Ferry made the story just as sensational.

That horrific Sunday in 1899 seemed to be the day that people's nightmares were coming true. So much of the public depended on passenger rail cars, such as in the Connecticut disaster, and trains and ferryboats and their associated gangplanks, as in the Mount Desert Ferry disaster. Such gruesome deaths were occurring as a result of doing commonplace things that were part of everyday life and assumed to be safe.

One difference in the disasters was the level of transparency of the two businesses involved. In the train car disaster in Connecticut, key personnel were secreted away, including the train conductor, who had survived the accident by jumping off the train. The speed of the train at the time of the accident had been in dispute.

In the Mount Desert Ferry disaster, Maine Central Railroad officials were cooperative with authorities. As had been pointed out by the *Boston Globe* during the inquest, all actions of the Maine Central Railroad had been done in public, and the site of the accident and the remaining broken gangplank were visible for all to see. The railroad had made available the employee responsible for the construction of the faulty gangplank to give testimony at the inquest.

The motorman of the ill-fated trolley car in Connecticut was arraigned on a charge of manslaughter in the disaster. He would plead not guilty. No charges appear to have been brought forth from the disaster at Mount Desert Ferry.

The visit of the North Atlantic Squadron in the summer of 1899 seemed to be cursed from the beginning. "The visit of the fleet this season has been greatly marred by the terrible drowning accident last Sunday.

Undoubtedly it has decreased the number of excursionists from the neighboring Maine towns. Still there have been crowds of sightseers, who have found untold delight wandering about, open-eyed over the big ships, asking questions of the genial, obliging officers of the day, and the sunburned tans ever ready to relate experiences and anecdotes connected with the recent battles they had been through," wrote the *Bar Harbor Record*.

The disaster at Mount Desert Ferry had a negative impact on the North Atlantic Squadron's visit to Bar Harbor, but another tragedy involving the squadron, just days later, would end the visit on a sad note, just as it had begun.

Wednesday, August 9, three days after the disaster, was the big day for the society of Bar Harbor's summer colony. The two main social events during the squadron's visit, both grand, were to be held in honor of the North Atlantic Squadron on that day. A large, formal dinner was being hosted by Charles H. Gramp of Philadelphia in honor of Adm. William T. Sampson and the officers of the fleet. After that, a formal dance would be held at the private club Louisberg, also in honor of Sampson and the officers. "It was one of the notable social affairs of the season," wrote the *Bar Harbor Record*.

On Wednesday afternoon, Mrs. Helen A. Sands, fifty-five, of New York ascended the gangway of the USS *New York*, anchored in Frenchman Bay. Mrs. Sands was a regular summer visitor to Mount Desert Island, spending her summers at Southwest Harbor. It was from there that Mrs. Sands had traveled that Wednesday to visit Admiral Sampson, presumably as his guest at the events planned for that evening.

Admiral Sampson was waiting on the deck of the USS *New York* for Mrs. Sands. She was about to grasp the hand of Admiral Sampson in greeting when suddenly she fell to the deck. She soon thereafter was pronounced dead. Mrs. Sands's remains were conveyed to New York that night. The dance and the dinner did go on, but without Admiral Sampson.

On Sunday, August 13, a week after their arrival, and a week after the disaster at Mount Desert Ferry, the ships of the North Atlantic Squadron pulled out of Frenchman Bay and left Bar Harbor at seven o'clock in the morning, headed to Newport, Rhode Island.

"The disaster at Mount Desert Ferry was only the first of two curses during that week-long visit," wrote the *Bar Harbor Record*. "Though victorious in war, the visit to Bar Harbor by the North Atlantic Squadron seemed to go down in defeat. It seemed cursed from the first."

Dr. George Phillips, who had been the first outside doctor to arrive at Mount Desert Ferry after the disaster, wrote a letter to the *Ellsworth American* a week after the event, summing up his reflections of that terrible day.

Dr. Phillips was well known in Ellsworth and Bar Harbor. He was a member of the Hancock County Medical Society and taught medical education to the public, addressing groups such as the Hancock County Teachers' Association and discussing "Health in the Schoolroom," or giving talks at the YMCA lecture room on "What we Should Eat and What we Should Drink." His talks were described as always well attended, interesting, and greatly enjoyed.

Dr. Phillips had offices in both Ellsworth and Bar Harbor. On Mondays, Wednesdays, and Fridays he could be found in Bar Harbor; Tuesdays, Thursdays, and Saturdays in Ellsworth; and Sunday was his day off.

He titled his piece, "Impressions of the Tragedy at Mount Desert Ferry Ellsworth, ME Aug. 16, 1899":

To the Editor of the American:

A week ago, last Sunday there occurred the worst and saddest accident in Hancock County since I can remember. I do not propose to describe it or write of it, at least not now; but to one who stood close to the matters of that day, with heart and ears and eyes open, there were things to be remembered for life. Men differ, I know, under such circumstances—some are dazed, benumbed; others, in spite of themselves, have vivid impressions that will never fade.

Amid all the horror and misery of it, there are some fine things to be cherished and remembered. Selfishness, miserable, craven cowardice there was, too plentiful, as there is always when five or ten scores of lives come instantly into the presence of death. But there were deeds that day that we are glad to remember, that make us know that total depravity does not exist, that lighten and gladden the gloom of that awful hour.

Those of us who had to do with the nearer view, saw many of these deeds that we shall keep with us, and we shall be kinder and a bit less faithless because of them.

A dear old lady had gone down. When she came to the surface her only thought was of dying soon and escaping the pain and misery of longer suffering. This was her wish and prayer. Beside her was a younger woman who, in her courage and strength, saw the hopelessness of the other and bade her be still. With words of cheer, with decisive and wise action, she placed the arm of the older over some fastenings, secured herself in alike manner, and finding the strength of her friend failing, never faltering in cheerful words, she gathered her other hand in her own, placed a foot beneath her head as she fainted, and for a half-hour continued by word and strength to support her, finally calling the rescuing party to "come and save this dear old lady." They went back for her—I hope. I would like to know that woman.

These things were multiplied many times. Another type is the nurse on the train, but not on the slip, herself ill and unfit for duty, who for many hours so worked in the bringing back of life and the care of sick, knowing its probable results, whose faithful help as I well know saved, with other means, surely two lives, and who is now suffering beyond endurance because of her work that day.

What could have been finer than the hundred deeds among the guests and proprietors at The Bluffs. I know of them better than most others. I would like to recount some of them—little things, no doubt more or less forgotten—but I dare not lest it seem fulsome praise. Surely the guests should have given up their rooms; no one doubts it. Surely our American humane instincts would bid at once the opening of the hotel by guests and proprietors. And it was done, even to the trunks and wardrobes of guests and landlord. The table, the help, the whole matter, were at the disposal of those who needed these things.

All this was done exactly as we expect the managers and guests of one of our good houses to do.

But there was more—so much more! The kindliness, the readiness to do the little things, the infinite number of happenings anticipating the wishes of these unfortunate guests, even in the case of the head of the house and others at considerable pecuniary loss and done so cheerfully. As I said above, I would like to mention some of these deeds and some of these people. But I am glad to know that men and women live who will do these things as I saw them done, and I feel a little better toward this old world since that day.

These are, of course, only types, examples, though true ones, of one side, the better side. I want to speak of another. I don't know him, nor does he know me, but I take it the man who saved more lives than anyone else in the terrible affair [Old Town Enterprise editor Chester W. Robbins] was the man in authority who by some chance happened there. It was a most fortunate thing that he was present. If he was a friend or even acquaintance of mine, I should hesitate to judge him as I do. I never had seen him.

In a small way I am accustomed to seeing men in peril and know a little of the value of a level head in danger. I had little time for accurate observation, yet I know, or at least believe, that a much greater panic was averted, because one man, with absolute authority, never faltered or hesitated. I was proud of him from the time I met him—quiet, calm as a summer morning, resourceful. I know that the little I did was better done because I met him that day.

It is well for those who carry with them and who must carry with them whether they will or no, the memory of that awful whirlpool of human life, to keep strongly to those things of which the above are examples. Let us get from this awful event, so far as possible, the strength that comes from seeing and admiring noble things.

Dr. George A. Phillips

The heroism of Bangor Fire Department chief John Mason was recognized less than a week after the disaster, in the August 12, 1899, edition of *Fire and Water*, a national magazine that reported on the emerging field of firefighting.

Chief Mason was seventy years old at the time of the disaster and had served on the Bangor Fire Department for approximately fifty years. He was described as having "seen all the fires here in the last sixty years, helped to stop thousands of them and looks fit for years of active service." He had recently been elected president of the Maine State Firemen's Association and would go on to be appointed the state inspector of fire under Maine's insurance commissioner.

Chief Mason was in the process of embarking on the *Sappho* with his wife when the gangplank broke. He was almost on the deck of the ship with his wife close behind him. As he felt the gangplank give way, Chief Mason made a desperate leap and laid hold of the rail of the steamer. His wife, however, went down with the other people on the gangplank. Chief Mason at once grabbed one of the ropes of the gangplank and reached it down to his wife, who seized it. Others in the water seized hold of her in a crazed attempt to rescue themselves at the cost of her life, and she was in imminent peril of losing the safety of the rope that her husband had extended to her. Chief Mason then descended the rope into the water and sustained her until they both were rescued. Mrs. Mason was badly bruised and suffered greatly from the shock, but was able to return home to Bangor with her husband that day.

Fire Engineering, August 12, 1899:

AN HEROIC FIRE CHIEF. A correspondent writes to FIRE AND WATER from Portland, Me., stating that he has it almost direct from a Maine Central railway official who was present at the Mt. Desert horror of Sunday last that "some magnificently heroic and effective work" was done by John Mason, former chief of the Bangor fire department, who was last week elected president of the Maine State Firemen's association for the ensuing year, and also chosen as delegate by that association to represent it at the forthcoming convention of the International Association of Fire Engineers at Syracuse, N. Y. Our correspondent says: "At the Ferry horror, Capt. Mason, after rescuing his wife, turned to and with the utmost coolness, at the imminent risk of his own life, saved many others. He is naturally a level-headed man, of sound judgments, and this, coupled with the experience of more than forty years in the fire department made his work very effective. There is no more modest man on earth than former Chief John Mason, and I suppose he would cuff my ears if he knew I was writing this to you, but he deserves a glowing notice at your hands, and, therefore, I send you the information."

Former Chief Mason's conduct speaks for itself and is its own eulogium. His already high reputation for bravery has been enhanced by his heroism and coolness in the midst of the horrors which surrounded him at such an awful crisis. Such "deeds of daring do" done in the cause of humanity far outshine those of the soldier or sailor, whose trade is war. And of such stuff are the heroic firemen of the world composed.

The *Sebenoa*, which had been at Mount Desert Ferry the day of the disaster, was involved in another rescue off the shores of Hancock just a month after the gangplank disaster. From a newspaper article dated September 7, 1899:

A party of young people, summer visitors at Hancock Point, six miles from Bar Harbor, had a very dangerous and unpleasant experience in Frenchman Bay today, by which they nearly lost their lives. But for the timely assistance of the ferry steamer Sebenoa, the party would all have been drowned.

As the Sebenoa left Sorrento this morning on the 9 o'clock trip, the wind blowing a gale from the northwest, a sailboat, some distance east of her course and about half way to Bar Harbor, was sighted, scudding before the wind, under bare pole and flying a signal of distress.

The Sebenoa hove to and a rope was thrown to the occupants of the sailboat. The occupants of the sailboat included a doctor from New York and his two brothers, as well as three students from Harvard College and a well-known singer at the time, Miss Mabel Monaghan of Boston.

The three young people started out from Hancock Point early this morning on their way to Ellsworth. They were advised not to attempt the trip, as the bay is very treacherous when such a gale is blowing.

The young people refused to take the advice, but before the boat was half a mile from shore the sails had to be taken in in order for the boat to live at all in the heavy sea and gale. The boat was nearly swamped several times and the position of the party was getting more dangerous every minute, as the boat was being blown farther out to sea and the storm was increasing.

Fortunately, their signal of distress was seen by the captain of the Sebenoa, who promptly went to the rescue. The young people were all thoroughly drenched and their yacht was half full of water when they were taken aboard the steamer.

A great deal of excitement was created among the passengers on board the Sebenoa, as it was feared the Sebenoa would not reach the sailboat in time to prevent a fatality.

When the young people were gotten safely on board, neither the passengers or crew spared any pains in caring for them.

Mr. George Southard of East Hampden, Maine, was a survivor who had a very miserable time after the disaster.

Mr. Southard had been badly injured in the disaster at Mount Desert Ferry, and also suffered from shock. He was one of the fifteen survivors required to spend the night at The Bluffs, too injured to move. At the time of the disaster, it was not known if he would live at all.

Less than a year after the disaster, in July of 1900, Mr. Southard was working for the Ashland Manufacturing Company at their mill in Ashland, Maine, about 150 miles north of his home in East Hampden. With Mr. Southard so far away at work, his wife, Nettie, was left home alone with the couple's three children. At the beginning of that year, Mrs. Southard had been in ill health, though the exact condition was not revealed. Six months later, in July, Mrs. Southard hanged herself in her East Hampden home.

"MADE QUICK END OF EARTHLY MISERY," read the head-line in the *Bangor Daily Commercial.*

Mrs. Nettie May Southard of East Hampden committed suicide Sunday forenoon by hanging. Despondency caused by prolonged ill health is the cause assigned for the act. She was the wife of George Southard, now employed by the Ashland Mfg. Co. at their mill in Ashland, and she leaves besides her husband, three children. Her age was 35 years.

For the past six months Mrs. Southard had been in ill health and it is said that the children, the oldest of whom is 17 years, had been cautioned not to leave her alone. She recently had seemed better than for some time, and as she had never by word or action indicated any desire to take her life it was not thought that there was any need of keeping a close watch over her. On Sunday morning, about 9 o'clock, the children did leave her alone for a time. At about 12 o'clock one of the children returned to the house and discovered his mother hanging by a rope in the hall upstairs. The body was cut down and efforts made at resuscitation, but to no avail.

Mrs. Southard had evidently climbed through a small opening leading into the attic, made a clothesline fast about the chimney and around her neck, and then lowered herself through the opening. Coroner Finnigan of Bangor was called, and after investigating the case he decided that an inquest was not necessary.

On October 4, 1900, a year after the disaster, Miss Nora McNamara of Bangor presented a gold watch to John Bell, the man who saved her life at Mount Desert Ferry. Mr. Bell was employed as an operator in the office of the Postal Telegraph Company in Bangor. The watch was an open-faced Waltham, was diamond-jeweled, and was accompanied by a handsome gold chain, having a charm set with diamonds and rubies. On the inside of the case was the inscription, "Nora to John, Oct. 4, 1900."

Of the most inspirational stories of the survivors of the disaster at Mount Desert Ferry was that of Miss Lillian Danielson of Brewer.

Miss Danielson had gone from the gangplank into the water with the other two hundred people that Sunday morning. After being rescued, her medical condition was serious enough that she was confined to The Bluffs Sunday night and did not return to her home in Brewer until the following day. The newspapers at the time listed her diagnosis as "nervous prostration," a diagnosis shared by many survivors. She was in critical condition when she arrived home in Brewer the following day.

For many months after the disaster, it had not been known whether Lillian would live at all. At first her Lmbs appeared to be paralyzed. Adding to Lillian's misery was the death of her sister in early March, seven months after the disaster. Mrs. Carrie Wheldon was only twenty-nine when she died of pulmonary tuberculosis, from which she had been suffering for some months. She left behind a daughter.

At the time of the disaster, Miss Danielson had been in charge of the Littlefield Clothing Factory on Parker Street in Brewer, which employed many people in the area. Due to her medical condition, Miss Danielson was not able to return to her position at the factory after the disaster. Freeman Littlefield, the proprietor, ran operations in her absence. Over the winter, however, Mr. Littlefield unexpectedly died.

With Miss Danielson unable to reassume her duties at the factory, the Littlefield Clothing Factory closed. Many in Brewer and Bangor were put out of work, in the middle of a harsh Maine winter.

Many other clothing manufacturing companies stepped in and offered to lease the closed factory. Satisfactory terms could never be finalized, however, because of one deal-breaker—the big clothing companies refused to sign contracts with the Brewer factory unless it was run by Lillian Danielson herself.

Miss Danielson was uniquely qualified to run the clothing factory. For many years before assuming charge there, she had worked at a factory owned by Mr. Littlefield in Winterport and was described as thoroughly understanding the clothing manufacturing business and all its details. "In fact, Mr. Littlefield used to say that she knew the business better than he did," said the *Bangor Daily News*.

The officers of the large clothing retailers who had done business with the Littlefield factory still believed in Miss Danielson, her fortitude to recover from the effects of the disaster at Mount Desert Ferry, and her ability to take control of the profitable Brewer clothing factory once again. During her recovery that winter, Miss Danielson received many letters and would be visited by representatives of A. Shuman and Company, of Boston, for whom the Littlefield Clothing Factory had previously made garments, urging her to reassume control of the factory. They told her they knew she could have the work done to suit them and they wanted her to have their contracts.

With excellent medical attendance and the best of nursing care over the winter, Miss Danielson was eventually able to sit up, and her physician said that it was but a matter of a few weeks before she would be able to move about.

During her recovery, Miss Danielson carefully considered the business propositions directed at her. She discussed the matter with her doctor, who assured her that it was but a matter of a few months before she would be able to go into the factory and look after the details as she had in the past. Ultimately Lillian made the decision to return to the helm of the Littlefield Clothing Factory in Brewer.

The announcement of her return to control of the Brewer factory in the spring of 1900 demonstrated the interest the community had taken in Lillian Danielson and her plight after the disaster at Mount Desert Ferry. Everyone had been in Lillian's corner. "It was announced on Tuesday that Miss Lillian E. Danielson had secured the Littlefield clothing factory in Parker Street and that work would begin there on next Monday morning. This will be gratifying news to all Brewer people in more ways than one. They will be glad to see this factory, which employs a large number of hands, once more in operation, and also to learn that Miss Danielson has so far recovered from the effects of the injuries which she received in the Mt. Desert Ferry disaster of August 6, last, as to be able to once again take an active part in business affairs," wrote the *Bangor Daily News* on April 11, 1900.

Until Miss Danielson was able to be in the building herself, the work in the factory was done under the direct supervision of Miss Mary J. Welch, who had been assistant superintendent there for several years until the plant closed over the winter. With Lillian Danielson living directly next door to the factory, Miss Welch made frequent reports to her during the day for instruction. "So that even though confined to her room, that energetic young woman will maintain a constant supervision over her business," wrote the *Bangor Daily News*.

Over the winter the families of the victims took care of the lost loved ones' affairs. Notices of estate probate appeared in the local papers. For some, the story of the disaster continued through the legal system for the next few years. The first of the lawsuits against the Maine Central Railroad would be heard during the April term of the Maine Supreme Court in 1900. Nine cases initially were filed by survivors of the disaster at Mount Desert Ferry against the Maine Central Railroad for damages related to injuries sustained in the accident. Six of those survivors were Lillian A. Danielson, Georgie A. Russell, Mary T. Sweeney, Annie B. Hammill, Mary L. Shorten, and Alonzo P. Oakes, all listed as being of Bangor. Miss Russell, who had been in New York under medical treatment for injuries sustained in the disaster, returned to Bangor to be in attendance during the hearing.

The court opened at 10:00 a.m on Tuesday, April 3, 1900, with Judge Thomas H. Haskell presiding. On Friday, April 19, the case of *Alonzo P. Oakes v. the Maine Central Railroad* was the first on the docket. The hearing began at 9:30 a.m. and lasted all morning.

Delia E. Wiley Oakes

Delia and Alonzo Oakes lived at 260 Ohio Street in Bangor at the time of the disaster. Alonzo, the son of Hudson and Lizzie Oakes of Foxcroft, Maine, was thirty-three years old and was employed as a clothing salesman by the Chapman Clothing Company of Bangor. Mr. Oakes was well known in the Bangor area and was politically active in that city.

Delia Oakes was a milliner, or hat-maker, which was a lucrative business given the fashion of the era, which dictated the wearing of hats by both men and women. Delia and Alonzo had a five-year-old son.

On the day of the disaster, Alonzo and Delia Oakes were in the company of Mr. and Mrs. George Wyler, also of Bangor. Whether the

Oakeses' son was with the party is unknown, though he is not mentioned in news reports from the time. The Oakes party was among the last of the people who fell into the water from the broken gangplank, thrown into the middle of the mass of people who were struggling for their lives. Mr. and Mrs. Oakes were separated in the fall. Alonzo Oakes fought desperately to get to his wife and save her, but instead Mr. Oakes saw his wife dragged down to her death by another person before he could make his way through the water.

Mr. Oakes was just barely saved from the wharf above. He was taken to The Bluffs, described as "almost crazed" after being rescued from the water.

After the disaster, Alonzo would bury his wife at the Maple Grove Cemetery in Bangor, in the Wiley plot, the family of Mrs. Oakes. The stone that marks the grave is large and impressive.

Following the tragic death of his wife, Alonzo Oakes was a desperate man. His health was deteriorating, he had a son to support, and his wife had been the main breadwinner of the family. Without her, he was in the position that many women of the time found themselves in when their husbands unexpectedly died—helpless.

Mr. Oakes's lawsuit against the Maine Central Railroad was for five thousand dollars for the death of his wife in the disaster. Mr. Oakes claimed that the accident was due to the neglect of the defendant corporation "in not providing a suitable slip for the use of its passengers in boarding its steamboats at the Mount Desert Ferry wharf."

Alonzo Oakes told the court he was suing the railroad in his capacity as administrator of Delia Oakes's estate solely for the benefit of his five-year-old son. W. B. Peirce, Esq., lawyer for Mr. Oakes, opened the case for the plaintiff, describing fully the accident at the ferry in which Mrs. Oakes lost her life. Mr. Peirce stated that Mrs. Oakes had contributed largely to the support of the child, and that, owing to Mr. Oakes's poor health, she would have continued to support the boy had she lived.

The witnesses for the plaintiff were Mr. Oakes, Mrs. C. B. Dexter, a sister of Mrs. Oakes; Lester R. Wiley, a brother; Margaret E. Clark, who was Mrs. Oakes's employer; and others, including physicians who had examined Mr. Oakes and found that he had tuberculosis.

The lawyer for the Maine Central Railroad, Mr. Woodard, admitted the railroad's liability in the death of Mrs. Oakes. The defense had no testimony to offer, and the case was heard simply on the question of damages. Mr. Woodard spoke only of the conditions that surrounded the child, and said that he thought that in ten years the child would have been helping the mother financially, had she lived, rather than the mother helping him. He asked the jury to consider the matter without prejudice.

The jury remained out about an hour and returned a verdict for the plaintiff in the sum of $3,500. "The matter is of some importance as it is supposed other similar actions are pending," wrote the *Portland Daily Press*.

The Maine Central Railroad appealed the award. Lawyers for the railroad argued to the court of appeal that under legal statute the damages could not be punitive, neither could they be awarded for the physical pain and suffering of the deceased or the grief and sorrow of the beneficiary. The sum given must be the present worth of the future pecuniary benefits of which the beneficiary was deprived by the wrongful act, neglect, or default of the defendant, argued the railroad.

Mr. Oakes's side argued that under the appropriate legal statute, to recover damages for the death of a person "caused by the wrongful act, neglect or default" of another, the earning capacity of the deceased, including not only physical ability to labor but the probabilities of obtaining profitable employment, is an element to be considered in estimating damages.

The court of appeals sided with the railroad in part, ordering Mr. Oakes to remit $2,500 of the $3,500 award back to the Maine Central Railroad within thirty days or face a new trial, in which Mr. Oakes would have to re-argue his case.

Two years after the ruling, the now eight-year-old son of Alonzo and Delia Oakes was an orphan.

Alonzo Oakes died in February of 1903 at the home of his mother, Mrs. Lizzie Oakes, on Spring Street in Foxcroft, Maine. He was thirty-seven years old. "His wife was among the unfortunate victims who lost their lives in the Bar Harbor calamity in 1899," noted the *Bangor Daily News*.

Besides his son and mother, Alonzo Oakes left a sister and several relatives. After the funeral, the body of Alonzo Oakes was forwarded to Bangor by train, where he was buried beside his wife.

Chester W. Robbins, thirty-three, editor of the *Old Town Enterprise*, was generally considered the main hero of the disaster of Mount Desert Ferry, and his name and story had been spread in newspapers from coast to coast. Leaving Mount Desert Ferry by train Sunday evening, Chester Robbins turned his efforts to publishing the next edition of his newspaper. This would be a difficult task—both Mr. Robbins and his wife had been in the disaster, as had his nephew. Chester W. Robbins was thoroughly exhausted from his rescue efforts and his prolonged submersion in the chilly Maine water. His nephew, Chester M. Robbins, had nearly died in the disaster. The entire family was also trying to emotionally deal with all they had seen and experienced that day.

Chester W. Robbins had been born in California in 1866 but lived in Maine most of his life. Mr. Robbins was a man who enjoyed travel and adventure. It was from a journey to the World's Columbian Exposition in Chicago in 1883 that he returned to Maine with a wife, Rachel, a southern girl of much charm. Chester Robbins himself was described as genial.

Five years after his marriage, Mr. Robbins founded the *Old Town Enterprise*. On March 3, 1888, the first edition of the weekly eight-page publication hit the state's newsstands.

Chester Robbins was very community oriented. He was largely instrumental in having the Maine State Legislature grant a city charter to Old Town, in 1891. He would also fight for small causes, using his skills at instigation and persistence to see the number of fire alarm boxes in the city of Old Town increased from four to forty.

Mr. Robbins was involved in real estate, at one time owning several properties near the train station in Old Town. Chester Street, which ran from Main Street to the Maine Central Railroad station, was named for him. Perhaps a sense of whimsy is seen by the fact that the street was given Mr. Robbins's first name, not his last. Several pieces of real estate near the station passed through Chester Robbins's hands before he decided to build what was later known as the Robbins Block on Main

Street. This building boasted a marble stairway that Mr. Robbins had bought in Boston from a wrecking firm, which had salvaged it from an old Boston mansion. The Robbins Block was eventually razed to make room for a parking area. Mr. Robbins also dealt in the sale of goods and novelties and could be depended on to supply almost any type of merchandise. He was famous for his beautiful calendars, which he published annually for the local merchants.

Chester Robbins also loved to travel. He would combine his love of travel and his skill at organization into annual excursions along the Maine and Canadian coast and parts of New England, which Mr. Robbins would personally host. As an excursion conductor, Mr. Robbins, standing tall and straight, wearing a goatee, gave off a commanding appearance. His skills in the role were described as most impressive, and generally very few incidents ever arose to mar his plans for those under his charge. His tours became quite popular with the people of the Old Town area and the Maine Press Association.

The next edition of the *Old Town Enterprise* would hit the newsstands a few days late, on Saturday instead of Wednesday. Mr. Robbins would call it a "Special Saturday Edition." "Subscribers who receive the Enterprise late this week will not wonder when they know that it is the first time since the paper was started, over eleven years, that our last forms were not on the press by Friday evening,' wrote Chester W. Robbins.

Extra help in our line is not available in Old Town on short notice, and three members of the Enterprise family being in the accident has had a bad effect all round, but we are thankful to have come out alive.

The Enterprise was handicapped this week. Mr. and Mrs. Robbins and Mr. Robbins nephew, Chester M. Robbins, were among the unfortunate ones who were precipitated into the water, and while they were fortunate in their escape from drowning, they are still unable to attend to regular duties. Mrs. Robbins received the most arduous injuries and although she was able to return home on the day of the accident, she is still confined to her bed. Chester M. Robbins has been unable to attend to his duties in the office and C. W. Robbins, though not seriously injured in the accident, has suffered considerably from the work of rescuing others, as he remained in the water until he saw every live body taken out. While unable to reply personally to the numerous congratulatory letters he has received from friends this week, concerning the work of rescue, he desires to express publicly his heartfelt appreciation of the many kind words that have been written and spoken.

Chester W. Robbins's own story, from the *Old Town Enterprise*, August 12, 1899, started with the headline: "Frightful Accident at Mt. Desert Ferry/The Slip Breaks down and 200 people slide into the water and under the wharf/twenty lives lost but should be thankfully considered a small number—the verdict of the jury."

On the front page of the newspaper was a very dramatic drawing, which had also been used in a few other newspapers. The drawing showed the scene of the rescue effort from the vantage point of the deck of the *Sappho* looking toward the wharf. It depicted rescue efforts in the pen, with people being pulled out of the water with ropes, ladders, and manpower, many shown as being unconscious.

The above picture is presented by the Bangor Daily News and represents the accident after nearly all the live bodies had been rescued from the water. You are looking at the end of the slip, which at the chain was some five or six feet above the water, while the broken end of course was in the water. The other portion of the slip where you see the ladder was only thirteen feet long and slanted a good deal more than the picture represents. The sides of the gangway were boarded down as far as the slip is ordinarily operated, but fortunately for some of us it was open below so that many came to the surface under the wharf and apart from the struggling mass of humanity which was piled on top of each other in the waters of the open slip.

The slip was 38 feet long by 10 feet wide containing 380 square feet and contained at the time of the accident over 200 people as they were surging on faster than the narrow gang plank, from the slip to the Sappho would permit the crowd to enter and find places upon the steamer.

It was a horrifying sight to see so many struggling for life, others passing beneath the surface, and while the writer was doing his best for those about him, to see life pass from those he could not reach. There were many who possessed wonderful presence of mind, a fact which is evident and proven by the small number of deaths which occurred, as follows.

It was here that Chester Robbins printed the correct "List of Deceased" at Mount Desert Ferry. "One of the most serious accidents which has ever taken place in Maine occurred last Sunday at Mt. Desert Ferry when a train load of about 1000 passengers were about to enter the steamer Sappho for a trip across to Bar Harbor, where thousands of visitors were expecting the warships of Uncle Sam's navy. Several hundred passengers had already passed on to the boat when with a buckle at first then a sudden splash about 200 people slid into the water."

Mr. Robbins was able to assist his wife and other ladies of the Maine Press Association to the pilings under the wharf, where they clung until a rescue could be made. Though his name and story had been told across the country's newspapers for the past week, the only issue Chester Robbins took issue with was the description of him stripping down to his underclothing in public, even though it was in the middle of a rescue effort.

Several were reached under the wharf by the writer and life preservers which were thrown in from the Sappho put around them while many others who had succeeded climbing upon the beams succeeded in pulling others and women up after them. It was under the wharf that this writer removed his clothing—not on the wharf as several papers have stated, which would elucidate that we escaped the first scenes and experiences.

Through the efforts of Messrs. Eben Hartwell of this city, R. M. Campbell of Ellsworth and others whose heroic work in saving lives has been favorably commented upon by the daily press, the ladies referred to were assisted up the ladder and taken to the rooms with others at the Bluffs Hotel.

The Enterprise cannot give in detail any adequate description of the heart-rending scene. Men worked bravely, and have been termed heroes, but heroics and courage were afterthoughts.

Twenty Maine Press Association members were on the slip when the crash occurred, and thirteen of them were precipitated into the water and all rescued. Chester M. Robbins, son of Rev. J. W. Robbins of Mexico, Me., who has been employed in the Enterprise office for a year past was also among the excursionists from Old Town and came very near being drowned, requiring the services of physicians and nurses most of the afternoon, and feels under deep obligation to Postmaster and Mrs. J. M. Oak of Bangor for kindness shown him at their room in the hotel.

Of the people from this city and vicinity who were in the accident only one death occurred, that of Mr. Joseph Murphy, one of our bright and promising young men who had many friends and was popular with his associates. Mr. Murphy had been married but a little over a year and leaves a widow and an infant son, his father, Mr. John Murphy, two brothers, John and Thomas, and a sister, Mrs. James Cavanaugh of Massachusetts.

The front page of the *Old Town Enterprise* featured a drawing of Mr. Murphy.

Mr. Robbins, a man of his word, also told readers of the *Old Town Enterprise* that he had not forgotten his promise to give a full report on the excursion he had conducted the previous week with the Maine Press Association. "It is always our intention to fulfill all promises and while two weeks have passed since the press excursion took place and most of our readers have been informed of the Bar Harbor accident in which the editor of the ENTERPRISE took quite an active part and which has rendered him only partially capable of fulfilling the duties to which his attention is usually required, it will not be surprising that only an abbreviated letter can be offered on the excursion," wrote Robbins.

Chester W. Robbins was hailed as a hero after the disaster at Mount Desert Ferry. His name and the story of his actions spread across the state and the nation. Wrote the *Ellsworth American*:

Mr. Robbins seemed clear-headed, fearless, and tireless in his work as lifesaver. He is an expert swimmer and does not know fear. "His work was almost miraculous," said an eyewitness. He swam under the wharf, pulling out this one and that one. He saved some who it seemed could not escape drowning. Mr. Robbins is a hero, and no mistake. The number of lives that heroic man must have saved, it is hard to estimate. Not only that, but his valor stimulated others to work harder. He is a hero, as well as a perfect gentleman. Mr. Robbins was as cool in that dreadful deathtrap as he was in engineering his excursion through Washington county, and the ladies and brothers of the press should feel proud of this hero. They should feel proud of him as a business man, proud of him as an entertainer, and proud of him as the noted hero in saving lives at Mount Desert Ferry.

Wrote the *Bangor Daily Whig and Courier*, "One by one he would take persons, tie a rope around them and let them go; and by the time one head reached the wharf he had another supported, ready to be lifted on to firm footing. It was estimated by other workers in the rescue that fully 30 bodies, conscious and unconscious, were brought out of the well in this way."

Wrote the *Bangor Daily News*, "Mr. Robbins has been termed the hero of the day, and evidence goes to show that he, if anyone, deserves this title. After a terrible struggle to save himself from going under, he turned his immediate attention to his wife, and it was with great difficulty that he rescued her, as two women were clinging to her from behind, and holding her down. It was only with the promise that they would be saved that they were induced to let go their hold. Mr. Robbins's word was good, and he rescued the two women, then turned his attention to others. It was only by his cool headedness and ability to act quickly in times of peril that about 12 souls were saved."

From the *Gardiner Daily Reporter Journal*: "The accounts credit Mr. Robbins, of the Oldtown Enterprise, who was the manager of the press excursion, with great work in saving lives. He assisted eleven women to places of safety. We are not surprised at the good report, for he is always doing more for others than for himself. I have known him for years and have loved and honored him more and more each year. He is a perfect specimen of nerves and muscle, tireless and lithe as a cat; mentally bright, of perfectly inexhaustible good nature, and with administrative ability enough to run a Cook's excursion. He never varies, never forgets, never gets out of patience; but never before has he been called to fish his party out of the briny deep. He needed no honors to endear him to his brothers and sisters of the press association."

A week after the disaster, Mr. Robbins was honored in the national magazine *Newspaperdom*, a weekly magazine out of New York that reported on the field of newspaper publishing. The editor of *Newspaperdom* had been sent many newspaper clippings regarding Mr. Robbins's heroics in the disaster. Under the headlines, "Honor to whom honor is due" and "Editor Life-Saver/A dozen persons rescued from drowning by a Maine Scribe," the article read:

> *"Hero" is an appellation often loosely applied. Few men have even a chance to earn it. But Chester W. Robbins, editor and proprietor of the Old Town (Me.) Enterprise, has a clear and undisputed title to the cognomen, that will command honor for him through life, and secure a place for his name through all time on the role of illustrious lovers of their fellow men. Such distinction dates of Sunday, August 6th, when Mr. Robbins was precipitated with a mass of struggling humanity into deep water by the breaking of the gangplank at MDF, between the wharf and steamer, and 20 men, women and children were drowned. The news of this terrible calamity horrified the entire world the next morning; but not so swift in its traveling was the story of Mr. Robbins's self-forgetful achievements in lifesaving, thorough which it is estimated that not less than twelve to 15 persons were rescued from the fate that befell so many of their companions.*

Editor Robbins as Tour Manager

Mr. Robbins has always been a devotee of editorial excursions. He never misses one of his state organization's outings and has several times participated in the extended trips of the National Editorial Association as a delegate. So markedly has he developed the traits of a good tourist that the Maine editors have often entrusted plans and arrangements to him, making him a member of the committee in charge. It was in this capacity that he accompanied, with Mrs. Robbins, the members of his state association on their trip the first week of this month. After the regular itinerary was covered, a party of 15 decided to extend their travels to Bar Harbor, and on this memorable Sunday morning joined hundreds of other excursionists at Mount Desert, to take a steamer for the noted resort, to see the warships and otherwise add to their experiences.

Cool-headed from the first Mr. Robbins went down close to the edge of the slip, fortunately. When he came up, he found himself under the wharf, with his wife and two other women, whom he helped to places of safety on timbers. He couldn't have been anything but perfectly self-possessed and thoughtful only of aiding others, from the very first. One after another he, being an expert swimmer and powerful withal, snatched from danger, with the aid of life-preservers flung from the steamer. Finding his movements impeded by clothing, he stripped his outer garments, and again devoted his best efforts to saving the panic-stricken and helpless. But in spite of all he and other brave men could do by all means in their power, twenty persons met their death in this frightful casualty, some expiring after being taken from the water.

The Maine Press Association met again on January 25, 1900, four and a half months after the disaster. This was the winter portion of their twice-yearly meetings. There were no tours or sightseeing during the winter meeting; this was a time to take care of association business.

Chester W. Robbins was honored by his colleagues in the Maine newspaper industry that day, not only by word, but by action. They would elect Mr. Robbins to the office of president of the Maine Press Association at the meeting.

This was the thirty-seventh annual meeting of the Maine Press Association. Outgoing association president J. M. S. Hunter addressed the crowd, noting the members of the Maine Press Association who had been at Mount Desert Ferry.

> *A few of our members have a greater cause for thankfulness, perhaps, than the rest; and it is a source of pleasure for us all to know that one of our members figures as the worthy recipient of our thankfulness and gratitude, for, through his bravery and good judgment, the lives of several were spared to their families and friends.*
>
> *The members of the Maine Press Association wished to officially recognize Chester W. Robbins and his actions that day in August.*
>
> *The awful disaster at Mt. Desert Ferry in July last will never be forgotten by those who were connected with it; nor will the fifteen of the members of the Maine Press Association forget, so long as their lives and memory are spared, the noble and unselfish efforts of our brother, Chester W. Robbins of the Old Town Enterprise, which resulted in saving so many lives on that awful day. It is fitting that at this time we, as an association, take proper action to express our gratitude to Brother Robbins. He was ready to take his life in his hands in order to save the lives of his friends. What greater or more noble act that this can be mentioned?*
>
> *I will recommend the appointment of a special committee of three to prepare and present at a subsequent session, to Brother Chester W. Robbins, some fitting testimonial of our appreciation of his noble and successful efforts in the saving of lives. And I also suggest that the regular order of business be laid aside so that this committee may be at once appointed and given suitable time in which to act on this important matter.*

The committee was at once appointed, and later in the day they reported back to the assembly with the following statement:

Your committee to whom was referred the matter of preparing a testimonial to Brother Chester W. Robbins for his heroic and successful efforts in saving lives at the Mt. Desert Ferry accident, has attended to that duty and asks leave to report, as follows:

This Association hereby tenders its sincere and heartfelt thanks to Brother Chester W. Robbins for the courage, fearlessness and ability displayed by him at the terrible accident at Mt. Desert Ferry last August, in saving the lives of members of this Association and others. Whether engaged in managing Press excursions or called suddenly to perform such duties as he took upon himself at the accident already named, in which he risked his own life to save others, Brother Robbins is always equal to the occasion and ready to perform any duty, whether pleasant or otherwise. His services on that terrible day at Mt. Desert Ferry can never be forgotten.

This report shall be spread upon our records and a copy of it furnished to Brother Robbins by our Secretary.

All of which is respectfully submitted by the committee. G. A. Quimby/L. H. Murch.

Following the reading and acceptance of this testimonial, President Hunter gave up his seat to the new president of the Maine Press Association. Chester W. Robbins gave a few brief remarks, which were characteristic of his reply whenever asked about his heroics during the disaster. "Men worked bravely, and have been termed heroes, but heroism and courage were afterthoughts. They worked as men should, with cool heads, calm and calculating minds, crowding much into little, and accomplishing results which afterward considered were marvelous in the extreme," said Chester W. Robbins.

Following his remarks, Mr. Robbins got down to business and began appointing committees to serve during the ensuing year.

Later in 1900, as the one-year anniversary of the disaster approached, Chester W. Robbins's name was raised as a possible candidate to the state legislature that coming winter. "Favorable mention is made of Chester W. Robbins, the energetic editor of the Old Town Enterprise, for the position," wrote the *Bangor Daily News* in July. "No man has evinced a greater interest in the prosperity of his town and state than Mr. Robbins, and his nomination would be met with hearty approval by those men who want an active and progressive representative at the State House during the coming session of the legislature."

The following month, instead of promoting himself, Mr. Robbins seconded the nomination for the incumbent representative for Old Town, David Carr. Mr. Robbins then made a few remarks and expressed his desire to assist Mr. Carr's candidacy in every possible manner.

Mr. Robbins continued to personally conduct his popular excursions. A year after the disaster at Mount Desert Ferry, he was guiding a group of approximately 150 people to Quebec and Montreal. Wrote Robbins in his newspaper:

> The *"personally conducted party"* which will make the trip to Quebec and Montreal August 14th, under the direction of CWR will be the largest that he has conducted in the four years that those trips have been so popular. Already the list includes names from Bangor, Ellsworth, Dexter, Foxcroft and Monson, beside a large number in Old Town who are contemplating the trip.
>
> For $23.00 C. W. Robbins of OT will provide your railroad ticket to Quebec, an excursion to St. Anne . . . he also provides sleeping car berth both ways for all who join his party . . . more? Yes, he pays all hotel bills at Quebec and Montreal and provides carriage drives for his party in both cities and throws in other interesting features that cause his friends to *"wonder how he does it."*

The year following the disaster, Mr. Robbins would take on additional responsibilities in Old Town by serving as a census-taker for the 1900 federal census. He would be appointed treasurer of Old Town's first Board of Trade the following year and would be one of three Republican candidates to the Maine State Legislature, a position he did not win.

In 1908 Chester W. Robbins sold the *Old Town Enterprise* to Mr. A. H. Brown, a resident of Old Town and a graduate of the University of Maine, Class of 1880. The newspaper continues to this day, now called the *Penobscot Times*.

Chester W. Robbins died on September 24, 1941.

The excursion that Sunday had not been the Maine Press Association's first trip to Bar Harbor via Mount Desert Ferry.

In 1890, nearly ten years before the disaster, E. H. Elwell, editor of the *Portland Transcript*, died at Bar Harbor of heart disease while on his way home from that year's Maine Press Association excursion. He was sixty-four years old and been in the newspaper business all his life.

In 1885, four years before the disaster, the Maine Press Association made a trip from Mount Desert Ferry to Somes Sound aboard the steamship *Sebenoa*. On board were George S. Rowell, the business manager of the *Portland Daily Advertiser*, and Judge Henry Maker, a most influential and highly valued citizen and local businessman from Hallowell.

The *Sebenoa* was built for service on the inland passage between Bath and the Sheepscot River, and the big waves of Frenchman Bay tossed the *Sebenoa* about in what was described as "the strangest fashion." Judge Maker was leaning upon the rail of the ship, at the gangway, when the boat lurched, the rail gave way, and Judge Maker would have gone overboard had not Mr. Rowell instantly thrown himself upon the prostate man. With help, both men were afterward drawn back to a safer position on the ship.

Judge Maker later presented Mr. Rowell with a handsome copy of William Cullen Bryant's *Library of Poetry and Song*, with this inscription: "George S. Rowell from H. K. Maker, in remembrance of prompt aid at a time of great danger. 1886."

"Bar Harbor has been sort of a hoodoo for the Maine Press Association," wrote the *Gardiner Daily Reporter Journal* after the disaster at Mount Desert Ferry. "On one trip there came near being a shipwreck, on another a member died, beside the last great disaster."

The Loss of Mount Desert Ferry

And so the dream of a number of planners, which began with the purchase of Mrs. Nathaniel Grant's land "for a song" by a Canadian man named Clergue, who later sold to the Maine Shoreline interests, and who in turn sold to the Maine Central Railroad, dissolved, the boom became bust; and Mount Desert Ferry reverted to its quieter, more residential existence.
—Sanford Phippen, Hancock Historical Society

The disaster at Mount Desert Ferry did not seem to have any long-lasting impact on the Maine Central Railroad, Mount Desert Ferry, or The Bluffs Hotel. Though the disaster remained in the memories of Mainers for years, it was not often talked about. Business continued through the Waukeag Line of the railroad to Mount Desert Ferry, the passengers continued their travels to Mount Desert Island, and The Bluffs Hotel continued its Sunday dinners.

Time moved on, and so did life. Capt. Edgar P. Dickson of Hancock, who labored from the deck of the *Sappho* to the point of physical injury during the rescue, continued taking passengers to Bar Harbor and the other towns in Frenchman Bay serviced by Mount Desert Ferry. Captain Dickson spent his last five years with the railroad serving as fleet commander, having general oversight and authority over the Maine Central marine service, not only in Frenchman Bay but on the Rockland, Stonington, and Sergeantsville routes as well.

Edgar Dickson had been one of the first Hancock residents to sign on with the Maine Central Railroad when it came to town in 1884. His first position was as mate of the *Sebenoa*, on the run between Mount Desert Ferry and Bar Harbor. Over his career, Captain Dickson served as the master of the ferry steamboats *Sebenoa, Norumbega, Samoset, Sieur de Monts, Pemaquid, Moosehead*, and of course the historic *Sappho*, with which his name would always be linked in history.

Many of the wealthy and powerful men and women from the cities extended a hand of greeting to "Captain Dick" upon their arrival by train at Mount Desert Ferry. Captain Dickson was a friend to everybody, and everybody was his friend. His unfailingly courteous manner in his dealings with the passengers of the steamships under his command made him the natural representative of the Maine Central Railroad to greet the well-to-do summer guests on their arrival to Hancock. The summer residents of Mount Desert Island and Hancock came to regard Captain Dickson as reliable and dependable, always ready to straighten out any tangle that might arise in any way on their passage over Frenchman Bay to their summer home. "In his official capacity, Capt. Dickson was proficient, thorough and painstaking, and having grown up with the service he knew every detail of it and its every need and responded promptly and resourcefully in every emergency," wrote the *Bangor Daily News*.

Captain Dickson was also one of the most well-known businessmen in Hancock, serving as a director of the Bar Harbor Savings Bank and the Clark Coal Company. A community-minded man, Edgar Dickson was also a Freemason and belonged to the Knights of Pythias.

Captain Dickson died twelve years after the disaster at Mount Desert Ferry, at the West Street home of James E. Foster in Bar Harbor. "Capt. Dickson almost literally died in the harness, for only last Monday he was at the boat attending to his duties for several hours," wrote the *Bangor Daily News* on August 8, 1911.

Captain Dickson's body was received in Bar Harbor by the crew of the *Sappho*, who escorted their late captain to Mount Desert Ferry. The remains were met there by a delegation of prominent Hancock citizens. Ultimately Captain Dickson's body would be escorted to the coastal town of Westport, Maine, one hundred miles south, for burial.

One of Captain Dickson's sons, Bert, later became the captain of the *Sappho*, and another son, Ernest, served as engineer on many of the steamers his father had mastered that sailed in Frenchman Bay. The steamship business was in their blood, and they came by it naturally.

In 1917, six years after the death of Captain Dickson, the *Sappho* was taken out of the service of the Maine Central Railroad, to be replaced by a newer, faster steamship. In the minds of the public, the new steamship could never really replace the *Sappho*. The elegantly appointed *Sappho*, an institution known so well to the travelers and residents of Frenchman Bay, host to two US presidents, was gone forever, and with her the era she had symbolized.

Things were beginning to change in the Hancock area in 1917. An income tax had been imposed four years earlier, which curtailed the uncontrolled wealth that paid for the opulence that Bar Harbor once symbolized. American was in its first world war. Henry Ford had invented the automobile as well as the assembly line that made its mass production and common availability possible. Automobiles were just starting to move into the transportation market at the time the *Sappho* was taken out of service, and ridership on the Waukeag Line of the Maine Central Railroad was just starting its decline.

A writer for the *Portland Sunday Press* wrote about the *Sappho*'s last trip out of Frenchman Bay, and the loss of an era that went with her:

> *I saw a ghost the other day. And in seeing that ghost I saw a host of others, men of other days, giants in the world of letters and of politics, men of affairs in the business world and thousands of others, some of whom have long ago gone to the other land beyond the shadow line we call death. The ghost I saw was the old Maine Central flyer Sappho, being towed up this harbor by one of the steam lighters that carry stone and sand that are used to build wharves and breakwaters along the coast. Time was indeed when the Sappho would have resented such an indignity as this, but those days are over forever. Today the once queen of the Penobscot Bay has a piece of canvas over her smokestack, her thunderous resounding whistle once heard never to be forgotten has*

been removed, some of her cabin windows are broken, others stuffed with boards, and her decks are a mass of blistered paint and broken canvas. As I looked at this steamer being towed to what may prove her last resting place, my thoughts went back to the famous picture by Turner of the old fighting Temeraire, being towed up the Mersey to be broken up, the glory of battle of the Nile and of Trafalgar not being sufficient to save her from the vandal's hands.

No battles have been fought around the Sappho. But for more than 20 years this boat plied the waters of Frenchmen's and Penobscot Bay between Mount Desert and Bar Harbor wharf and was the only link between the outside world and the beautiful summer homes of those who were then Maine's greatest and the greatest not only of this, but of other nations. I can see the well-remembered face and stalwart form of Capt. E. P. Dickson standing beside the wheelhouse as the boat prepared to start out from the ferry wharf, laden with the beauty and fashion of the wealth and distinction of this land on its way to the Harbor.

No figure stands out more prominently than that of James G. Blaine, Maine's and the nation's greatest public man of his time. I see, too, Benjamin Harrison, President of the United States, Henry Cabot Lodge, then a congressman, now a senator from Massachusetts. Mr. Lodge was an alert, thin, red whiskered young man then. Today his locks are silver and his form much more rotund. President Harrison and also Mr. Blaine wore those famous white, tall hats that have gone forever.

I can remember Dr. S. Weir Mitchell, one of the leading alienists of the country and one of its best writers. I see him now, tall and stooping, with long, gray hair and a straggling gray beard, as with his professional air he walked about greeting again his friends of former years, pausing ever and again to drink in deep breaths of the strong salt air that came straight from the vast deeps.

Haskett Derby is another whom I well remember when I think of the Sappho. Dr. Derby came to be one of us during his later years, but for a long time he was a regular summer visitor at Bar Harbor, and his trips to and from on the Sappho linger well in my mind. Dr.

Derby in those days was a stalwart man with strong face, and a professional reputation that was worth a golden fortune.

I remember Sir Julian Bauncefote, that well remembered and most satisfactory of our British ambassadors. I remember other foreign diplomats for in those days, Bar Harbor when Mr. Blaine was there, was the nation's summer capital, and where the President and the secretary of State went, there also went the ambassadors and the ministers and their office staff.

But best of all I remember Payson Tucker. Who is there that is a suitable age in this state who does not remember him? He was Maine's greatest railroad man, born and brought up in our midst, learning his business on our lines and afterward building up the magnificent system to be handled by others in such a way as to be virtually the only railroad in the northeast that pays dividends in times of financial trouble.

Payson Tucker loved the Sappho. The steamer was built largely under his personal direction at Bath. The engines were built by his direction and were of the best. In her day nothing in these waters could touch the Sappho. I see Frank Jones who was for a time great in railroad circles. Mr. Jones had a place nearby and he made frequent trips on this steamer. Mr. Jones was a man of mark by his appearance in any company and once seen he would never be forgotten. Charles William Eliot, he being almost the only one out of that goodly company now left alive, Robert Amory, De Grasse Fox, Dr. Burton Harrison, Joseph Iasigi, the Biddle family of Philadelphia, William Gardner, Francis Lynde, Dr. George Fox, a worthy representative of a most worthy name and ancient lineage, Johnstone Livingston, F. M. Weld, J. Montgomery Sears and the members of his interesting family, Rev. Christopher Starr Leffingwell, one of the most picturesque looking men I ever knew, and all the rest gone, most of them to that borne from which no traveler ever yet returned.

There were hotels in Bar Harbor in those days. The Rodick, the old West End, the Louisburg, which is about the only one left that anyone could recognize today, and all of the goodly company that used to throng their spacious halls, fill their dining rooms and their ballrooms, whose summer gaiety enlivened the streets and whose comings and goings made so much for this old boat.

As I looked at her coming up the harbor, swinging around and tying up at the wharf battered and dingy and old and perhaps out of date, I could not help but remember the lines of the poet referring to the likeness between old ships and old men and the people that once were but no longer are. It carried me back to those piping days when despite all that is said and written now Bar Harbor was in its prime, both as a summer resort for people who went to secure rest and refreshment, from close communion with nature in all its savage wilderness along the rock-bound shores. But where also the great men of the world assembled and over the social cup of tea worked out a great many problems of finance and statecraft, the full import of which it may take generations yet to properly unfold to the public. There were giants in the land in those days and most of them during the season found their way to Bar Harbor and they went to and from the island on this steamer which if it could talk and tell the story, could a tale unfold that would be of such absorbing interest that no man would stop until he had read it all.

But steamers like men change and those that are the great ones of one generation become the least of the next. They grow old and wear out and the places that once knew them know them no more. In the case of this steamer, it has been replaced by newer and larger and in some respects better boats. But it will never fall to the lot of any of them to carry such a distinguished multitude of great people as fell to the lot of this old vessel which, unless all signs fail, is shortly destined to go to the junk heap simply because no use can be found for her whole.

Mount Desert Ferry would remain in operation another thirty-two years after the disaster and another fourteen years after the loss of the *Sappho*.

There is always a better mousetrap waiting just around the corner. In 1884 Mount Desert Ferry had been the better mousetrap, improving transportation to Mount Desert Island and transforming an entire region in the process. The age of gilded railroad passenger service to Bar

Harbor via Mount Desert Ferry would have another twenty years after the disaster without real competition. No transportation arrangement could improve upon the rail and ferry service that Mount Desert Ferry provided.

In the early 1900s, just as the Maine Central Railroad was launching the *Moosehead* and the *Rangeley*, the newly invented automobile was starting to become available, not just to wealthy hobbyists but to the everyday working person. The *Moosehead* and the *Rangeley* would be the last two passenger ships ever built by the Maine Central Railroad.

At first, automobiles were not allowed on Mount Desert Island. As more and more of the wealthy visitors to the island acquired and wanted to use their new automobiles, the laws started to change. Soon each island town had different laws regarding their use on public roads. Bar Harbor was a holdout in the battle against automobiles, not allowing their use until the start of World War I.

The death knell for ferry service in Hancock was symbolically tolled in 1919, when John D. Rockefeller brought his summer party of guests from New York to Mount Desert Island in five automobiles rather than by private railroad car through Mount Desert Ferry. This marked a definitive change in the transportation choices of those wishing to visit Maine's most popular tourist destination.

Ferry service in Frenchman Bay deteriorated rapidly between 1917 and 1925. During the early 1920s there was a general decrease in passenger traffic and revenue on the Mount Desert branch of Maine Central Railroad's Waukeag Line, resulting in the discontinuation in 1924 of the "around the hills" ferry service from Mount Desert Ferry to Seal Harbor, Northeast Harbor, and Southwest Harbor, because the volume of traffic had dropped below the financial break-even point. This left only the steamship *Norumbega* to provide service from Mount Desert Ferry to Bar Harbor, Hancock Point, and Sorrento.

With the number of passengers continuing to decrease, in 1925 the Maine Central Railroad announced its first major cutback to the number of trains traveling daily to Hancock. By 1926 the railroad was providing bus transportation from the Ellsworth train station to Mount Desert Island for the out-of-state passengers of the Bar Harbor Express who wished to arrive on the island faster than could be done on the ferry. In June of 1927, Mr. D. C. Douglas, the vice president and general manager of the Maine Central Railroad, addressed the Bar Harbor Board of Trade, telling them that passenger and freight numbers had declined steadily and it was a "very remote possibility" that Bar Harbor train and ferry service would be discontinued in the future.

"The Frenchman's Bay boat service is a much less important thing now than it was in 1914, but it still fulfills a definite function and will be continued," wrote the *Bar Harbor Times* in an editorial on June 13, 1928. "There is one feature of the route that will never change; it will always be a beautiful scenic route to MDI and that alone will probably keep it in existence."

By 1930, only the *Pemaquid*, the smallest and oldest of the twentieth-century steamships in the Maine Central Railroad fleet, was left on the run from Mount Desert Ferry to its limited stops in Frenchman Bay. Train schedules at Mount Desert Ferry had gone from a high in 1914 of seven trains per day down to two per day. The *Pemaquid* was hauled out of Frenchman Bay for maintenance at the end of the following season and never returned.

In 1931 the causeway to Mount Desert Island was completed. The Maine Central Railroad knew that this was the end of Mount Desert Ferry. In May of that year, representatives of the railroad attended a meeting in Bar Harbor in which they outlined the details of the unprofitable steamboat service to Mount Desert Island. In place of the steamers, proposed the railroad, would be luxury buses from Ellsworth to Bar Harbor for all train passengers, and other over-the-road transportation for all freight.

The meeting was attended by two hundred people. Opposition to the plan was voiced. Nothing changed. The headline in the *Bar Harbor Times* on May 6, 1931, told the end of the story: "Maine Central Will Discontinue Frenchman's Bay Boat Service."

On Labor Day 1960, the Bar Harbor Express made its final run from New York to the awaiting bus coaches at the Ellsworth railroad station.

It simply was no longer profitable for Maine Central Railroad to operate the passenger train at all.

In 1967, E. Spencer Miller, president of the Maine Central Railroad, discussed the loss of rail service in the area:

> *In common with many others who look into the future, I see a time when, in large sections of the country, the highways are going to become glutted and the great attraction of moving freight over them in single vehicles, or moving passengers over them with one or two people being carried in a vehicle powered by an internal combustion engine, is going to become non-existent and may even become limited by imposition of law . . . one train operating into a metropolitan area could easily accommodate 800–1000 people and therefore supplant somewhere between 500–1000 automobiles, eliminating all of the congestion and all of the air pollution which they cause. We of the Maine Central Railroad believe that those things are going to happen and our state of mind is simply this: We are in the planning stages and thinking about this. We went out of the passenger business pursuant to public desire as evidenced by the fact that each of our trains by 1960 was handling less than half a bus load. We are willing and anxious to get back into that business when the pendulum swings to such an extent that it will be the desire of the people once again to have the comforts and reliability of passenger train service, in addition to the great public need to eliminate the uneconomic expense of super highways, and the pollution of the air which a multiplication of vehicles on them necessarily produces.*

A few years after the Bar Harbor Express made its last run, the Maine Central Railroad was bought and incorporated into a larger railroad company. Its name lives now only in history.

With the decision of the Maine Central Railroad in 1931 to bus all passengers from Ellsworth to Mount Desert Island came the closure of Mount Desert Ferry. It was the sad end of an era for the people of Hancock.

The timing of the closure could not have been worse for the town and its surrounding areas. A worldwide economic depression, the worst ever known, had begun two years previous to the closing of Mount Desert Ferry and lasted a full decade. Many Hancock residents had either been employed by the railroad at Mount Desert Ferry or provided goods and services to the large operation there. Replacement jobs just were not available in the remote area of Hancock. "So many people worked at the ferry. They couldn't get jobs around here like before," said Sanford Phippen. "All of the people who worked at the Ferry, of course, found themselves like so many other people across America during the Depression, unemployed."

Maine Central Railroad's decision to build Mount Desert Ferry forty-seven years previously had brought economic prosperity to the small town of Hancock and changed its way of life, seemingly forever.

Mount Desert Ferry is often only thought of as the small spot of land on McNeil Point that housed the train station, ferry wharf, and hotel, but a more extensive support system just a few miles before reaching that spot had added considerably to the industry of Hancock.

During the summer there were many trains, as many as seven or eight a day, most of them long and full. In Mount Desert Ferry's heyday, dozens of Hancock residents worked there—on the trains, the steamer boats, or in the hotel. Many local residents were employed as "truck men," workers who loaded and unloaded cargo from the steamboats. Truck men were in high demand.

While the wharf and train station at Mount Desert Ferry were the support system for Mount Desert Island, "the yard" was the support system for Mount Desert Ferry. The yard was located a few miles before the train and ferry station, on shore land next to the railroad tracks. In the yard was the vast locomotive barn, which housed the train engines. There was a large turntable used to rotate the giant engines in the proper direction for travel. The support for the turntable was built in the ground, with its circular surface at ground level. The "basement" of the turntable still remains on the former grounds of the yard.

There were other structures and facilities at the yard, including sheds and water towers. A large amount of water was required by the railroad to create the steam that powered its engines. Maine Central Railroad bought a spring in Hancock just to supply the extra water, and its pump house still stands today.

Large railroad crews worked at the yard, some there simply to maintain the Pullman cars of the Bar Harbor Express, cleaning them inside and out.

"That was a tremendous installation down there for a town of this size," Hancock resident Monroe Moon told the Lois Johnson Historical Society of Hancock. Mr. Moon had worked for the railroad at Mount Desert Ferry.

The yard was an active place, especially for a small rural town. The short road that led to the yard, Cinder Road, had several houses along it. On the other side of the yard, closer to Mount Desert Ferry, was the Mount Desert Inn, a hotel patronized by more blue-collar guests, including some employees of the railroad.

Hancock resident and Maine Central Railroad employee Fred Grant shared his recollections with the Lois Johnson Historical Society of Hancock. Mr. Grant said he remembered that in the mornings there would always be a railroad brakeman outside at the yard, "sitting there all forenoon" cleaning the kerosene lamps that were hung about the waiting room and station at Mount Desert Ferry. Outside in the yard would be the "car cleaners" and other railroad workers, who were mostly local Hancock people, including Frank and Ellen Murphy, Archie Gatcomb, Morris Moon, and many others.

Many of the rail workers lived for the summer in the camps that were built around the train yard. Mr. Goldsberry, the local Pullman agent, lived nearby and served dinners for the railroad crew. Also staying at the yard would be the staff of the private Pullman train cars stored there, generally a chef and a porter, who were separate from the household staff of the cars' owners. Generally, these men were brought from the car owner's personal staff from New York or Philadelphia and stayed in the railroad cars, ready at a moment's notice should the car's owner wish to take a trip.

A number of Hancock people remembered that the train porters who worked on the private Pullman cars, many of them African American, also lived in the cars, spending the Maine summer nights playing cards in the yard. During the day, the porters would buy chickens, milk, eggs, and cream from the nearby farm of Minnie and Kate Grant. Every summer morning one of the porters would run into the Grants' yard calling, "Miss Minnie! Miss Minnie!" Returning to the yard, they would cook the chickens in a barrel and have a barbecue. Frank Murphy, a well-known clam-digger, would bring his fresh harvest to the camps for sale.

Many Hancock residents, though not directly employed by the Maine Central Railroad, made their livings from Mount Desert Ferry.

Samuel Johnston delivered the mail to the station. To keep warm in the winter, Mr. Johnston would cover himself with a "buffalo blanket." Children would try to jump aboard his horse-drawn carriage and were warned, "No one is to touch the U.S. Mail."

Frank Colby delivered eggs, milk, and butter to Mount Desert Ferry, as did Walter Clarke, who also delivered vegetables in the summer. Walter Clarke started a bakery business in his Hancock home, which was also used as a general store.

Kate Grant operated a tearoom and restaurant at the ferry. Freeman Grant opened a store of "groceries and confectionary" at the site in 1903. Two additional stores, operated by R. W. Grant and I. H. Foss, were also opened to serve the people at Mount Desert Ferry.

Harvey and Vester Carter used to take in boarders, as did Frank and Laura Colby, whose house for years was a very busy place. Laura Colby was noted for her delicious and generous servings at mealtime.

Ernest Dickson built his house as well as an adjoining store, operated by his wife, Lola, next to Mount Desert Ferry. Ernest was chief engineer on most of the Frenchman Bay steamers, all of which his grandfather, Capt. Edgar Dickson of the *Sappho*, had been master of at one point or another. The Dicksons were an entire family of seagoing men and were very respected by the other men who worked on steamboats all along the Maine coast. Famous Mount Desert Island summer resident Henry Ford, inventor of the automobile and the mechanized production system, used to spend the forty-minute steamship ride across Frenchman Bay down in the engine room with Ernest, talking of matters of mutual engineering interest. Ernest judged Henry Ford to be "a very smart man."

Mount Desert Ferry was simply a way of life in the town of Hancock.

Among its extensive facilities, Mount Desert Ferry proper and the yard made up its own little city. Like any city, Mount Desert Ferry had its own post office. Mr. Ivory L. Wardwell, who was at Mount Desert Ferry on the day of the disaster, was the first station agent and postmaster in 1884. After Wardwell's death, Ernest Abbot was appointed agent and postmaster. Minnie Grant ran the last post office out of her house.

Three years after the station was built, growth was significant enough in Hancock that the Mount Desert Ferry Schoolhouse was built in 1887. Prosperity was in such abundance at Mount Desert Ferry after its opening that plans were made to capitalize on the area's success. In 1900 a casino was planned for Hancock, but never seems to have materialized. A plan was also drawn up for a housing development near The Bluffs. Buena Vista would have been built on land just west of the area between the station at Mount Desert Ferry and the yard. The fifty-six acres of land would have been subdivided into twenty-eight lots, each containing two or three acres. A map of the proposed development, drawn by a Boston mapmaker, clearly indicates Maine Central Railroad's proximity to the development and its convenience to Boston. It can be assumed this subdivision was planned to be the summer residences for people south of Maine. This plan also never materialized.

As famous Mount Desert Island summer resident Henry Ford was spending his voyage across Frenchman Bay talking in the engine room with Hancock resident Ernest Dickson, ironically it was Mr. Ford's invention and mass production of the automobile that would cost Mr. Dickson his job, as well as the jobs, the economic support, and the new and accepted way of life of the people of Hancock.

Passenger and freight traffic had already been steadily dwindling at Mount Desert Ferry when the Maine Central Railroad discontinued service there in 1931, favoring the transportation of passengers of the Bar Harbor Express on buses across the new causeway to Mount Desert Island, and the passage of freight over the same road. Mount Desert Ferry, the golden goose that had made possible the growth of Bar Harbor,

Mount Desert Island, and the town of Hancock, was suddenly gone, never to return.

"And so, the dream of a number of planners, which began with the purchase of Mrs. Nathaniel Grant's land 'for a song' by a Canadian man named Clergue, who later sold to the Maine Shoreline interests, and who in turn sold to the Maine Central Railroad, dissolved, the boom became bust; and Mount Desert Ferry reverted to its quieter, more residential existence," wrote Hancock historian and author Sanford Phippen.

By the time Mount Desert Ferry was closed in 1931, The Bluffs Hotel had already been gone for sixteen years.

The Bluffs had become a fixture in Hancock after its construction. The residents of Hancock worked at the hotel in the summer to earn money for the winter. Farmers and shopkeepers in the town provided The Bluffs with various goods and services. The regular guests and returning staff would look for one another every season.

A few people from Bangor had set up private summer homes along the shores of Hancock before Mount Desert Ferry was even an idea. The construction of Mount Desert Ferry, which provided easy access to the town of Hancock via rail and steamboat, had prompted a building boom for upscale resort hotels in the town, where there had been none before. By 1887, three years after the ferry was built, four hotels were operating in Hancock, including The Bluffs, The Tarratine, the Crabtree House, and the Robinson House.

The Tarratine Hotel was already in operation when The Bluffs was constructed. Housed on the coast along Hancock Point just a few miles south of The Bluffs, The Tarratine was popular and well patronized, and the list of applications for its rooms was always long. Cottages had been built outside the hotel to handle the ever-growing list of patrons.

The building of The Bluffs sparked a competition between the two resort establishments. As The Bluffs was just starting to take shape on the small hilltop at Mount Desert Ferry, across town The Tarratine was being remodeled and refurbished, with the addition of more sleeping rooms, new dining rooms, and an office. The following year, the management of The Tarratine announced it would enlarge the hotel to twice its current capacity. A year later The Bluffs constructed a number of nearby spacious cottages with verandas and balconies. In the summer of 1889, the Tarratine added a pavilion replete with a dance hall, library, and billiard room. The Bluffs countered that same season with the building of tennis courts and the hiring of a landscape gardener.

"Rivalry raged between the proprietors of these two imposing structures," wrote Anne Pomroy in an unpublished paper titled "Hancock, Maine: 1880–1889 Early Influences of the Tourist Industry on a Small Coastal Community."

In the end, The Tarratine would outlive The Bluffs.

The disaster at Mount Desert Ferry seemed to have no negative effect on business at The Bluffs. Despite the accident in August, proprietors Peter Cuddy and George Bemis said that the 1899 season had been a financial success.

In the spring of the following year, it was announced that Mr. Bemis would move on to run another seasonal resort in Maine and Mr. Cuddy would run The Bluffs on his own. At first Mr. Cuddy had been silent on plans for the upcoming season. "Regarding the Bluffs at Mt. Desert Ferry, where Messers. Bemis and Cuddy entertained so large a number of visitors last year, nothing definitely is known, but without doubt the house will be opened since it has begun growing in popularity as a nearby resort, where businessmen can easily go to pass Sunday," wrote the *Bangor Daily News* in the spring of 1900.

News soon spread that The Bluffs would not only open for the season, but would open earlier and be bigger and better. "The Hotel Bluffs, at Mount Desert Ferry . . . will be opened rather earlier than usual—on June 20, when the summer train schedule on the Maine Central will take effect. The hotel will be greatly improved in many respects, all the rooms on the first guest floor being arranged in suites, while the grounds will be further beautified and new walks laid out. Many applications for rooms for the season have already been received and Mr. Cuddy looks for a prosperous season at this pleasant resort," wrote the *Bangor Daily News*.

Mr. Cuddy and a crew of men arrived in May at The Bluffs to put the place in readiness for the season and make the promised improvements. When they were done, the hotel had a new incandescent gaslight system, which provided illumination in every part of the hotel. New suites of rooms were prepared with all the conveniences of the age. A special arrangement with the Maine Central Railroad had been made whereby guests of the hotel could travel to Bar Harbor and back on Wednesdays and Saturdays for twenty-five cents. The year 1900 was one of the best seasons The Bluffs ever had.

"At the Bluffs they are enjoying an unusually prosperous season, and Cuddy informed the Bangor Daily News representative yesterday that there was not an available room in the house and that he has been turning away guests for the past ten days, and that many of the guests will remain well into September," wrote the *Bangor Daily News* on August 6, 1900, the first anniversary of the disaster at Mount Desert Ferry.

Though it sounded as if business was always good at The Bluffs, behind the scenes the hotel reportedly failed to make money. The proprietors of the hotel changed quite often. In 1892, seven years before the disaster, the hotel was reported to have been closed for the entire season.

"Enquiries are being made by quite a number of Bangor people as to whether The Bluffs at Mount Desert Ferry will be opened this year, as they desire to pass part or all of the summer there if it is to be. For various reasons it was closed last year. It would seem that this excellent hotel, so well located, ought to pay the owners and it would accommodate quite a large number who have spoken of taking rooms if it is open this year," wrote the *Bangor Daily Whig and Courier*.

In 1906 The Bluffs would be put up for sale. "[F]ully furnished, good chance for a live hotel man. Bargain. Address T. F. Moran, Bar Harbor."

Seven years later The Bluffs would be closed for good. The building would sit empty for a few years before The Bluffs was taken down in 1915, thirty years after having been built.

Automobiles were first starting to arrive on Mount Desert Island at the time The Bluffs closed, which caused some passengers to bypass Mount Desert Ferry entirely. The real cause of the demise of The Bluffs, however, ironically was the train that made The Bluffs hotel so convenient to travelers.

The trains arriving at Mount Desert Ferry landed literally over the water, looking directly across Frenchman Bay at Mount Desert Island.

The views and the nature of Mount Desert Ferry are breathtaking. The site was, and still is, magical.

The guests who stayed at The Bluffs, however, were looking for a quiet alternative to Bar Harbor. Mount Desert Ferry seemed the perfect place for that, with the grandeur of Mount Desert Island just a look away, and a trip to the island within just a one-hundred-yard walk from the hotel to the ferryboat.

It was that one hundred yards that made all the difference. The extravagant coastal resort hotel was simply too close to the railroad tracks. The convenience of Mount Desert Ferry was the demise of The Bluffs. Several times daily, the long, loud trains chugged into that peaceful, secluded spot, belching thick black smoke from the time they arrived until the time they left. Thousands of loud, excited passengers transferred daily from the train to the ferryboat and vice versa. Tons of freight was moved from the train to the ships that waited to deliver it to Mount Desert Island. The train station was necessarily located at Mount Desert Ferry, but it would be the train station that prevented the enjoyment of the quieter summer that The Bluffs tried to offer.

The closing of The Bluffs was also attributed to the growing popularity of other coastal resorts, including other spots in the town of Hancock, such as The Tarratine, as well as neighboring Bar Harbor.

The last proprietor of The Bluffs was Capt. Billy Grant, of Hancock, from whose family the land for Mount Desert Ferry had been purchased. Captain Grant also ran two stores there. The Bluffs would be torn down by its new owner, Frank Moore.

According to the January 16, 1915, edition of the *Bar Harbor Times*:

Frank R. Moore of Ellsworth has bought all the Hotel Bluffs buildings at Mt. Desert Ferry, including the hotel building, two cottages and stable. The buildings are on land leased of the Maine Central Railroad and will be removed. The purchase also includes all the furniture and furnishings of the buildings. This Mr. Moore has already removed to Ellsworth and is selling off. One of the cottages, also, he has already sold, together with the stable. It is probable the other cottages will be sold and removed. The hotel will be torn down and the timber sold on the spot or taken to Ellsworth. The removal of the Bluffs marks the passing of the last vestige of an attempt to boom the Maine Central terminal as a summer resort. After a few seasons of fair prosperity, the summer people passed it by for Bar Harbor and the other island resorts, or to join the cottage colony at Hancock Point.

The Bluffs had been a part of the history of Hancock. Many people had set foot in the beautiful place since its construction thirty years previously, while others had only set eyes on the magnificent structure. Watching the demolition of The Bluffs was painful for the people of Hancock. They wanted mementos from the place—large or small. Some of the cottages that adorned the grounds of The Bluffs, including the one in which the inquest had been held, were sold or torn down. Several of the "Bluff's cottages" were bought and moved to other parts of town. One was purchased by Hancock resident Galen Dow, who as a boy worked as a bellboy at the hotel. The boards of some of the cottages went into the building of other homes or structures around Hancock.

The *Bar Harbor Times* kept its readers informed of the developments involved with the demolition of the structure. *Bar Harbor Times*, January 20, 1915: "Mr. and Mrs. Alonzo Lee have recently purchased of Mr. Moore the piano from the Bluffs Hotel for their daughter, Miss Gladys Lee."

Bar Harbor Times, February 6, 1915: "Work has been begun on tearing down the Bluffs Hotel. Mr. Moore has Mr. Treadwell of Lamoine in charge of the job. Mr. and Mrs. Treadwell are keeping house in one of the outer buildings which used to be the icehouse while the hotel is being torn down. Mr. Moore was here one day last week on business. It is understood the cottages have been sold out and will be removed as soon as possible."

Don Marston was a boy growing up in Hancock after The Bluffs had closed but before its demolition. In the summers he would go fishing at the wharf at Mount Desert Ferry after the steamers had departed. When the fishing was slow, Marston would go explore The Bluffs. Her size was still majestic on that small hill at Mount Desert Ferry, but her appearance betrayed her. The building sat empty and in disrepair.

"I prowled around it and imagined its colorful past," wrote Marston. "During those years between 1913 and 1916 I often heard the words "tragedy' and 'disaster' mentioned. At the twix age it didn't seem possible such words meant HERE, at Mount Desert Ferry."

Don Marston would return to Hancock as an adult, long after The Bluffs and Mount Desert Ferry were gone. He decided to find out the story that had been behind the whispers he heard as a child. Soon he knew the story of the broken gangplank, the twenty dead, the horror of the sights and sounds of that Sunday morning in August 1899.

"Small wonder that in 1913–1916 people still spoke of that Sunday at Mount Desert Ferry as a 'tragedy' and talked of it in hushed tones," wrote Don Marston in the *Lewiston Journal* on January 25, 1964.

Despite the extensive national coverage of the disaster at Mount Desert Ferry, the story was soon forgotten. The crux of the story had unfolded and been wrapped up in forty-eight heart-wrenchingly efficient hours. The accident occurred on Sunday morning, and by Tuesday morning the inquest verdict had been read and the dead were being buried. One year after the accident, the *Bangor Daily News* was one of the few Maine newspapers to remember the disaster. "It was a year ago today that the terrible accident at Mt. Desert Ferry occurred, in which a score of people met their death and many more were seriously injured," wrote the paper.

Ownership of McNeil Point, the land that housed Mount Desert Ferry, has changed hands over the years since being owned by Maine Central Railroad. At one point it was used by the Standard Oil Company, who in 1942 erected two big storage tanks on the location, where oil tankers would dock at the old ferry wharf and unload. This operation ceased in the 1950s, and the property was bought by Dan Cushman, who had been an employee of the oil company. Mr. Cushman would use the land that housed the cottages of The Bluffs to build his own summer rental cottages.

Rumor has it that during Prohibition, from 1919 to 1933, Mount Desert Ferry was used for rum-running at night.

The property on which Mount Desert Ferry proper and The Bluffs was located remains privately owned, currently by a marine service company. The Town of Hancock has discussed the possibility of purchasing the property, given its access to the water, its beauty, and its history.

Phil and Karen Johnson owned the property at the turn of this century. In the June 2000 edition of *Out and About Down East Maine*, the couple talked about the property they owned, and the history it contained. The Johnsons built a house and ran the boatyard in the area that once housed Mount Desert Ferry. The couple told Anne Porter, the author of the article "When Trains Ruled, Hancock Bustled," that their house came with a history that lent an extra dimension to their life on McNeil Point.

The couple said that people still dropped in at the property, accessible only by a narrow dirt road that blends in anonymously with the other narrow back roads of rural coastal Maine. Some of the visitors to the property were people who had worked at the once-thriving port. Some had been on the train crews; others rode the steamers that left many times a day to and from Mount Desert Ferry. Many just remember having Mount Desert Ferry as part of their lives, having fished at the spot or done business with the kitchen of The Bluffs.

"The people that used to work here—of course, they're now old men," Phil Johnson said. "They're spread out all over the country and they want to see where they used to work one more time."

In 1990, Nan Lincoln of Mount Desert Island was approached by Patrick Riley, who had just retired from his job with AT&T in Portland, Maine. With time on his hands, Patrick, one of five brothers, had decided to track down the details of an old family story with which he had grown up. The story was of the heroism of Patrick's grandmother, Blanche Hourihan Riley.

Patrick and his four brothers had heard a story throughout their lives that their grandmother, as a young woman, had survived a disaster on the water in which a number of people had drowned. They knew the event had happened near Bar Harbor sometime in the latter half of the 1890s.

Patrick Riley called the *Bar Harbor Times* and asked if anyone knew what that disaster might have been. Mr. Riley spoke with Ms. Lincoln, the Arts and Style editor, who was able to confirm that the disaster of which Blanche Riley had often spoke was the disaster at Mount Desert Ferry.

Patrick, along with three of his four brothers, would later arrive in Bar Harbor. With the help of Ms. Lincoln and the Bar Harbor Historical Society, the Riley family was able to put together the pieces of the family story.

Blanche and Tom Riley had emigrated to Bangor from St. Johns, New Brunswick, just a year before the disaster. To show their patriotism, the young couple traveled on the 8:25 a.m. excursion train that Sunday morning to pay their respects to the victorious North Atlantic Squadron. The couple was described as being excited about the excursion.

Blanche and Tom arrived on the 8:25 excursion train with the other passengers and headed for the gangplank. They were soon separated in the excited crowd. Tom would make it to the gangplank, while Blanche was still on the wharf. Suddenly there was the sound that sounded like a cannon being fired.

In her story to her children and later her grandchildren, Blanche would tell about the terrible moment when she saw her young husband tumble into the water and disappear under the pilings of the wharf. That horror was short-lived, only to be replaced by a worse one. Blanche was one of many who would be accidentally pushed from the wharf into the water by the crowd of people behind her.

According to the Riley family story, Blanche's choice of dress helped save her life that day. She wore a heavy dress, a tightly woven, sprigged taffeta skirt rather than a lightweight, cotton summer shirtwaist. Her skirts filled up with air during the fall, and the heavier weight maintained that air in the water. With the extra buoyancy she was able to paddle to help, with several other ladies clinging to her ballooned skirt.

After being pulled to the safety of the wharf, Blanche looked frantically in the pen for her husband. She could not find him. Blanche implored one of the men involved in the rescue effort to check under the wharf, where she had last seen her husband as he fell into the water. The rescuer finally found Tom, wedged lifelessly among the pilings under the dark wharf. Tom's body was pulled ashore, and the rescuer told Blanche that her husband was beyond saving.

Blanche Hourihan Riley was described as having always been a strong-willed woman. She had also been hiding a secret—she was pregnant with the couple's first child.

The strong-willed mother-to-be was not going to give up as easily as had the rescuer. Immediately she began giving commands to nearby people on the wharf, ordering several young men to bring over one of the large wooden barrels of flour. She insisted they roll her lifeless husband over the barrel.

For the first few minutes it was of little use. As the men continued their effort under the command of Mrs. Riley, the water at last spilled out of the lungs of her supposedly lifeless husband. He began gasping for air.

Blanche and Tom Riley eventually took one of the trains out of Mount Desert Ferry on Sunday, arriving home in Bangor, where Blanche would nurse her husband through double pneumonia. Before long he was back to his regular health, and six months later the first of their five children was born.

When Tom and Blanche Riley's grandsons visited Maine in 1990, they took a trip to McNeil Point in Hancock to see for themselves the site where their grandparents' story had unfolded. "[T]he descendants of the people who were part of the events of Aug. 6, 1899, cannot stand on that now quiet shore without hearing the ghostly cries of desperation mingling with the mew of gulls wheeling overhead," wrote Nan Lincoln.

"We all went out together. On the way we saw the earthworks for the train tracks, and at the site the blackened stumps of the pier pilings sticking up out of the water. We stood there quite a while in silence, picturing that long-ago scene of terror. For the three strapping Riley boys, it must have been especially moving knowing that had their grandmother not survived, they would not be standing there," said Nan Lincoln. "It's a haunting place when you know the story."

Evidence of the once-thriving Mount Desert Ferry can still be found in Hancock, if one looks hard enough for it.

"A recent walk down Ferry Road to Grant's Hill in Hancock shows almost no sign of the bustling train station and hotel that defined Mount Desert Ferry at the turn of the twentieth century. If one looks closely, a remnant of a pier can be seen. Otherwise, it is a quiet and beautiful point on the coast of Maine, now occupied by a marine service business," wrote Brook Ewing Minner in the book *The Bar Harbor Express: A Most Elegant Travel Option.*

The train turntable and the few other remnants of the yard are still tucked in a sparsely wooded area along the water, along with a few new and beautiful houses, a few miles before the site of Mount Desert Ferry. The walls of the turntable's basement are still there. In the center is a small concrete slab with four iron rods sticking up out of it in a square configuration. This was what turned the giant locomotives on a large table so that they would be pointed the correct direction for the trip back to Bangor by way of Ellsworth.

Years after the ferry had been closed, there was another fatal tragedy at Mount Desert Ferry when the daughter of Walter Moon was playing at the old turntable and was crushed to death.

Other remnants of Mount Desert Ferry remain. In the woods of Hancock along the abandoned track stands a sign with a railroad marker. The remains of the original tracks can be seen and are featured at the location of the former Washington Junction station, now a public rest area and cultural point along Route 1. One spur of the original Maine Shoreline Railroad is now a walking trail.

Between the yard and McNeil Point remains the pug hole, a small area where the Maine Central built a short train trestle to cross a little cove. The railroad loaded the area with two mounds of dirt for the bridge supports but left a small section for water to continue to come in to shore. The pug hole was a favorite swimming hole of Hancock youth in the summer. The water that slowly came in with the high tide would hit the bare land and be warmed by the heat that the land had absorbed, making it a warmer-than-usual swimming spot in waters that are normally still chilly even in the summer.

The building that housed the Mount Desert Post Office still stands today. One old sign that reads "MT DESERT FERRY" hangs on the wall of Hancock resident Ruth Maynard. The boards that make up the sign came from one of the old ferry buildings.

The only real vestige of Mount Desert Ferry at the privately owned McNeil Point is the strip of barren earth that runs down the center of the marine service yard and serves as its driveway. This is where the short section of railroad track that took the train to the wharf lay. The far end of the driveway, where passengers had once come around the final corner to arrive at Mount Desert Ferry, is now woods. If one did not realize that railroad tracks had once run through the woods onto that small area, one would not know they were driving on history.

Only after turning around and starting back toward the entrance of that short strip of land, however, can one appreciate the view that greeted the hundreds of thousands of passengers, rich and poor alike, who rode the trains of the Maine Central Railroad to Mount Desert Ferry during its forty-seven years of service. In front of the passengers stood the hills and mountains of Mount Desert Island and the sparkling blue water of Frenchman Bay. A long-lost rustic lighthouse in the middle of the bay completed the welcoming scene for the travelers of the railroad. Regardless of the amount of money in a person's pocket, the view from Mount Desert Ferry was priceless.

Upon seeing that view, it becomes more understandable why it hastened the hearts and spirits of the 1,300 people on the 8:25 train that Sunday morning in August as it rounded the corner and pulled in to Mount Desert Ferry, with the historical and elegant *Sappho* waiting to carry them into that view and make them part of the adventure it represented, just as it did for everyone else, even if only for one day.

Appendix
Lists

LIST OF VICTIMS

George. H. Bennett, Bangor, age 35.

Mrs. G. H. Bennett, Bangor, first name unknown, age unknown.

Mrs. Ellen Horn Billings, Bangor, age 68.

Irving Bridges, Hancock, age 31.

Albert Colson, Levant, age 40.

Clifford Cushman, Corinth, age 25.

Mrs. Lillian Sleeper Derwent, Bangor, age 23.

Charles W. Downes, Ellsworth, age 13 or 14.

Mrs. Bertha Curtis Estey, Ellsworth, age 31.

Ora M. Lank, Danforth, age 28.

Miss Blanche Lewis, Hampden, age 19.

Melvin McCard, Corinth, age 31.

Margaret Mower, San Francisco, age 67.

Joseph Murphy, Old Town, age 30.

Mrs. Minerva Murray, Brewer, age 23.

Mrs. Delia Wiley Oakes, Bangor, age 33.

Mrs. Addie Tripp Stover, Ellsworth, age 47.

Miss Grace Sumner, Bangor, age 15.

F. E. Sweetser, Portland, age 31.

Miss Elizabeth Ward, Bangor, age 19.

Maine Central Railroad

Franklin Wilson, President.

Morris McDonald, Superintendent.

A. A. White, Division Superintendent.

Theodore Dunn, Chief Engineer (structural).

Capt. Edgar P. Dickson, Hancock, *Sappho.*

William W. Jellison, Hancock, Freight Agent out of Mount Desert Ferry.

Ivory L. Wardwell, Hancock, Station Manager at Mount Desert Ferry.

Frederick Sanborn, Train Conductor (conductor of the 8:25 train out of Bangor).

John S. Heald, Bangor, Claim Agent.

F. M. Grover, Claim Agent, Boston and Maine Railroad.

William Witham, Lisbon, Foreman of Bridges.

Doctors and Nurses

Dr. Daniel Brown, Ellsworth and Brockton, Massachusetts.

Dr. D. W. Bunker, Bar Harbor.

Dr. C. D. Edmunds, Bangor.

Dr. C. A. Gibson, Bangor.

Dr. George R. Hagerty, Bar Harbor.

Dr. Lewis Hodgkins, Ellsworth.

Dr. Nathan C. King, Ellsworth.

Miss Roberta Logie, Nursing Student, Bangor.

Dr. W. C. Mason, Bangor.

Dr. Daniel McCann, Bangor.

Dr. E. A. McCullough, Bangor.

Dr. William McNally, Bangor.

Dr. Charles C. Morrison, Bar Harbor.

Dr. Elmer Morrison, Bar Harbor.

Dr. E. T. Nealley, Bangor.

Dr. Ora Pease, Old Town.

Dr. George Phillips, Ellsworth.

Dr. J. K. Phillips, Bangor.

Dr. Watson S. Purington, Bangor.

Miss Harriet Rolfe, Nurse, Bangor.

Dr. Eugene B. Sanger, Bangor.

Dr. W. H. Simmons, Bangor.

The Misses Stewart, Nurses, Bar Harbor and Philadelphia.

Dr. Frank Whitcomb, Orono.

Gangplank Survivors

There were an estimated 200 people who fell from the gangplank at Mount Desert Ferry at the time of the accident. Fifty more were reported to have been pushed into the water immediately after the breaking of the gangplank. Out of those 250 people, 20 died in the disaster. Below is the list of 100 survivors of the disaster. Combined with the 20 who perished, this accounts for 120 of the 250 people who went into the water that day, almost half. Hopefully the other 130 names are not lost to time.

Charles H. Adams, Bangor.

Mrs. Charles H. Adams, Bangor.

Horace Ashley, Sullivan.

Louise Bartlett, Orrington.

Julia Billington, Ellsworth.

Horace E. Bowditch, Augusta.

Mr. and Mrs. Lincoln G. Bragdon and two children, Bangor.

Louise Bridges, Ellsworth.

Rev. and Mrs. George H. Brooks, Ellsworth.

Joseph Cobb.

Mr. G. R. Collier, Boston.

Mr. and Mrs. A. W. Curtis, Ellsworth.

Miss Lillian Danielson, Brewer.

Miss Ettie Davis, Ellsworth.

Mabel Davis, Ellsworth.

Mr. J. H. Deahan, Bangor.

Mr. George Derwent, Bangor.

Eugene Dudley, Bangor.

Mrs. Herbert Dunning, Bangor.

Mrs. James Dunning, Bangor.

Mrs. Dutyl, Bangor.

Miss Ida Edminster, Bangor.

Hollis Estey, Ellsworth.

Kate Fahey, Bangor.

Charles F. Flynt, Augusta.

Ida Flynt, Augusta.

Ludella Fogg and his aunt, Bangor.

Arthur E. Forbes, South Paris, Maine.

Miss Grace Gatchell, Old Town.

Howard Gillie, Bangor.

Edmund Phinney Greenough, Portland.

Annie B. Hammill, Bangor.

Alice Haskell, Pittsfield.

Charles B. Haskell, Pittsfield.

Etta Haskell, Pittsfield.

Louis O. Haskell, Pittsfield.

Harry Lancy, Portland.

Mr. and Mrs. Patrick Leonard and two sons, Bangor.

Anna Loring, Portland.

George D. Loring, Portland.

George Lowell, Ellsworth.

Mr. and Mrs. John Mason, Bangor.

George Mattox, Bangor.

Miss Nora McNamara, Bangor.

Elmer Nichols, Bangor.

Alonzo P. Oakes, Bangor.

Mr. and Mrs. Jesse H. Ogler, Camden.

Mr. and Mrs. P. O'Leary, Bangor.

Mr. and Mrs. Lysander Palmer, Bangor.

Charles H. Parsons.

Albert Peterson, Bangor.

Mary Peterson, Bangor.

Peter H. Peterson, Bangor.

Carrie S. Pomeroy, Ellsworth.

Nellie Jenness Purington, Bangor.

Dr. Watson S. Purington, Bangor.

Maud Raymond, Ellsworth.

Blanche Riley, Bangor.

Tom Riley, Bangor.

Chester M. Robbins, Old Town.

Chester W. Robbins, Old Town.

Rachael Robbins, Old Town.

Georgie A. Russell, Bangor.

Miss Mary L. Shorten, Bangor.

Miss Lena Smith, Exeter.

Walker B. Smith, Bangor.

James H. Snow, Bangor.

George Southard, East Hampden.

George Spaulding, Orono.

John H. Stone, Bangor.

Miss Mary T. Sweeney, Bangor.

Fredrick M. Thompson, Portland.

Mrs. F. H. Thompson, Portland.

Fred Tuck, Bangor.

William Vance, Providence, Rhode Island.

Gertrude Veazie, Bangor.

Ella Whitcomb, Orono

Dr. Frank Whitcomb, Orono.

Robert Whitcomb, Orono.

Herbert A. Whitmore, Bangor.

Charles. E. Williams, Portland.

Mr. and Mrs. George W. Wyler, Bangor.

The Bluffs

George Bemis, Proprietor.

Peter Cuddy, Proprietor.

Mrs. James K. Chamberlain.

Abbie A. Fairbanks, Bangor.

Capt. Henry N. Fairbanks, Bangor.

Miss Nora L. Fairbanks, Bangor.

Augustus Hand, New York.

Susie Hand, Ellsworth and New York.

Freeland H. Libbey.

Mr. and Mrs. William L. Miller, Bangor.

Mr. and Mrs. J. M. Oak.

Mr. and Mrs. E. C. Ryder.

Gen. and Mrs. Joseph S. Smith.

Miss Ethel M. Stratton.

Mrs. Irene Stratton.

Inquest

Dr. Dorpheus L. Fields, Ellsworth, Coroner.

John Bunker Jr., Hancock County, County Attorney.

L. F. Hooper, Hancock County, Sheriff.

Bennington C. Addition, Bangor, Lawyer.

Charles B. Drummey, Ellsworth, Lawyer assisting Hancock County District Attorney.

Hannibal E. Hamlin, Ellsworth, Lawyer for Maine Central Railroad.

Jury

James Butler, Hancock.

Henry Eppes, Ellsworth.

George W. Googins, Hancock.

William F. Grant, Hancock.

S. C. Moore, Hancock.

Nelson Stewart, Hancock.

Witnesses

Abbie A. Fairbanks, Bangor.

Capt. Henry N. Fairbanks, Bangor.

Nora L. Fairbanks, Bangor.

William W. Jellison, Hancock.

Ethel M. Stratton, Bangor.

Ivory L. Wardwell, Hancock.

William Witham, Lisbon.

Sources

Bangor Daily Commercial, Bangor, Maine.

Bangor Daily Whig and Courier, Bangor, Maine.

Bangor Whig and Courier, Bangor, Maine.

Bar Harbor Record, Bar Harbor, Maine.

Bar Harbor Times, Bar Harbor, Maine.

Boston Globe, Boston, Massachusetts.

Buffalo Review, Buffalo, New York.

Courier, Waterloo, Iowa.

Daily New Era, Lancaster, Pennsylvania.

Ellsworth American, Ellsworth, Maine.

Ellsworth Enterprise, Ellsworth, Maine.

Fire Engineering, Indianapolis, Indiana.

Fitchburg Sentinel, Fitchburg, Massachusetts.

Gardiner Daily Reporter, Gardiner, Maine.

Kennebec Journal, Augusta, Maine.

Lincoln, Nan, Mount Desert Island, personal interviews.

Maine Central Railroad, poster advertising train excursion to Bar Harbor, 1899.

Maine Coastal Living.

Marston, Donald, *Lewiston Journal*, January 25, 1964.

Middletown Daily Argus, Middletown, New York.

Minner, Brook Ewing, *The Bar Harbor Express: A Most Elegant Travel Option*.

Modern Swimming, "How to Resuscitate a Drowning Victim," 1916.

Mount Desert Herald, Mount Desert Island, Maine.

New York Journal, New York.

Newspaperdom, New York.

Old Town Enterprise, Old Town, Maine.

Out and About Down-East Maine.

Oxford Democrat, Paris, Maine.

Pen and Pencil: Bar Harbor and Mount Desert Island, pamphlet, (New York: Liberty Printing Company, 1886).

Phippen, Sanford, *The Sun Never Sets on Hancock Point: An Informal History* (Hancock, ME: Historical Society of the Town of Hancock, 2000).

Phippen, Sanford, Hancock, Maine, personal interviews.

Pomroy, Anne, "Hancock Maine: 1880–1889 Early Influences of the Tourist Industry on a Small Coastal Community" (unpublished paper).

Portland Daily Press, Portland, Maine.

Reading Times, Pennsylvania.

Sandusky Star-Journal, Sandusky, Ohio.

Spokesman-Review, Spokane, Washington.

Star-Gazette, Elmira, New York.

Tolkes, Bryant Franklin, *Summer by the Seaside: The Architecture of New England Coastal Resort Hotels* (Lebanon, NH: University Press of New England, 2008).

Vital Records, State of Maine.

Waterville Mail, Waterville, Maine.

Whitney, Deane Spurling, "A History of the Maine Shore Line Railroad" (master's diss., University of Maine, 1961).

York Daily, York, Pennsylvania.